The American Utopian Adventure

SERIES TWO

BY THEIR FRUITS

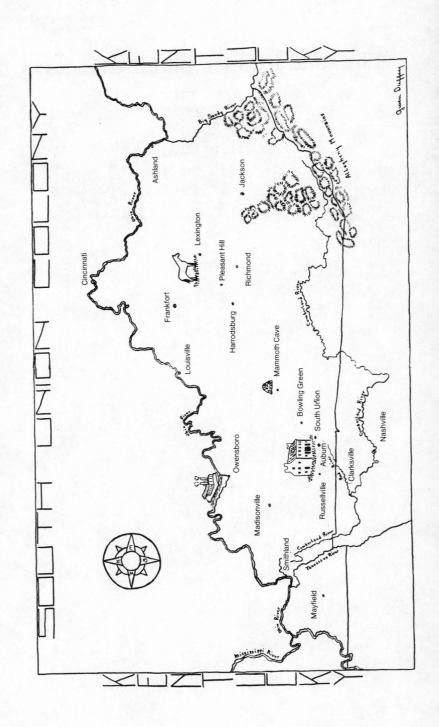

BY THEIR FRUITS

The Story of Shakerism in South Union, Kentucky

By JULIA NEAL

PORCUPINE PRESS

Philadelphia 1975

First edition 1947
(Chapel Hill: The University of North Carolina Press, 1947)

Reprinted 1975 by
PORCUPINE PRESS, INC.
Philadelphia, Pennsylvania 19107
By arrangement with The University of North Carolina Press

Library of Congress Cataloging in Publication Data

Neal, Julia.
   By their fruits.

   (The American utopian adventure : series two)
   Reprint of the 1947 ed. published by the University
of North Carolina Press, Chapel Hill.
   Bibliography: p.
   Includes index.
   1. Shakers--South Union, Ky. I. Title.
BX9768.S8N4 1975   289.8'09769   74-26579
ISBN 0-87991-003-8

To

My Mother and Father

and

To

Sue

Great, great-granddaughter of Eldress Harriet

ACKNOWLEDGMENTS

EXCEPT for the original stimulus given by Professor Gordon Wilson, this study might never have been started. Without the invaluable criticism given by Professor Roy Cowden, it would probably never have been completed. To both of these I wish to express sincere gratitude.

Further appreciation is due Mrs. Frank Moore and Miss Elizabeth Combs, of the Kentucky Library staff, for their consideration and help; to Mr. Robert Hulen, Mrs. Bland Arnold, and Mrs. Elizabeth Wilson Daniels (deceased) for the use of primary source material; and to Mrs. O. S. Bond for the use of many of the photographs which accompany the text.

I am especially grateful to Mrs. Gwen Duffey for the friendly interest shown both in the editing of the manuscript and in the preparation of the map.

M. J. N.

CONTENTS

ILLUSTRATIONS

I

MOTHER ANN

IN 1736, THE YEAR GEORGE WHITEFIELD preached his first sermon to an English congregation, there was born in Manchester to the wife of the blacksmith John Lee a baby girl, who was named Ann. By the time Ann reached the age of twenty-two and joined the religious society known as the Shaking Quakers, Whitefield had earned his reputation as a fiery preacher of the Methodist doctrines and had already made five of his seven visits to America. It was after one of these trips that the evangelist visited Manchester and preached with his usual persuasiveness to a large congregation. Seated among "Whitefield's hearers" at that service was Ann. Whether in England or America, those who attended a Whitefield service were greatly stirred by the revivalistic preaching; Ann was no exception. Being a young Englishwoman whose world included little more than Toad Lane and the factories where she had worked, she was further excited by the evangelist's accounts of America and of the charities he had established there.

It was in 1770 that Ann, like many others of her period, began to feel herself personally guided by divine revelations. The first of these manifestations caused her to testify that "no soul could follow Christ in regeneration while living in the gratification of lust"; and the second one, in 1774, revealed to her that she was to go to America, where, according to her revelation, the second Christian church would be established. Immediately Ann began to formulate the doctrines of the com-

1

munal religious society which she felt called upon to establish in America.

Not only Ann but eight others declared that they too had been directed by spiritual manifestations to go to America, and they made ready to sail May 19, 1774, on the *Mariah*. In the group were several of Ann's family: her husband, Abraham, to whom she was unhappily married, her brother William, and a young niece Nancy. It was fortunate for their cause that another of the group, John Hocknell, was as prosperous as he was enthusiastic, for none of the others had sufficient funds, and it was Hocknell who paid their passage.

During the eleven weeks at sea the emigrants held daily services, singing, dancing, and preaching with such vigor that Captain Smith threatened to throw them overboard unless they stopped their noisemaking and their testifying against the wickedness of his crew. Part of the time they spent discussing their future problems: where they would live, whether they would find work, and how long it would be before they could establish their proposed community. Had they known they were to be caught up in the Revolutionary War, they would have had real cause to wonder whether or not they, as English subjects, would be tolerated by the warring colonists.

Another problem about which they should have been greatly concerned, but did not seem to be, was that they were making the crossing in a ship condemned as unfit for a voyage. Even when an evening storm brought high seas and a wind which wrenched loose a plank of the ship, the group remained confident, but the captain "turned pale as a corpse, and said they must all perish before morning." It was Ann who stepped forward and addressed the ship's officer: "Captain, be of good cheer; there shall not a hair of our heads perish: we shall arrive safe in America. I just now saw two angels standing by the mast, through whom I received this promise."

But Ann had more to offer than mere verbal encouragement. In a few moments she and her companions were busy aiding the sailors at the pumps, and there they stayed until a large wave struck the ship with such violence that "the loose plank instantly closed to its place." The manner in which the little group met the emergency impressed and softened the captain so much that he forgave Ann for her exhorting against the wickedness of his men. In gratitude he is reported to have given the group "free and full liberty" and to have said that he would not be afraid to sail through Hell's Gate with them at any time.

On the first Sunday afternoon in August the *Mariah* docked in the New York Harbor. Eager to see their new surroundings, Ann and her companions disembarked and began their sightseeing by marching in a body up the middle of Pearl Street. Sitting outside the doorway of their Pearl Street house and watching the approaching parade were the Cunningham family, whose casual interest turned to amazement when the marchers came to a sudden halt before them. They were even more startled when the short, thick-set feminine leader stepped directly up to Mrs. Cunningham, called her name, and announced: "I am commissioned of the Almighty God to preach the everlasting Gospel to America and an angel commanded me to come to this house and make a home for me and my people."

Whether the Cunninghams were more awed by the angelic message or by Ann's penetrating blue eyes and dignified bearing is not known, but it is known that "without any words" all nine were taken in and given a home until they were able to provide living quarters of their own.

Fortunately for the Cunninghams the newcomers soon began to find work. Ann and her husband moved to a household on Queen Street, where Abraham worked as a journeyman at his old trade, and Ann washed and ironed for the employer's family. Also leaving the Cunninghams was the seventy-year-old John Hocknell, who was so pleased with his new country and new religion that he returned to Cheshire, sold his property, and brought his Methodist family to join the proposed communal experiment.

All the Hocknells and their neighboring family, the John Partingtons, arrived in Philadelphia on Christmas Day one year later. Upon reaching New York, Hocknell learned that Abraham had been very sick and that he and Ann were suffering severe poverty. He also learned that during Abraham's convalescence he had spent so much time in public houses that he had "soon lost all sense and feeling of religion."

As the months went by the new English recruits and all of the original group, except Abraham, worked and saved, looking forward to the time when they could establish themselves as an independent community.

Because she had taken the position of leader, directing the group's activities, formulating the doctrines, and holding the religious services, Ann had come to be known as Mother Ann. Furthermore, in addressing their leader as Mother, Ann's followers were declaring their belief in the duality of God, a doctrine which had given them the name of the United Believers in the Second Coming of Christ. They believed that just as the male and the female are exhibited throughout the animal and vegetable kingdoms, so God had appeared also in both forms. The first appearance had been "in the male in the man Jesus; the second had been in the female—in Ann Lee." It was further believed that Christ had made his second appearance in the form of Ann because of her Godly life, her self-denial and humility, her patience and wisdom, as well as her long suffering and intense labors for mankind. Mother Ann readily accepted her role as "the spiritual partner in the line of the female. To such as addressed her with the customary titles used by the world, she would reply, 'I am *Ann* the *Word*,' signifying that in her dwelt the word."

A second major doctrine held by Mother Ann and her coworkers was that of direct communication between Christ and His Believers. In stressing that every Believer is a witness of Christ and that he receives all instruction, reproof, and counsel directly from Him through the indwelling of His spirit, they were contradicting the widely accepted belief that God speaks invariably through the Scripture. Even so, they staunchly upheld their belief and pointed out that the inward presence of the spirit would free an individual from all former ceremonies and forms of worship, that through the spirit the individual would discover the "corruption of a fleshly nature" and would begin to count it a "distinguishing privilege to preserve his body in sanctification and honor." To preserve one's body in sanctification and honor was to practice celibacy, and those who came into the full fellowship were to live lives of innocence and purity, practicing "entire abstinence from all sensual and carnal gratification."

The same self-control would deliver a man from every branch of evil, such as "pride, covetousness, anger, and hatred"; consequently, he would grow into "a peaceable, gentle, kind, and loving spirit who could live with others from one year's end to another without feeling a hard thought, much less expressing a hard word." When freed of such evil impulses, a Believer should be ready to accept the practical principles, such as honesty and integrity in all words and dealings; humanity and kindness to both friend and foe; diligence in business; and prudence and temperance in all things. All true Believers were expected to be frugal but not parsimonious; to keep clear of debt by discharging all just dues, duties, and equitable claims as seasonably and effectually as possible; to extend charity to all children, educating them in useful knowledge and science; and to provide suitably for all the sick and aged. Because peace was considered an important divine precept, all converts were to abstain "from war and bloodshed, from all acts of violence towards their fellowman, and from the party contentions and politics of the world."

Even though the Believers accepted and stressed the principle of direct communion between Christ and His followers, they practiced the principle of oral confession of sins to God before living witnesses. Any man who wished to confess his sins could do so to an elder, and any woman to an eldress. Such a confession to the ministry was to be in the same spirit as to a confidential friend.

Among the teachings of Ann none was more readily accepted than that concerning the economic virtue, that is the belief that religion glorified work as well as worship. Two of Ann's most frequently expressed admonitions were: "Put your hands to your work and give your hearts to God," and "Do all your work as though you had a thousand years to live; as you would, if you knew you must die tomorrow." She gave specific instructions to both the women and the men. The women were to keep the family clothes clean and decent and were to wash on Monday; they were to keep a clean house because spirits would not live where there was dirt; and they were to provide places for all their things so that they might be found by day or night. The men learned that every faithful man would "go forth and put up his fences and plough his ground in season." In Mother's religion godliness did not lead to idleness.

After two years of putting their hands to work and giving their hearts to God, the Believers felt ready to organize formally their community. Consequently, the group—with the exception of Ann's husband, who had found himself another woman and had denied the cause altogether—bought a tract of land and established their first colony at Nishayuna, seven miles northeast of Albany, New York.

Naturally the new plan for living attracted attention. As more and more people inquired about the experiment and many accepted the principles, the English Believers found themselves in awkward circumstances, for the more conservative church people began to accuse Ann of witchcraft; whereas, many patriots, stirred with revolutionary zeal, accused the entire group of treason. Such accusations caused Ann and the other leaders to be imprisoned more than once. But, as is usually the case, the persecutions served only to increase the ardor of the group.

They began to travel throughout the New England territory, opening the testimony to all who cared to listen. Riding about on these missionary trips, they often sang. On at least one occasion Mother leaned from her carriage and called to the men who followed on horseback, saying, "Brethren, be comfortable. Brethren, be joyful."

"We will, Mother," responded the brethren, and then the entire group went on, "singing very joyfully till they arrived at David Green's." Frequently the outdoor singing was so vociferous that the Believers "were accused of making disturbance and of breaking people of their rest, by singing and shouting along the road at a late hour of night."

Many of their early songs have been described either as being wordless or else as being composed of some strange jargon or "unknown mutter." Thomas Brown, in an account of his seven years among them, reported that the assembled Believers "always sang tunes without words." That many of the tunes were lively is learned from his further statement that the principal objection "people far and near" made against the Believers was their "dancing and singing jig tunes and hornpipes, particularly on the Sabbath under the pretence of worshipping God." At least one group was fired upon while they were singing, the bullet passing close to the principal singer as he stood near a window. Yet he continued with his song and the service went on to its natural conclusion.

Although Brown's firsthand account stresses the lack of song texts, one is inclined to question the complete absence of texts when he considers that the first Believers, who came from England, had their national heritage of folk singing. It is also known that the New York and Connecticut singing Baptists had their own tradition of denominational hymns—hymns which had been published as early as 1766 under the headings: On Baptism, On the Lord's Supper, and On Various

Occasions. Also, it is probable that some of the American members were acquainted with even earlier hymnals: those of the different sects in Pennsylvania and New York; those containing the English compositions of Watts, Wesley, and Whitefield; or perchance the odd 1763 hymnal printed in the language of the Delaware Indians.

Among the original English group no one enjoyed music more than Ann's brother William. Before leaving England, William had been an officer in the king's royal guard, belonging to the regiment of Oxford Blues. No doubt he knew many ribald texts which could be sung to lively martial tunes. But after coming to America, he delighted in "divine songs for which he had a remarkable gift," and his strong voice was often heard in music described as being "melodious and powerful."

William's love of singing was evidently a family trait, for Ann was also a lover of music. From the beginning she made singing and dancing an integral part of the religious services. At one of the first services held in their new country, Ann and her followers "had a joyful meeting and praised God in songs and dances." Another early meeting was described as being one of "shaking, trembling, speaking in unknown tongues, prophesying and singing melodious songs." Occasionally at the church services only Ann sang. It is related in the *Testimonies* that at a certain meeting in 1781 she "began to sing with great joy and love, and gathered the people around her, and her countenance was very beautiful and glorious."

Once Ann sat in a chair almost all day and sang "in unknown tongues, the whole time, and seemed to be wholly divested of any attention to material things." But at other times she "uttered expression in her own language" even though the text might be little more than an ejaculation or a simple refrain. Frequently she walked the floor making "melodious songs by divine inspiration." Once she sang, "Now Mother is come! Mother is come now," saying it was the song she knew John Bishop had in his heart.

Under Ann's missionary direction, the communal religious faith began to spread throughout the East. By 1792, only eighteen years after the Believers had landed in the States, they had established eleven separate societies: two in New York, four in Massachusetts, one in Connecticut, two in Maine, and two in New Hampshire.

On September 8, 1784, the active leadership of Ann came to an abrupt end with her death. The forty-eight-year-old feminine leader had been in America only ten years, yet so strong was her influence that up to the present time her leadership has never been overshadowed by that of any of her successors. At the time of her death one of the elders who was greatly "gifted in vision" testified that when the breath left her body he saw in vision "a golden chariot drawn by four white horses which received and wafted her soul out of sight." Ann herself saw "Brother William coming in a glorious chariot" to take her home. In the thoughts of her devoted followers nothing less than a glorious golden chariot would have been appropriate for Mother's last journey.

Succeeding to the position of leader was Elder Whittaker. Whittaker did his best to meet the responsibilities of the position, but his first major project failed utterly. Perhaps the elder's plan was too ambitious for the young society and required too much of some of the new converts.

It was Whittaker's plan to spread the gospel in foreign lands; accordingly, he ordered a two-hundred-ton ship built at the town of Rehoboth. The ship was christened the *Union*, but from the beginning the name was a misnomer. In consequence of a bitter contention between Morrel Baker and Noah Wheaton as to who should be captain, the ship did not set sail as a missionary vessel. Instead it was fitted out as a merchant ship, and as such, voyages were made "to Hispaniola to Havanna to Hispaniola to Charleston to Savannah to Hispaniola to Boston." The cargo consisted of horses and flour rather than "gospel" as originally planned.

Because the conduct of the merchantmen "did not comport with their profession," the venture was given up and the ship was finally sold in the Boston harbor. Whittaker readily admitted that the building of the *Union* had produced no gain for the Church either economically or spiritually.

Ann, too, had thought often in terms of new and larger missionary fields. Shortly before her death she had predicted a great revival, saying: "The next opening of the gospel will be in the southwest; it will be at a great distance and there will be a great work of God." Accepting the predictions without question, Mother's followers waited twenty years before reports finally came from the far-off states of Kentucky and Ohio that an unprecedented revival was sweeping throughout the new West. Learning that the revival was already in its fourth year, the New York leaders hurried to dispatch missionaries.

It was on New Year's Day, 1805, that those appointed— John Meacham, Issachar Bates, and Benjamin Seth Youngs— set out from New Lebanon, Columbia County, New York, to open the testimony on the western frontier.

II

THE KENTUCKY REVIVAL

THE ATMOSPHERE OF RELIGIOUS EXCITE-
ment which permeated the western territory in the early
nineteenth century had begun in Logan County, Kentucky,
along the Gasper and Red rivers and had spread throughout
the Cumberland territory of western Kentucky and Tennessee
into northern Kentucky and Ohio. The "great manifestation"
or revival spirit was in contrast to the marked lull and apathy
which had previously existed among the western church people.
This fact is affirmed in the journal of John Rankin, a Presbyterian minister of Tennessee.

Rankin was the son of Irish immigrant parents who had
come first to Pennsylvania in the 1740's and had moved later
to North Carolina in July, 1775. As a child, young John had
been thoroughly trained by his Calvinistic mother in all the
catechisms, creeds, and psalms; and as he grew older, the books
which were offered him for information and entertainment
were also highly Calvinistic, stressing always the practical
duties of religion.

It was in January, 1796, that the thirty-eight-year-old
minister preached at Gasper River. He recorded in his journal
that during his stay he could not discover a single individual
who seemed to have any knowledge of a living religion or any
desire for it. The frontier minister's observation is not a surprising one when it is recalled that in those years Logan
County was often referred to as "Satan's Stronghold" or as

11

"Rogues Harbor". It was Peter Cartwright who described the county as being the refuge for counterfeiters, horse thieves, murderers, and notorious outlaws.

Two and one-half years later Rankin returned to Gasper to assist in a four day sacramental meeting. Such meetings usually began on Friday when the congregation came together to sing, to pray, and to hear sermons in order to prepare themselves for the reception of the sacrament on Sunday. Rankin immediately sensed an improved religious attitude. Inquiring, he learned something of what had occurred the summer before when two young brothers, preachers on their way across the pine barrens to Ohio, had turned aside to attend a sacrament meeting on Red River. One of the young ministers had been invited to preach and had done so with such "astonishing fervor" that "tears ran down faces and one, a woman in the rear of the house, broke through order and began to shout."

The crowd had lingered after the regular ministers left and had listened to the second brother shout and exhort. Again, many were greatly affected. From then on the people of Logan County became increasingly aware of the improved religious conditions of their community.

When Rankin began to deliver a sermon on regeneration, he was astonished to find that his own lack of animation of the past five years seemed to give way to a love for the people and his tongue was loosed. Such manifest emotion on the part of the minister had a great effect on his hearers, who immediately began expressing themselves in an external demonstration. The fervor became so noticeable that even after the congregation was dismissed, the majority of the people sat with bowed heads and trembled in silence. At times some of them burst into tears of sorrow.

Such an occasion called forth many inquiries on the subject of religion. It also resulted in Rankin's being called as teacher of the Gasper congregation. The minister moved from Tennessee to Kentucky in December, 1798, where during the next

year he ministered to this flock and visited neighboring congregations as well, preaching whenever he felt led to do so.

In August of 1799 there were again noticeable results at
the Gasper sacrament meeting. Many people fell under conviction, and others called on their neighbors to pray for them.
In the regular services held nearby at the Big Muddy River
meetinghouse, the minds and hearts of men and women were
agitated also. Especially was this true at the next sacrament
when Rankin preached from the text: "Beware therefore lest
that come upon you which was spoken in the Prophets; Behold,
ye despisers, and wonder and perish: for I work a work in
your days, a work which ye shall in no wise believe, though a
man declare it unto you." (Acts 13:41-42)

It was in June, 1800, that the principal members of the
three "awakened congregations"—Muddy, Gasper, and Red—
met together at the Red River meetinghouse. Included in the
union congregation were "citizens of every description and
also two zealous preachers from the state of Tennessee in
whom we could confide." Gathered at the little church, the
large number of people expected "to see the strange work and
to take part in the labors of the day."

The occasion as witnessed by Rankin is described in his
personal record: "The surrounding multitudes sat & heard
with reverence and awe, with increasing solemnity depicted on
their countenances through the meeting; at the conclusion of
which, a part of the people went out of the house, in order to
return to their places of residence—a large part remaining
on their seats in contemplative silence: But wonderful to be
seen & heard; on a sudden, an alarming cry burst from the
midst of the deepest silence; some were thrown into wonderful
& strange contortions of features, body & limbs frightful to
the beholder. Others had singular gestures with words & actions
quite inconsistent with presbyterial order & usage—all was
alarm & confusion for the moment.—One of the preachers a
thorough Presbyterian being in the house beckoned me to one

side, & said, in evident perturbation of mind: What shall we do! What shall we do!? He intimated some corrective to quell the confusion.—I replied: We can do nothing at present—We are strangers to such an operation—We have hitherto never seen the like; but we may observe their cry, & the burden of their souls—This prayer is both scriptural and rational, and therefore it is most safe to let it work; lest in attempting to root out the tares, we should root out the wheat also. ... At this instant the other preacher from Tennessee, a son of thunder, came forward & without hesitation, entered on the most heart-stirring exhortation, encouraging the wounded of the day never to cease striving, or give up their pursuit, until they obtained peace to their souls." The congregation left the meetinghouse for their homes to think and talk about the next gathering, which had been announced as a sacramental meeting to be held early in July at Gasper River.

Naturally the news of the unusual affairs began to spread and the successive meetings grew larger in attendance, swelled by those who came from curiosity, by those who came seriously to benefit their souls, and, in addition, by those formal Presbyterians, many of them from Tennessee, who came to judge "whether it was a delusive spirit emanating from the Prince of Darkness of which they were very apprehensive."

The members at Gasper, by working overtime, managed to finish shingling their new meetinghouse the night before the gathering was to take place. The workmen made temporary seats and thoughtfully spread the shavings over the floor to prevent the dust from soiling the people's clothes. So extraordinary were the events of the meeting that it is well to see the account from the journal of an eye witness, the preacher Rankin. He wrote:

"On Friday morning, at an early hour, the people began to assemble in large numbers from every quarter, & by the usual hour for preaching to commence, there was a multitude collected, unprecedented in this, or any other new country of so sparse a population. The rising ground to the west & south, of the meetinghouse, was literally lined with covered wagons & other appendages—each one furnished with provisions and accommodations, suitable to make them comfortable on the ground during the solemnity. . . . At the accustomed hour public worship was introduced in due order & was attended with solemnity, & deep impression thro' the day, & even through the night religious exercises continued with but little impression. . . . On Monday, the last and great day of the feast, the public cry and proclamation of the spirit came forth. . . . Towards the evening of said day inquirers began to fall prostrate on all sides and their cries became piercing and incessant—Heavy groans were heard, and trembling and shaking began to appear throughout the House:. . And again in a little time, cries of penitence and confessional prayer sounded thro' the assembly—Toward the approach of night, the floor of the meetinghouse was literally covered with the prostrate bodies of penitents so that it became necessary to carry a number out of doors and lay them on the grass or garments if they had them. The night was beautiful; heaven & the elements seemed to smile on the occasion. Some found peace through the night, others continued in tribulation. All set out for their homes Tuesday morning."

Rankin not only commented upon the strange effects of the meeting on the congregation but mentioned also the noticeable change on the part of the Presbyterian ministers. The ministers no longer spoke in sectarian language, he wrote, but rather they were now in unison with the gospel of salvation. Here in the Kentucky wilderness was found a parallel case to that of John Cotton when his acceptance of Puritanism first became apparent to his Cambridge University congregation through the changed literary style of his sermon. The change in religious views on the part of both Cotton and the wilderness preachers was to be seen clearly when their sermons were found to be out of harmony with their former education.

The first camp meeting was followed by similar meetings everywhere. The next month at nearby Edwards Chapel, a Methodist Quarterly Meeting surpassed the first meeting in both numbers and excitement. The crowds continued to grow, reaching the peak of twenty thousand at the 1801 Cane Ridge camp meeting in northern Kentucky. People were quite willing to drive long distances to gatherings that offered both religious and social satisfaction.

Generally, the meetings were held in a clearing near a little church, which could not hold the congregation but could serve as the preachers' dwelling. Usually at the opposite end of the clearing was a rude platform from which the ministers could address the people as they sat about on stumps, fallen logs, or on the ground. Around the edge of the clearing, the wagons, loaded with provisions and bedding, would be lined up in orderly rows. At times when the mothers were actively participating in the services, they would leave their babies in the wagons or else would place them behind a protective log or tree root. The camp meetings were most impressive at night when the glare of the camp fires, the blackness of the surrounding wood, the loud entreaties of the ministers, and the anguished cries of the sinners all added to their strangeness.

The revival fires were not limited to any one denomination. In fact the frontier Methodists and Presbyterians began to hold union preaching and communion services, with the Baptists joining them in the preaching services only. All the preachers spoke with renewed life and zeal. Extended demonstrations became more and more a part of the surging enthusiasm manifested at the meetings all over Kentucky and in the adjoining states. Those under conviction took more and more to dancing and to bodily exercises, which came to be known as "the rolling exercise, the jerks, and the barks." Respectable people fell on the floor confessing their guilt of every sin. Sometimes individuals fell into trances that lasted for hours, sometimes even for days and nights. Coming out of the trance, they always exclaimed rapturously their praise of God for this evidence of His grace, and often they predicted future events.

There was Betsey Berry, eighteen years of age, who announced that the Kingdom of Christ was near at hand, but that the revivalists were not in it. According to Betsey's message the people of the Kingdom were yet to make their appearance. This she professed to know as a result of a vision she had experienced in 1802. Then there was George Walls, who was said to have spent an entire Sabbath in 1804 under the operation of the spirit. He became convinced that the new Jerusalem Church would be built near the head of the creek where later the South Union Shaker colony was to place its buildings.

Such accounts can be paralleled by the recorded revival stories from other parts of Kentucky as well as from other states. There is the story of A. Dunlavy of Ohio, "who had never before been exercised but who was taken with the shaking and jerking . . . from that to dancing which continued for four hours with scarce any intermission." Frequently an entire group found themselves in exercise, "putting their heads together about a foot from the floor, chattering as with unknown tongues" or expressing their new found zeal by sitting in a circle and playing button.

That such widespread manifestations would grow out of their first camp meeting had not been foreseen by the Gasper River elders. They had hoped only for an increased membership and a deepened spirit in their own church; they had not anticipated that the spirit of revivalism would mean a re-examination of all the church doctrines.

Soon many of the leading ministers found themselves in "disagreement with their church, believing that an honest hunger for righteousness which the established church had failed to satisfy was at the root of all the mysterious manifestations." Those examining the established beliefs further agreed that divine revelation came directly to each individual and

that every person could understand spiritual things without
"any written tenet or learned expositor." In accord with their
faith in the rights of man the revivalists began to apply the
names of "brother" and "sister" to all members, poor or rich,
black or white. They also introduced the custom of giving
each other the right hand of fellowship, a part of the service
in which everyone could participate. Another of the new features was that the members stood alone and prayed individu-
ally. At times the separate petitions were offered simulta-
neously and it is said the praying could be heard at a great
distance.

The revivalist Richard McNemar did much toward directing
the people's minds against the established church order by a
sermon which he preached at Watervliet, Ohio, in 1802. The
climax of the sermon was a demonstration in which he broke
two staves, one of which he called the church creed and the
other, the order of church government. The demonstration of
stave-breaking was greeted with "unbounded enthusiasm"
even though Kemper, a rigid Calvinist, was preaching simul-
taneously to the same congregation.

Contests between the rival groups were common. At an Ohio
camp meeting in 1803 sermons were delivered alternately by a
Calvinist and three liberal Presbyterians. The crowd itself was
divided between the old and new doctrines. Feeling ran high.

Separation between the revivalists and the staid church
people was inevitable. In 1802 a division came in the Presbyterian church. A new presbytery, known as the Cumberland
Presbytery, was organized for the purpose of licensing and
ordaining men who could not meet the educational qualifications set up by the older presbyteries. It was thought that such
a step was justified in view of the increased demand for preachers which the revival had created. Ministers so approved were
referred to as "illiterate exhorters with Arminian sentiments."
In 1803 the Transylvania synod charged some of its own ministers with preaching erroneous doctrines. Five of the men

under suspicion withdrew and organized the new Springfield Presbytery. But when the leaders realized they were actually forming a new denomination, they dissolved the presbytery and drew up a last will and testament. Witnesses to this will were the leading revivalists, Richard McNemar and Barton Stone, and Robert Marshall, John Dunlavy, John Thompson, and David Purviance.

In the document it was willed that "the power of making laws for the government of the church, and executing them by delegated authority forever cease; that the people may have free course to the Bible." It was further willed that "candidates for the Gospel ministry henceforth study the holy scriptures with fervent prayer, and obtain license from God to preach the simple Gospel *with the Holy Ghost sent down from heaven,* without any mixture of philosophy, vain deceit, traditions of men or rudiments of the world." In their enthusiasm for their new religious views, those drawing up the will included a final item directed to all the "sister bodies," suggesting that they "read their Bibles carefully, that they may see their fate there determined and prepare for death before it is too late."

By 1805 it was evident that two new denominations had been launched in the West. Those separating from the Calvinists in southern Kentucky and in Tennessee were known as Cumberland Presbyterians. Those in northern Kentucky and in Ohio were called Christians or, more popularly, New Lights. It was early in the same year that the communal-minded United Believers or Shakers introduced their faith in this western country.

III

SHAKERISM COMES TO THE FRONTIER

THERE WAS A CONSIDERABLE STIR OF EX-
citement in the New Lebanon village at three A.M. on New
Year's morning when Meacham, Bates, and Youngs left on
their western journey. Neither the early hour nor the bitter
cold discouraged the villagers from getting up to wish the men
Godspeed as they drove away on the sleigh which was to take
them the first sixty-two miles. For the rest of the long and
hazardous journey the men were to walk and lead the horse
which would carry their baggage.

Before leaving home the messengers were given a letter of
counsel and instruction in which they were reminded of the
many dangers which confront anyone called upon to carry the
gospel to a dark world, and they were admonished not "to look
or listen after the affairs of the world nor the news or reports
that mankind are so full of, & do not concern the salvation of
the soul ... nor to be looking after the curiosities or new things
that are pleasing to nature, for it will have a tendency to lead
the mind away from the gospel." The emissaries were further
warned about disputing the gospel with any insincere person,
for such argument would be of no avail.

There was also a pastoral letter which was to be carried
from the New Lebanon colony to the future converts in Kentucky and the other frontier states. Written December 26,
1804, this letter had been signed by four of the New Lebanon

leaders: Stephen Markham, Ebenezer Cooley, David Meacham, and Amos Hammond.

Although the easterners were provided with $5,467 in missionary funds and were fortified with official greetings and instructions, there still must have been considerable conjecture as to their probable reception in the frontier country. But most likely their wildest suppositions as to possible opposition and persecution did not prepare them for what they met when their mission began to be too successful to go unnoticed by members of rival faiths.

Approaching Kentucky through Pennsylvania, Maryland, Virginia, and Tennessee, the Believers arrived at Matthew Houston's house at Paint Lick in Garrard County, Kentucky, on the Sabbath, March 3, 1805. On the evening of their arrival they spoke to a small group of the Reverend Houston's Presbyterian congregation. Four days later at the Paint Lick meetinghouse they publicly opened the testimony to the entire congregation. Although Houston was not to accept the new faith for some time, he was, nevertheless, willing to have his members hear the visitors' exposition of their principles.

The frontiersmen listened attentively as the easterners outlined their points of faith and their principles of practical living; and many of them who had already accepted much that was new and had discarded much that was old, found the eastern teachings challenging. Others were put into an inquiring frame of mind.

After a few days at Paint Lick, the evangelists continued their journey to Lexington. From there they went into Ohio, going first to Cincinnati. On Friday, March 22, they arrived at Turtle Creek at the home of Malcolm Worley, where they stopped to "rest the soles of their feet." The rest was well deserved, for in two months and twenty-two days of travel the men had covered 1,233 miles.

Interested in any mission that would bring men so far on foot in such cold weather through such wild country, Worley and his wife spent most of the night sitting with their visitors before a roaring fire and discussing with them their beliefs. "Now and then Mrs. Worley rose and snuffed the guttering tallow dips and poked the wick out wide so that the flame would be larger and Mr. Worley heaped the wood on the fire." Gathered around the fire also were the nine Worley children, some listening, some sleeping.

For his day Worley was a well-educated man. Because of his education and his greater-than-average wealth, he was a prominent citizen in his community and was a leading person in the Turtle Creek Presbyterian Church, which had become a New Light Congregation. Having heard the travelers' testimony, Worley was anxious to have his own minister, Richard McNemar, meet the missionaries; so early the next morning he sent word for the minister to come and meet the guests. The entire Saturday was spent in discussing "the most interesting points in religion." McNemar wrote later: "I judged them to be men of honest principles, singular piety, & a deep understanding in the things of God, and as such I determined to treat them so long as their deportment was correspondent. . . . I was rather disposed to hear and learn of God, than to shut out everything that was not included in my little sphere of knowledge."

The visitors asked the local minister whether "the rules of the meeting would permit them to speak" at his church service the next day. Said McNemar, "I was sensible the spirit of the revival, as well as that of our wholesome government, imposed no restrictions on any from hearing whoever they chose."

Speaking at the close of the regular service, Benjamin and Issachar set forth their beliefs and read the pastoral letter from the New York church. On Wednesday of the following week their host, Malcolm, became the first Believer in the West. Bates, who had gone to Kentucky a few days before to attend a camp meeting, regretted that he was not present to rejoice with his co-workers over their first convert.

Almost a month later, on April 24, Preacher McNemar also "opened his mind and united with the Believers." The majority of his New Light or Christian congregation followed their minister into the new order. By the third week in May, there were forty Believers who assembled at David Hill's house and "for the first time in the Miami or Western country went forth in the worship of God in the dance." The dancers made their own music by singing newly composed stanzas, such as,

> Brother cast your anger off,
> And every passion bury;
> Come in and share the fatted calf,
> And let us all be merry.

or

> My robe is new, my crown is bright,
> I'm happy, blest and free;
> I feel as little as a mite,
> As lively as a bee.

Worley's large and comfortable log house became the nucleus for the settlement Union Village, which was to become the center of all the western organization and which was to give two future colonies the names West Union and South Union because of their geographical relation to the pioneer settlement. Ohio was in her second year of statehood when the missionaries established their first western community and began their program of planned visits to the chief centers of revivalism throughout the state.

As soon as the brethren started their missionary program, they began to encounter pronounced opposition. While seeking to advance their testimony around Turtle Creek, they were present at a church service when the minister prayed (perhaps not so much for the information of the Lord as for that of the missionaries) that God preserve the innocent lambs from the ravening wolves that were going about the country in sheep's clothing. The brethren soon became accustomed to hearing themselves accused openly of evil doings. They also became so accustomed to the derisive epithet "Shaker" that they accepted it and began referring to themselves almost altogether as Shakers rather than as United Believers.

Leaving their Ohio converts, Meacham and Youngs went back into Kentucky in late June and followed along the evangelistic paths around Concord, Cane Ridge, Paint Lick, and Shawnee Run. During the late summer and early fall, they were again confronted with the evident distrust shown by the New Lights and by the more conservative groups. The Reverend Barton Stone (whom the brethren privately called the Arch Enemy of the Cross) was loud in his censure against the Shakers as land seekers, pointing out that any one joining the group must immediately give up his land and that it was their purpose to separate a man and his wife in order to get hold of the property. It may have been in order to disprove this accusation that the missionaries took part of their funds and bought some rich land in Bourbon County upon which they settled several families who needed help.

The general distrust felt for the Shakers continued in both Ohio and Kentucky, and it was expressed in various ways. The brethren were denied the right to speak publicly in many places; they were not allowed the privilege of defending themselves when they were accused of evil practices; traveling in strange country, they were seldom given proper direction. Property damage was inflicted by breaking the windows in the houses, by destroying the orchards, tearing down fences, and by burning the community buildings. Now and then the ears and tails of their horses were cut off. The early successes around Turtle Creek were protested by opponents who organized a mob that threatened to break up a service with staves and hickory clubs. Another mob burned the Believers' preaching stand which had been built to accommodate the growing crowds.

As further persecution the opposers held up all of the eastern views for mockery. Especially was this true of the belief in celibacy. Once when he was traveling near Lancaster, Kentucky, Benjamin was stopped by three men and accused of ravishing a young woman.

"If you say you have no desire for women, we shall examine you and see if you are as other men," taunted the accusers. "They tell us you have been altered!"

Benjamin answered calmly that it was not so, that he was not without temptation, but that he had "power over those things." The men continued to taunt and threaten Benjamin until the unexpected sounding of a trumpet in the woods frightened them away.

The principle of celibacy as held by the Shakers has not always been understood correctly by the general public. It was not, as an elder once explained to William Dean Howells, that the Shakers believed marriage sinful, but rather that they believed with Paul that those who married did well, yet those who did not, did better. In other words, the Shakers recognized two creations: the old and new. They taught that Adam had inaugurated the old—marriage and generation; whereas, Jesus Christ had inaugurated the second—virgin purity and regeneration. A true Believer fixed his hopes on "an eternal soul life, not an eternal physical life."

Naturally, the doctrine of celibacy, practiced by an otherwise practical people, provoked much comment and inquiry, and the leaders were called upon to answer such questions as: Why be celibate? What will become of the world? Does not nature require the use of the reproductive organs?

One elder responded that he failed to see that "the bringing to an end of this wicked world would be a great wrong. Most nominal Christians believe it will come to an end in a much less merciful way." As for not using nature's means for reproduction, the elder argued that when a farmer raises a thousand bushels of corn he does not feel that he is required to plant every grain of it because it has reproductive organs. Perhaps the Shaker viewpoint is best reflected in John Rankin's statement regarding his own parents: "My parents after a suitable acquaintance entered into that civil connection natural to the human family, who design living according to the order of the first Adam." Such a statement is not a condemnation.

The Shakers had their own ideas as to who were the apostles of a false doctrine. But remembering the admonition given them upon leaving the East about useless arguing and being so definitely in the minority, they answered their acrimonious accusers in a temperate way. Once when they had been forbidden by Stone to preach, Benjamin replied mildly, "I am sorry to see you abusing your own light." However, they did not have to be on such close guard when they wrote in their diaries; in the following entry, the use of the word "spurious" must have given the writer some relief. "November 25, 1805 Barton W. Stone, the great preacher of a spurious gospel, shut his door against us."

Even though many of the former Presbyterian leaders, such as McNemar, Rankin, and Houston, had joined the ranks of Shakerism, there were still left the vigorous Baptists to raise their protests. As late as October 9, 1808, a crowd of some two thousand people came to the Shaker grounds because a Baptist minister had made public appointment "to preach without permission in the Believers' stand." Nevertheless, the Shakers withstood the intruder and denied him the use of their stand; thus he was forced to move off about thirty rods. There he "held forth in a wagon on the resurrection." But since the larger part of the crowd stayed at the Believers' stand, the Shakers felt they had gained some ground.

Probably the huge crowd had gathered only out of the frontiersman's lust for excitement; yet it took more than this lust or even idle curiosity to cause one hundred and thirty spectators in May, 1809, to listen to John Dunlavy address the Believers almost three hours and then to remain seated to listen to additional twenty-minute and thirty-minute talks by

Houston and Youngs. There is evidence that such long services did not continue to be the custom of the Shakers, because a later writer put a notation into the same record, as he was copying it, saying that he thought the whole congregation must have been preached dry by that time.

To assist in combating the opposition and to aid the growing work, three new workers had come out from New York in July following the March arrival of the first three. Among the new workers was Elder David Darrow, who was appointed to serve as first elder in the West. The arrival of the helpers allowed Issachar Bates to make a September journey back to the mother colony that he might report on the progress of the work and secure more money. Issachar, who was past fifty, was to become the most traveled Believer of his day. In the decade 1801 to 1811 he traveled, mostly on foot, 38,000 miles and heard the confession of 1,100 converts.

In May, 1806, nine other New York workers, six of them women, came west. In all, twenty-two were sent out from the parent colony to help organize the western societies. Among the women who came in 1806 was Sister Prudence Farrington, who died the next year and was buried "under an oak in the wilderness of Ohio." In a poem, which was bad but no worse than numerous others of the popular epitaphic verses of the time, Bates eulogized the "precious sister."

> She lived without sin, and died without fear;
> She's not as she's been, and yet she is here.

The arrival of the new workers made it possible not only to enlarge the work in Ohio, but to open new work in Indiana, and to send a larger number of workers to follow up the early efforts in Kentucky. Gradually the Shakers began to win more tolerant notice everywhere. In Kentucky large numbers began to come to the meetings.

"Jan. 25, 1806—*At Cane Ridge*—We tarried at James Smith's—Eld. Benj. & Richard McNemar attended a Meth-

odist meeting where one Arskin preached. After meeting one
Elai Nunn invited Rich. to come to his house, & one Amos
opened a door for Benj. to preach at his fathers—both were
accepted. In the evening upwards of 100 people assembled to
whom Eld. B. & R. spoke with freedom for about two hours.
The people were very attentive & a number appeared under a
conviction of the truth. . . . Jan. 30—Rode ten miles to S.
Bonta's—Spoke in the evening to about 30 persons, who came
mostly out of curiosity to see dancing.—After speaking we
sang hymns, new songs and danced—& dismissed."

The record for May 25, 1806, states that Brother Benjamin spoke to an estimated crowd of from six to eight hundred
for three hours while he stood on a log and the people sat on
rails in the wood near Matthew Houston's. The service did
not close with the three-hour sermon for the audience had still
to hear the testimony of Matthew and of John Woods, "a
young preacher of respect among the people." John, as well
as Matthew, was a new Believer. The meeting closed finally
with the singing of the hymn: "When the Midnight Cry Begins—O What a Consternation."

At a June meeting four hundred crowded into the barn of
Elisha Thomas to watch the Believers worship in songs and
dances. Thomas, who was one of the three first converts in
Kentucky, lived near Shawnee Run, owning 240 acres of land
there. This gathering was followed by a larger one at which
a thousand people filled Sam Bonta's barn. On this second occasion, the spectators came from the neighboring towns of Dan-
ville and Lexington and from Shelby county. The meeting was
marked by some disorder, the principal offender being a young
man who attempted to trip several of the dancers. Following
the meeting, the brethren heard the confession of a Negro, the
first such confession in Kentucky.

The missionaries were gratified by the growing interest expressed in the Shaker beliefs. They were further pleased at a
meeting when one of their new converts, Henry Bonta, honored

them with a footwashing ceremony. Beginning with Benjamin, Bonta went from one New Lebanon brother to another, pulling off their shoes and kissing their feet. Bonta was joined by William Gordon, and together the two kissed the feet of the men as they put on the shoes again. The meeting ended in singing and dancing.

The dignity and propriety practiced by the first Kentucky converts did much to gain favor for the cause. For example, when Benjamin set out for Mercer County, Shakeress Betty Buchanan, who was also going, "went by herself on another road to give no occasion." Then there was the good impression made by Elisha and Henry when they left home to buy a load of salt. Staying overnight with strangers, they "knelt at the table before and after eating". Their hostess, Mrs. Tobias Wilhite, was pleased to entertain men who did not neglect their religious devotions while away from home on business. Soon after the visit, the host and hostess, as well as the twelve children "mostly grown," joined the Believers.

As Shakerism became stronger in upper Kentucky and Ohio, the little bands lost part of their decorum and began to show an intolerant attitude toward individuals who had continued to hold to the formal practices of the established churches. Even those ministers who had left the established churches and had accepted Shakerism were sometimes subject to treatment designed to purge them of any former beliefs to which they might still subscribe. In November, 1806, when some of the Kentucky Believers were visiting at Union Village, there was a service in which Anne Bruner felt herself to be under the exercises. She went among the spectators and took the former Presbyterian minister Matthew Houston by the hand and invited him to get down low. Obeying, Houston seated himself on the floor, but Anne insisted that he go lower. After he had prostrated himself she took a candle, held it to his face, and asked him if he loved the light. Sally Shields joined in the humbling of the minister by asking him to preach a sermon.

When he refused, Sally and Anne pushed him into a corner and bowed around him in derision. At another ceremony, Richard McNemar was humbled by being rolled in the dust and dragged over the floor. Such treatment was administered in order that the former "vain philosophy & systems of divinity" might be "brought down into the dust." When McNemar began to quote scripture in self-defense, he was silenced.

"Not a word out of your mouth," said his humblers. "You have explained away the sense of the scripture long enough—your head knowledge shall have an end—not a sentence out of your mouth!" Thereafter the self-appointed humblers took McNemar down the second time. "After this the sign of Esau and Jacob closed the scene." Such ceremonies must have had the desired effect, for it was not a great while until Houston and McNemar were considered outstanding Shaker leaders, who assumed much of the responsibility shared previously by the three easterners.

Indeed, McNemar quickly became one of the most valuable of all the western converts. Educated in both Greek and Latin, he was an able writer. In 1807, only two years after joining the Shakers, he had written and published *The Kentucky Revival*, the first Shaker book to appear in the West and the second work to be written and approved by the American societies. In addition to the history he promoted hymnology, writing many of the songs himself, and he started the periodical *The Western Review*, serving as "the projector, editor, typewriter, and pressman." It has been said that "Wherever the hand of Richard McNemar was felt literature and dissemination of the truth, as he understood it, were brought to the front." Publishing began with him two years after the founding of Shakerism in the West. His death was the practical ending of such activity among the Ohio Shakers.

McNemar's interest in hymns resulted primarily from his revival experiences when he had felt the power of the lively songs which the revivalists had substituted for the Calvinistic psalms and for the "allowed" Wesleyan texts. These songs, composed by the New Light ministers or by the members of the congregations, were set to the Scotch and English ballad tunes, and they employed the repetition and refrain also common to the ballad.

From the time of their arrival, the eastern leaders had been aware of the frontiersman's evident love of singing. They noticed that his songs were livelier than any they had known before and that he sang them with lustiness and complete abandon. What they soon came to realize was that the frontier revivalist, removed as he was from the Puritan singing of New England, was further advanced in the English practice of setting religious texts to jig tunes than were the religious singers of the East. Bates, who had been a fifer in the Revolutionary army and who had some talent for making verse, and Meacham, who as the son of a leading Baptist minister had spent his childhood among the singing Baptists, were both particularly aware of the power of the revival music. They, along with McNemar, were quick to seize the new song style as a means by which the Shaker doctrines could best be presented.

Such ready acceptance of the western music is an indication that the three easterners had perhaps more background for the unconventional songs than has generally been accorded them. At any rate, they encouraged the new converts to draw upon their strong musical inheritance to create their own hymns and marching songs in the spirit of their new religion. Many of the resulting songs were adaptations of the widely accepted revival hymns.

When the new body of western Shaker music was introduced in the East, the older colonists were favorably impressed, and in 1812 there appeared the first printed edition of a Shaker hymnal, published under the title of *Millennial Praises*. Many of the western hymns which appeared in the collection were the compositions of McNemar. It was not until 1833 that 'a western hymn book was published, and it was then that Mc-Nemar, using the *nom de plume of* Philos Harmoniae, published his *Selections of Hymns and Poems.*

Another Believer who spent part of his time in writing was the "scholarly and indefatigable" Benjamin S. Youngs. His comprehensive work of theology, entitled *The Testimony of Christ's Second Appearing,* was begun in July, 1806, and was completed April 10, 1808. The thirty-three-year-old author spent the winter months in a little north garret, where he wrote without the benefit of library materials. The spring and summer months he spent in his usual missionary endeavors. During the first summer, however, Youngs took time from his missionary work to write out a prospectus which had to be sent to New Lebanon for approval before the real work could be started in the fall. Published copies, priced at $2.00, were ready for the December, 1808, book market. It was always pointed out with pride by the Shakers that Thomas Jefferson "read it 3x3" * and pronounced it "the best ecclesiastical history that had been written and that if the principles contained in that book were maintained and carried out it would overthrow all false religions."

By the fall of 1807 the Shaker cause in the West was well established, having been greatly strengthened by the publication of the first Shaker books, by the creation of a body of songs peculiar to the faith, and by the addition of other eastern workers, as well as by such able frontier leaders as McNemar and Houston.

* Three cheers repeated three times.

IV

THE PROPHECY FULFILLED

THE WESTERN TERRITORY WITH ITS RAP-
idly changing concepts of democracy, its complete es-
pousal of the natural rights of man, and its recent baptism of
revival fever presented a great challenge to the socially conscious Shakers, who were representing a new religion based on
a communistic plan. Knowing how easily all of their recent
converts might be swept over to some newer faith and realizing,
too, how important it was to gain more converts while the revival spirit was still burning intensely, the leaders worked very
hard to keep their groups intact and to add others to the faith.
Hence, they made many long missionary journeys throughout
the territory which they had visited earlier and also planned
trips into the country not yet reached.

Among the most ambitious of the trips made to visit Believers was the 235-mile journey from Miami, Ohio, to Busroe,
Indiana, made in January, 1809, by Bates, McNemar, and
Youngs. Traveling with knapsacks on their backs, they went
through what was almost pathless Indian territory except for
the distance which they traveled along the Wilderness Road
to Vincennes. As they plodded over the muddy or snow-cov-
ered ground, the men were cheered by the tree markings which
had been left by other travelers and hunters who had preceded them.

Each nightfall the three missionaries provided beds for
themselves by cutting timber and splitting boards, covering

these with brush and their blankets. To allay, at least partially, the cold of the January nights, they kept a fire burning
at their feet. Not only did they find it necessary to combat the
extreme cold, but there was also the continual rain which made
it extremely difficult even to build a fire. In addition, the rain
added the problem of high streams and back water. Youngs'
diary contains the statement that they "waded a stream thigh-
deep." For a man who was never very strong and who weighed
only ninety pounds at the time, such an undertaking was an
arduous task. Reaching the Muskacatack or White River, the
men found it covered with ice. Bates, who volunteered to test
the thickness of the ice, tied poles to his feet and stepped out,
only to be plunged into the cold water. It was then evident
that nothing could be done except to make camp and wait for
the ice to become thicker.

As the time of the journey was being extended, the food
supply was running low. Being resourceful men of the
frontier, they began a search for supplemental food and were
soon rewarded by finding a foxhole where part of a wild turkey
had been left. Discovering the meat to be fresh and good, the
men dressed the fowl and cooked it for breakfast. They secured drinking water by melting some of the snow which by
that time had fallen to the depth of six inches.

The travelers waited several days, hoping that the river
would freeze over sufficiently to bear them. But as the days
passed, the ice did not thicken. At last they spent three hours
building a raft on which to cross the swollen river, but when
the river itself had been crossed, there was still five miles of
back water to be crossed. After spending the night on beds
made of bushes laid on the snow, they started early in the
morning to walk over the cracking ice of the backwater. When
they finally cleared this obstacle, they were so exultant they
expressed their joy and thankfulness by stopping on the first
knob to sing and dance. After continuing thirty-three additional miles, they realized that going any farther in the bitter

cold and rain would be disastrous; so they began looking for temporary shelter. Upon sighting a cabin, they called and were answered by what Youngs termed "the pleasant sound of a dog's barking," and it was even more pleasant to be welcomed by the settler McCoun and his wife, who furnished them a hearty breakfast of fresh, tender bear's meat and venison served with corn bread and coffee.

Upon leaving McCoun's house, the Shakers were in more settled country; so they were able to eat and sleep at the homes of the wilderness dwellers. They even dried themselves at the fires of the Miami Indians, whom they met soon after crossing the Wabash River. Standing around the camp fires, the mission-minded Shakers tried to talk to some of the natives but had little success in their attempts. Earlier in the trip they had passed other camps and had seen many Indians along the road, but as they continued across the Indian territory, the travelers became aware of a tension between the Indians and the white settlers. They began to feel that some sort of trouble was imminent.

When the last lap of the journey was completed, the Busroe Believers received the brethren warmly, poulticed their feet, and provided every comfort. But Youngs wrote, "Our greatest comfort was to find their steadfast faith in the gospel." To be able to rejoice with these Indiana Believers in their steadfastness and to carry such news back to the other frontier members was, after all, sufficient pay for the treacherous expedition which had lasted sixteen days.

This particular trip was probably one of the most hazardous of all the journeys attempted by the Shaker evangelists in the early years; but even so, it was only one of the many routine trips made by the ministers to the scattered bodies of Shakers over all the wide western country. In addition to these trips of encouragement to the young converts scattered throughout Ohio and northern Kentucky, there were other trips made into new territory to promote the Shaker teachings.

Before the Indiana trip Bates and McNemar, accompanied by Matthew Houston, had already gone to southwestern Kentucky to the Gasper River neighborhood. There at the headspring of frontier revivalism, they had witnessed the full fruition of Mother Ann's prophecy that there would be a great work of God in the gospel in the southwest.

It was October 17, 1807, when the experienced Bates and his co-workers reached Gasper and found lodging at the home of the local minister, John Rankin. Even though the emissaries were received hospitably by the minister, the leaders of the New Lights at both Gasper and Muddy rivers at first refused the visitors the privilege of preaching in their pulpits; however, some of the other members extended invitations to the brethren to come and preach in their homes. As early as the second day of their visit, John Sloss, of the Gasper vicinity, invited the Shakers to come to his house and hold a preaching service; a few days later, George Walls asked them to come to his home twenty-five miles away on Drakes Creek. From the very beginning, it was evident to Bates and his helpers that the people of Logan County were more receptive to the Shaker testimony than the people had been in upper Kentucky and Ohio. In the second week of their visit, the brethren heard the first confession, that of John McComb. During the next two days five others "opened their minds", one of whom was the minister Rankin. By the end of the first month there were twenty-six new Believers.

For the next eighteen months Gasper was a mission station to be visited at regular intervals by the Ohio and upper Kentucky leaders. Although Benjamin S. Youngs was to become the principal leader there, he did not see the settlement until May, 1809, when he came with the Shawnee Run ministry on an inspection trip. It had been necessary for Youngs to postpone his first visit until after his manuscript was ready for the printers in the winter of 1808. With the beginning of the year 1809 he resumed his missionary leadership by going first on the difficult trip to Busroe, Indiana, and by going next to southwestern Kentucky where he entered at once into an extended missionary program. Using Gasper as his base he made trips into Hopkins and Ohio counties, visited towns along Green River, and followed the Cumberland River into Tennessee and back into western Kentucky. Youngs and his companions were particularly happy with their reception in Madisonville, Kentucky, where they accepted an invitation to preach in the Hopkins County courthouse. While there they were entertained at the Dane McGary house near town and were pleased with an urgent invitation to come again.

Even though the opening of the Gospel was given a favorable reception in the Gasper territory, it was not received without some open opposition. As late as October, 1810, three years after the first appearance of the Shakers at Gasper, the barn filled with the Believers' fall harvest was set on fire. The fifteen-hundred-dollar loss of wheat, flax, and fodder, as well as the loss of harness and saddles, was a severe setback for the struggling young community. But the frontier Shakers were undaunted, and in September, 1811, in face of opposition, the Gasper body was organized into a regular society. The organization of the new western community was modeled on Joseph Meacham's eastern plan. Before joining the Believers, Meacham had been a preacher and leader in the 1799 Baptist Revival in Connecticut. After Elder Whittaker's death, when he became the principal leader, he worked out and submitted a plan for dividing the communities into two orders.

The First Order was the non-Communal class, or Gathering Order, organized to accommodate those "who received the faith and came into a degree of relation but who chose to live with their own families and to manage their own temporal concerns." As members of the First Order their privileges were those of religious worship and spiritual communion.

The Second Order or the Communal body was composed of those who signified their intention of entering the full Shaker

relationship. It was divided into three classes called Families—
the First, Second, and Third. The First or Novitiate Family
included all probationary members who were "under the special
care, direction, and instruction of the church family elders,"
and who were "fitted and prepared for advancement in Shakerism or were permitted to return to the world if they found that
they were not in full sympathy."

In the Second or Junior Family the members had the same
standing as those in the Novitiate except they were not embar-
rassed by matrimony. In the Junior Family the members could
retain ownership of their property as long as they desired. If
they chose to donate its use to the society, they could reclaim
it at any time.

Belonging to the Third Family, which was known also as
the Senior or Church Family, were all those who had entered
freely and fully into a united interest, who had given all their
property into the common holdings, and who expected nothing
in return should they ever leave the faith. It was always the
policy, however, to give to each departing member of the
Church Family possessions in proportion to that which he had
brought or to equip him with the necessary property for beginning life anew on the outside. A further privilege held by
the members of the Church Family was that they could make
regular wills concerning the final disposal of their possessions.

In general, the Gasper organization was based on the eastern
plan. Their most noticeable departure was in not providing
specifically for the non-Communal class. On at least two occasions the ministry was petitioned to provide quarters for
such members. Both petitions were granted, but the tone of the
journal entries is indicative of the feeling of the Gasper society.

"Dec. 3, 1819—*Looking over the Left*—As they can bear
nothing else, it is agreed and settled for Sam'l Steele & his
wife Ruth & daughter Fannie to live in a cabin by themselves—
Balky Horses to be sure!... Apr. 30, 1821—Robt. Pearce

wrote from Sangamon County that he could get his family to come to the Shakers if they could all live together—Thinks his wife Leah will agree to Shaker plan later—We agree to build a log cabin for their present accommodation."

Though they did not follow exactly the eastern plan for the non-Communals, the Logan county Shakers did provide for all the families in the Communal Order—the Novitiate, the Junior, and the Senior or Church families. As the community grew and houses were erected, the family groups became identified with the houses they occupied. Thus the Novitiate Family became the East Family; the Junior became the North; and the Church Family became the Center. It was not long before the Church or Third Family became known as the First Family because of the position they occupied. The term "third" had been applied by the easterners to indicate that those belonging to that group had taken the third or final step into the full Shaker fellowship. The Gasper journalists took further liberty with the original eastern terms by using the terms "family" and "order" interchangeably.

In addition to the three regular families as planned by Meacham, the Gasper society organized still others. There was the Black Family which included the Negroes who had accepted the faith, and there was the School Family, organized in 1812, to care for the children, none of whom could be accepted as regular members of the society. Living with their caretakers in a separate dwelling were those children whose parents had accepted the church relationship, those whose parents had sent them to be educated by the Shakers, and those who, for one reason or another, had been accepted as the charitable charges of the society.

As time went on, other family names began to appear in the society records. These referred to small groups from one of the larger families who were sent out to some part of the large farm to be responsible for the clearing and cultivation of some tract; for example, there were the East Section Family, the Drakes Creek group, and the Black Lick or Watervliet Family. The latter group lived three miles from the regular settlement. It was their duty to care for the work at the sugar camp and to cultivate the farm of 1,140 acres, part of which lay along Black Lick Creek.

Those who were appointed to the first Gasper ministry and who were to have full charge of the new society were Benjamin Seth Youngs, Joseph Allen, Molly Goodrich, and Mercy Pickett. After two years had passed, the Ohio ministry came and bestowed the titles of elder and eldress upon Benjamin and Molly. Throughout all the writings of the Shakers, these titles are used in referring to the leaders, but the members themselves were instructed not to use the terms in addressing the ministry; for as Elder Eades later explained it, these were terms indicating position rather than being distinguishing marks by which the ministry would be considered above the rest. This was only one of the many democratic policies which would give longer life to the Shaker enterprise than to many other similar communal attempts of the early nineteenth century.

The newly appointed ministry took up their duties at once, and all through the early fall they were busy effecting the full organization. Among the things demanding early attention were the assignment of members to the different families and the appointment of the family leaders. Each family had both its spiritual and temporal leaders who were responsible for the welfare of their respective families. Those responsible for the spiritual life were usually elders and eldresses. Those in charge of the temporal affairs came to be known as elder brother and elder sister.

In accord with the plans of the new ministry, the Church Family moved into a new frame house and had as their spiritual leaders John Rankin and Francis Whyte and as their temporal leaders Samuel G. Whyte and Absolom Chisholm. The North Family occupied a brick house formerly owned by

Jess McComb, a recent convert. McComb was appointed spiritual leader there, and he was to be aided by Sally Eades, with Thomas McLean and Sarah Robinson serving as the temporal guides. John Rankin's house was used for the home of the East Family, and the four leaders were Samuel Eades and Susan Robinson, spiritual, and Samuel Shannon and Priscilla Merifield, temporal. In the Black Family there were thirty Negroes, their leaders being Neptune Whyte and Betty Freehart.

Each family was to farm and carry on its own industries. The aggregate income of each group would go into its own coffer, and it was expected that each group would become self-supporting. At certain times, however, all the families pooled their resources to buy more land or to meet some other expense of the society at large.

Every one in a family was to do as his share of the work anything that was assigned to him. The emphasis placed on communal sharing of tasks can be seen in the elder's statement, when being highly pleased at the activity, he wrote, "Everybody is doing something now a days." The leaders themselves were not exempted from the general work. Harvey L. Eades, who was to become a recognized western leader, served in many different capacities: as ox driver, shoemaker, seed grower, tailor, teacher, often as journalist, and during the days of much construction as carpenter. In the capacity of carpenter, he planed the white oak planks to be used in the Center House.

As further evidence that the educated group were also assigned menial tasks is a journalist's comment on himself. "Oct. 1827 I Milton H. Robinson, an appointed cow feeder & with great reluctance I now proceed—to duty." Two months later the journal contained notice of a new appointment for Robinson. "Water Hauling—I, Milton H. Robinson am changed today from cow feeding to Water Hauling."

Sharing equal responsibility with the Shaker men in the new community program were the women. Years before Susan

B. Anthony was to stump the country for women's rights, the female members of the United Society of Believers were accorded their equal rights and responsibilities. As Shaker women they had the unique privilege of seeking religious and economic guidance from members of their own sex. They, too, found themselves with many changes of duty. When Elder Benjamin made one of his numerous visits east, Eldress Molly was expected to keep the journal in Benjamin's absence. Evidently, Molly grew tired of her responsibility for she wrote: "N.B. Now, if good little Eld. B. don't come home soon I mean to quit keeping this journal, see if I don't! Molly."

All individuals joining the society signed some kind of formal agreement. Those in the Church Family, later known as the First Family, signed an agreement to "dedicate themselves and their all"; those in the Junior and Novitiate Families signed an agreement whereby they could retain their property but could not take anything for their work. The pact of agreement was always drawn up between the new member and the trustees of the society. Taken from the written agreement of Sarah Lynn, the following paragraphs typify the terms of agreement signed by most of those outside of the Church Family. It will be noticed that Sarah was joining with her children.

"Wherefore the said Sarah Lynn agreeably to her own faith and understanding & being desirous as a member of said Society to devote her time & talents for her own & the general good of the same both agreed and voluntarily of her own free choice doth covenant agree & promise, firmly, by these presents, to conform to the rules & principles of said Society, & that she will never bring any charge against the s^d [said] George and Eli, nor against any other members of said Society on account of any labor or services that ever have been done by her the said Sarah or by any of her children while living with said society or within any of its rights and privileges.

"And the said George & Eli likewise agree & promise . . .

that the said Sarah & children, in sickness or in health so long
as she & they remain members of said Society & conformable
to its rules & principles shall receive a sufficiency of comfortable
food & lodging & raiment, shall enjoy the mutual rights &
privileges of said Society—and that no charge of debt or
blame nor any demand whatever shall be made or brought
against the s⁴ Sarah on account of any kindness services or
benefits which she the said Sarah in health rendered while
remaining member of said Society as aforesaid—"

The said Sarah, being unable to write her name, made her
mark, as did most of the converts during the first twenty or
thirty years of the Gasper organization.

When Benjamin Price and his wife, Peggy, joined in 1812,
their property, valued at eight thousand dollars, consisted of
money from the sale of lands, oxen, horses, sheep, English
cattle, wagons, saddles, oil, white lead, salt, cotton, iron, and
other similar items. Going into the full church relationship,
Peggy and Benjamin turned over all their property to the
United Society because they believed that all men had "an
undoubted and inalienable right, given them of God, to be at
full & entire liberty to choose their own religion & to give or
withhold, as they please, their services or property for its
support." So "being of lawful age . . . and free from the just
demands of any other person or persons whatever," Peggy and
Benjamin dedicated their property to the society in consideration of their love, union, and attachment "for the support &
increase of the gospel . . . and . . . for the good objects of charity & such other charitable & benevolent uses & purposes as
the gospel may require." Such dedication of their property
did not remove the Prices' right to draw up a will in which
they could make stipulation for division of their property after
death.

It happened that January 31, 1822, was a day set aside
for all the Shaker brethren who had families and property to
make their "wills, assignments, and donations." According to

this plan, Price wrote his will, in which the chief bequests were as follows. The daughters, Maria and Peggy, were to receive sums of $1,000 and $500 respectively for their own free use and disposal after they were twenty-one. The society was to receive $1,500 "towards the building & finishing the meeting house & its appurtenances" and "$500 towards procuring of water in the village."

Many of the wills made the society the chief beneficiary. One such will was that of Robert Houston, which had been drawn up on May 20, 1816. The faulty spelling seems evidence enough that Houston wrote his own will, rather than having the more educated elders do it. It reads as follows:

"In the name of God Amen. I will that my soul and Spirit shall remain in the Gosple wheather in the body or out of the body—& as to my temporal estate I will it all to the Trustees of this society at South Union called Shakers for the use of the Gosple which I believe they have & that the said Trustees shall pay all my lawful debts if any—

"My will further is that if my Natural Heirs in there lifetime should call for any of the Estate above that they shall have two hundred dollars each except John Alexander & Sally now called Lucy.

"This done in health and soundness of mind."

Polly Mecom willed the society all of her "temporal property, gained by honest industry," which consisted of "one good horse, called Button, one good cart, comfortable clothing etc." These bequests were so made because of "the love & kindness of said Society" manifested towards her and because of "the confidence and good faith" in which she held the society.

During the year 1811 many meetings were called by the ministry in order that instructions could be given to the young society. The first regular worship service as a full-fledged society was held on October 8, in the frame meetinghouse built the year before on the north side of the great road. At the church meetings many plain discourses were delivered against "fallen, proud, selfish nature." It was a common procedure to have two sermons at the service—one for "the world", the other for Believers. On one such occasion J. Dunn, who later was to turn into a frequently mentioned backslider, spoke to the world; and so pointedly did he reprove a young woman that she went away offended. By Christmas Day of the first year, the society had advanced far enough in the instructions to keep the day in songs and dances and to have what the recorder called a "pretty lively" time.

The Shakers were interested also in giving the best secular instruction possible to the children in their care. The year 1810 had seen not only the construction of a meetinghouse but the erection of a frame schoolhouse as well. This little frame building stood far into the twentieth century as a tribute to the care given the village buildings at all times. A dinner was held that year for the school children, and between seventy and eighty children were present and were "remarkably hearty." Among the school children were two mulattoes referred to as the "yellow boys." A year after the school house was built, two North Union emissaries—Malcham Worley, the first western convert, and Joseph Stout—spent six months in Kentucky establishing the order of schools at Gasper and Shawnee Run. By 1812 there were one hundred children and eighteen adults living in the School Order which had been moved to the grove. The Shakers, always interested in the best modern methods of doing things, began using the Lancastrian school method as early as January, 1819, only a short while after the system was first practiced in America.

As further indication of the colony's development into a fully organized society, Brother Benjamin began the first official Gasper *Journal* on January 7, 1812. Although the community record was officially started on this date, it included happenings prior to its opening date. A copy of John Rankin's personal record, as well as copies of the personal accounts kept of the early happenings in upper Kentucky and in Ohio, and a compilation of all the personal records of the Gasper members kept prior to the beginning of the official journal were included. The neatly written journals contained a full account of all spiritual and temporal affairs at Gasper; daily weather reports were also included. In general the house books were kept clear of the journalists' personal affairs; these were reserved for individual diaries. But at least one Shaker brother projected himself into the society annals when he made no other entry for the day except the following: "Wed. 28 *I must remember this evening for particular reasons best known to myself* . . . Milton."

With the beginning of the official journal, the organization of the society into families, and the opening of the testimony throughout the surrounding territory, the Gasper community looked forward to launching its first great program of expansion.

V

TAKING ROOT

AFTER THE GASPER COLONY HAD EFFECTED its organization, the first great program of expansion was launched. Because the community was to be essentially agrarian, one of the first steps was to acquire large tracts of farming land. By 1813 the young community had acquired 2,581 acres in addition to its original acreage. The land, purchased at an average of $6.25 an acre, was usually to be had for a down payment and a promise of three yearly payments. Much of it was uncultivated and had to be grubbed before crops could be planted.

The elders seemed to take great pride in recounting how speedily the work went on in face of difficulties. One reads such comments as: "March 9, 1813 Grubbing: Twelve Brethren commence on 32 acres. Finish in 15 days," and "March 12, all hands great and small—aged, middle aged and youth—went to the new meadow ground to work today." Sometimes as many as "three dozen schoolboys" would be assigned to the task of burning the brush off a newly grubbed field. Because they were needed in the work, the larger boys were given only a half-day's schooling during the busy farm seasons. The time of cornplanting and oat sowing, and the harvest seasons for wheat, hemp, and flax were all busy ones.

Those assigned to gardening were always pleased to have their products "come in" early. Nowhere is this pride more apparent than in a July, 1812, entry, when it was thought to be sufficiently exciting and important just to record for the daily account: "*Roasting ears*   The first green corn today."

Looking forward to their canning industry, the villagers planted seven hundred apple trees southwest of the Center House grounds and more than four hundred peach trees along the creek. Already trees on their land were a source of income, for the maple sugar industry was in full swing. A sugar camp had been established on the Black Lick tract where in March, 1813, eight hundred pounds of sugar was taken at one tapping.

Just as they felt pride in the productivity of the garden, so also did the Shakers find pleasure in "the peach trees in full bloom" or in all "the fruit trees along the Creek shining green." Being fully cognizant of their agrarian interests, the journalist found it important to list disasters too. Perhaps a late frost had killed the beans, or the rust had attacked the wheat.

Not any less ardent were these backwoods people in the industrial side of their community life. Two of the earliest industries were shoemaking and sawmill work. The neighborhood soon began to patronize the Shakers' new mill, the first log being brought by their neighbor William Harris. Business increased so rapidly that in July, 1812, the foundation was laid for a second sawmill. Two years later the Shakers had, in addition to the sawmills, both a gristmill and a fulling mill. Also, they were operating a tanyard and a stone shop. After the school children were moved into one building, the vacated cabins were all turned into shops needed for the stone cutter, the wheelwright, the blacksmith, and the carriage maker.

The erection of the milldam had required considerable time and effort. Much time had been spent in digging and filling the ditch, and further time had been consumed in rebuilding the wall which had broken more than once while the construction was under way. When the wall had been finished finally, the millstones had been set. These stones had been secured by the Shaker stonecutters who had spent a month at the Goose Creek quarry near Louisville. It had taken eleven days for five men using two wagons and thirteen horses to transport the large stones to South Union. Because the mill could not be reached without a new road, the Shaker engineers blazed one through the thicket south from the milldam site to meet the "great road" running from Russellville to Bowling Green.

In keeping with the enlarged building program, the men had set their first brick kiln in the fall of 1811, only a month after the society was formally organized. From this kiln came all the common and stock bricks to be used in the construction. The first brick house to be built was a dwelling for the Church Family; the second was the meetinghouse, constructed on "the south side of the great road."

During the fall of 1813 the sisters sometimes conducted the services alone because the brethren were too busy burning brick for the new meetinghouse to attend those being held in the frame buildings. Once before, the women had conducted the service in order that the men might go ahead with the raising of a sorely needed barn. One must admire the Shaker propensity for giving attention to whatever was most urgent. Perhaps in no other way is one better aware of the equality of work and worship in the Shaker mind than in their willingness to turn from religious to industrial matters or the reverse if the occasion demanded. "October 25, 1813 *Sweet Potatoes* Young Brethren quit cutting stone for the Meeting House to save the Sweet Potatoes." Besides the cutting of stone and the burning of bricks, there were nail cutting and shingle making to think of. Upon one occasion the men worked so consistently that they finished twelve thousand shingles in nine days.

In addition to the work at home it became necessary to send some of the workers on long trips to secure things which could not be had nearby. For example, the coal banks owned by the society in Butler County, Kentucky, had to be visited for the winter's supply of coal; fur hats had to be brought from Red Banks; and salt was often purchased in Ohio. Many trips were made to the iron works in Pittsburgh. Here were purchased such things as bar iron and castings, "nailor shears", blacksmith tools, kettles, pots, stoves, and sawmill cranks, as well as articles of glass and steel. When it was impossible to procure certain metal articles, the Gasper farmers were left to devise substitutes. In April, 1812, it was recorded that wooden hoes were being used for covering the corn.

As the Shakers began to get an economic foothold, they were destined to feel an increased amount of civic opposition. Both the Ohio and Kentucky legislatures passed a law aimed against the Shakers. In Kentucky it became constitutional to grant a divorce on the grounds that the husband or the wife was joining the Shakers. The party not joining obtained all the property and all the children in the family. "Feb. 8, 1812 Another display of the Dragons power. An unconventional law was passed by the Kentucky Legislature today. Whereby a divorce is allowable by one of a party joining the Shakers & the part not joining obtains all the property & children of the family! *Oh! Kentucky! Noble Ky!* how art thou fallen." Further civic opposition came from the Logan County court which sent a committee to condemn the "seat for the sawmill." These court actions of 1812 and 1817 were only the beginning of a long list of proceedings instigated against them.

The divorce law involved the Gasper Shakers in a prolonged court case regarding William Boler, who had joined the society in 1808. Through the Barren County court Boler's wife brought suit to have possession of the land and of their son Daniel. Through the astuteness of either Boler or the Shaker leaders he deeded his land to the society and took his child to the head society in New York before the court decision could be rendered. The boy Daniel grew up in the East and became one of the leading Shaker ministers of later times. The case was finally transferred to the Logan County court, and nine writs of habeas corpus were served at Gasper by John Morton of Russellville. As he recorded the legal case, an elder could not refrain from expressing his personal opinion: "Barking up

The Center House Well, a favorite stopping place for
both the Rebels and the Federals.

The 1810 Schoolhouse.

Arched doorways in Center House hall.

Interior of Center House.

the wrong tree, friend Morton. The Child whose life Herod seeks has been gone a whole year since." In light of his religious attitudes (he) wrote further: "Like the many words and wonders of the Almighty—what his enemies intended for harm; the Lord turned into good for his people and his cause. So be it. How useless to fight against God."

But further difficulties were to be experienced. Beginning on December 16, 1811, there was a series of earthquakes that continued as late as 1815. The first, which came at five minutes past one A.M., is described as being heavy. Another came at twenty minutes past seven, shaking trees and buildings; and during the remainder of the day there were a few more. Again on December 31 two shocks came during the night which caused the recorder to write, "So quaked off the year 1811." It was probably much later that he learned as the year 1811 quaked off, the large Reelfoot Lake had been formed in western Kentucky and Tennessee. According to the 1813 house journals the earthquakes are recorded as having been felt on thirteen days and the remark is made, "It seems as though our little ball might be shaken to pieces quite easily."

But in spite of all opposition and difficulties, the Shakers began to enjoy a growing reputation as a people who were establishing a successful communal enterprise. Naturally the village had many visitors, and travelers made it a point to get to Shakertown at nightfall. "1812 *Strangers* I have omitted to notice the fact that we have daily, almost, strangers to entertain. In the two nights past we have had twenty-eight strangers. This morning twelve horses were saddled before the door."

But there were other things to be considered besides physical expansion and the entertainment of guests. The rumors of the War of 1812 soon became a reality. "Sat. May 17, 1812 War! War Rumours! Distressing prospect before the Believers. Indian murders in Ohio. . . . July 18, 1812 War declared against Great Britain the 18 June."

The Believers at Busroe were caught in the Wabash Valley action between the United States Army and the Indians, and the three hundred members temporarily deserted their settlement to join the Union Village in Ohio. Later some of these same refugees came to the Kentucky societies. Sixteen teams of horses and oxen were used in moving the fleeing Shakers across the backwoods country to Gasper.

By the early part of the next year many of the Shakers were being drafted for action in the war with a penalty of one hundred dollars to be paid for not going. The village was also disturbed by the companies of soldiers who came to camp at their spring. Usually the soldiers, moving in groups numbering between four and five hundred, camped and moved on quietly, but sometimes they were a disturbing element. Once, a body of forty militia came searching for Indians who had been reported to be in the Shaker meeting the day before. Another time the usual quietude of the village was broken by some drunken soldiers who raced their horses up and down the Shaker streets. "Sept. 1816 Horseracing in our streets: a lot of drunken soldiers now horseracing in our streets & no way to prevent it—distressing very." Here then is a foreshadowing of the Civil War days which the society was to know—those days when the troops of both armies would be marching through and stopping for food, days when the Believers would be accused of harboring refugees and slaves.

Not only was the period of 1810 to 1815 a time of uneasiness because of the war, but the young community was beginning to feel the loss of its power through financial reverses. The record for October 8, 1813, gives a rather dark picture of the young Utopia. "*Distressing, Very!* Low and distressing times in these days—Weak handed and many sick—Grain to buy & from 10-30 miles to Mill—Winter coming on—No shoes— No leather—no shoemakers if we had—no money anywhere— with which to purchase—no blacksmith—& the society $14,000 in debt."

The very fact that the Logan County Believers had been able to buy land on credit to the extent of a $14,000 debt was an indication of the regard in which they were now held as contrasted to the distrust of five or six years before. Faced as they were with debt and financial reverses the leaders of the group found it was necessary to raise some money. Two of the men went to Vincennes to sell some horses, and William Johns sold 454 acres of his own land at $6.00 an acre to add to the treasury. But still hard times seemed to continue. "October, 1813 Fodder all exposed in the fields. No wood to burn and scarce a hand to get any. Winter near. . . . November 29, 1813 Heavy trials—deep involvement and low state of subsistence. No mechanics nor mechanical branches for support and heavier still existence of evil spirits."

Elder Eades, writing many years later, gave his own personal testimony as to the dark days, for he wrote of the pinching he had felt in his stomach and how he, a six-year-old child, had only half as much mush and milk as he craved. But even in such times as these, the shrewd business sense of the Shakers caused them to go ahead and put three coats of paint on the roof of their new brick house. Although possessed of little actual money, they demonstrated the long view in their business judgment.

The darkest days had passed by the time of the 1814 wheat harvest when the one-hundred-acre wheat crop was divided among three hundred people. In addition to a third of an acre of wheat for each person in the community, there was an acre of corn for each one. The supply of meat for the winter consisted of three beeves and twenty-eight hogs; and so when the year drew to its close, an elder could write: "Believers now in good health and prosperity."

The next year's January census gave the number in the society, "little & big, black and white", as 330, the school group being the largest with 159 individuals. This, the practical-minded leader pointed out, meant "almost half children to be clothed & schooled." Now that "the world" brought their children to the society and left them after signing papers of indenture, the school group had been greatly increased.

When an elder wrote of the distressing times of 1813, he deplored the presence of the evil spirits which were so easily recognized in the behavior of many of the members. Many people who had been attracted primarily by the novelty of communal living were finding that the tenets set forth by the serious-minded leaders demanded too much of them. "Jan. 8, 1813—Robert Gray took off his family by violence and threats. He took all his plunder with him and *more too*." "October 11, 1813 *Taken away:* Old Adam Kirkindale took off his children by force. Polly the eldest goes weeping." Others who were having trouble holding to the doctrines did not leave, but they did find it necessary to reinstate themselves by confessing publicly again and again. According to Youngs there were two men and their wives who particularly needed discipline. In copying the journal, a later Shaker added his own comment: "Father B. The flesh is a thing that puts some people in a bad fix even in the year 1870."

But no one seemed to have more difficulty in holding to the new beliefs than did Joseph Dunn. At the beginning of his life as a Shaker, Dunn had been so enthusiastic as to stand up in public meeting and reprove one of the spectators at the service, but later he was playing the role of chief backslider. "Nov. 15, 1812 Joseph Dunn made public confession today in meeting and begged another privilege. After meeting he and his wife Ann confessed and were received again.... May 13, 1813 Wrathy, rather, Gone. Jo. Dunn today forced off Anne and all the children. So if Anne would not go—he would take the children—bind them out and then come and be revenged by burning every house and barn. The man who he got to take him away asked him if he was not afraid God would kill him. Poor Anne went away bitterly." There were other times when Dunn was either "fixing for his trinity—world, flesh & Devil" or he was coming back from his worldly excursions. At the final leave-taking the keeper of the journal was so exasperated as to resort to punning: "The last of Dunn. Dunn has done it." It can be noticed from the dates, November, 1812, and May, 1813, that Dunn was what the Believers came to call a "Winter Shaker". Coming in the fall, leaving in the spring, he could well be the ancestor of "The Hired Man" of twentieth-century fame. The so-called "Winter Shakers" were numerous enough to be a difficult problem. Sometimes they were detected and asked to leave. Such was the case of one woman who bragged that she intended to stay only until spring. An eldress, upon hearing the woman's expressed intention, sent her off in the middle of February.

To protect themselves against unjust future claims from the transient members, the businesslike trustees requested those leaving the Novitiate and Junior orders to sign a statement to the effect that they had received the full amount of all their property which they brought with them. If the members who were leaving had little to claim, they were given enough to help them become established elsewhere. Such was the case with Margaret Smith who signed the following: "Received of Eli McLean one of the Trustees of the United Society called Shakers at South Union one Bed & furniture & six dollars as a present having no demand against said Society."

Corruption of the religious life at Gasper was in evidence in many other ways. Enthusiastic though they were, the orthodox Shakers were dismayed when some of their own society went off on the tangent of a meatless diet. The fad of dieting which developed later in community life was not then general. Long before Bronson Alcott advocated the vegetarian diet at Fruitlands, some of the Shakers had become fanatics. "May 19, 1813 No meat. Poor good Willie Jones. Now too good to eat meat. . . . May 27 *Troubles* Troublesome times—troublesome souls. No meat eaters. Live forevers! False revelations, notions, heresies, devilment!" At first the ministry displayed forbearance for the weaker members, but finally they felt "forbearance ceasing to be a virtue." So they spoke sharply, emphasizing the fact that all who chose to go to the world had that liberty.

In addition to debt, war, and a show of fanaticism and weakness on the part of some, there was yet another factor to add to the distress of the young community. This new problem was the famous cold plague of 1814 and 1815. During the spring of 1814, one third of the South Union members were sick, their names filling four pages of a large journal. Of this number twenty died, some of whom were buried on the same day they died. Reports came from all over Kentucky indicating the disease to be widespread, with the death rate much higher elsewhere than it was at Gasper. This plague was another of the many epidemics, including smallpox and yellow fever, which America experienced before the days of preventive medicine. In the fall of 1815 the cold plague was again experienced with fifty of the Shakers sick at one time. The third week of September brought more than its share of sorrow, for during the week there were four deaths, three of them occurring on one day. Two days later one of the school children burned to death. "Sept. 30, 1815 Desolation and Deep Distress, Blacksmith shop desolate, no sound of the hammer on the anvil! Fulling mill desolate—no cloth on the bars! Brick yard forsaken by all but a few boys. . . . Oct. 1, 1815 *Meeting* heavy, harps mostly hung on the willows. Sadness and distress on account of the great sickness."

Yet in spite of all the difficulties stemming from the war and sickness, as well as from weakness and fanaticism, the earnest leaders exercised their authority and held their services regularly. Soon there was evidence that the religious zeal was reviving. "May, 1815 *Meetings* are powerful of these times— quite a revival attended with various exercises—*A War* against the *Beast of Whore*—many hymns & verses composed the past week—Opening of minds—Meetings all seem both interesting and profitable. In every family Solid impressions increase—also with deep mortification & convicted for Sin. God speed the work!" The growth of the religious spirit continued, and on a June Sabbath of the same summer the meeting was described as free and unrestrained, "the Believers carried on in the good old way—dancing, clapping hands, etc."

The religious development continued. By 1816 the Gasper members were following the Holy Order Worship, which had been introduced early at the parent colony of New Lebanon by its inspired author, Father Joseph Meacham. Although the Holy Order had been practiced sometime at Union Village and Pleasant Hill, it was only introduced at Gasper in September, 1816. Since 1813 Gasper had been called South Union to indicate its geographical relation to Union Village, Ohio. The change had been made official in a letter written on May 1, 1813, to Mother Lucy Wright of New Lebanon.

So the first ten years passed with their portion of failure and success. Those in authority had many problems to face; the lay members found many topics to discuss. One can easily imagine two sisters, in the dairy perhaps, who stopped their butter molding long enough to whisper about Crazy Polly Johnson's "cutting up and putting herself at the head of the meeting at the North House and playing the wild generally." No doubt there was speculation in the kitchen about Old Milly Price, who went hazelnut hunting and stayed lost in the woods two days; or about little Milton Robinson, who was taken to the Sulphur Springs to cure him of the "scald head." Probably there was conjecture as to what cured Andrew Barnett of the spider bite after all. Was it the Black Snake root, the sweet oil, the drafts of raw onion to the hip, or the hartshorn? Naturally the men had the most to say about the folly of Robert Johns' trying to tread the spokes of a wagon wheel in motion. One should not take unnecessary risks, they certainly must have agreed; and Johns had paid dearly for his folly by getting a broken leg.

The first major disaster which the society suffered was the loss of their sawmill by fire. "Oct. 14, Tues—1817—*Fire! Saw Mill Burned*—At two o'clock in the night a terrible outcry of fire was sounded—I looked out and beheld the Sawmill in flames beyond redemption. Grist Mill—Fulling Mill & Stone Shop all exposed. Fire however confined to saw mill. *Courage*— This same day all hands turn out to getting timber to rebuild it. This is good—Molly." Six weeks later the mill was running again. The co-operation which made speedy restoration of the sawmill possible marked all the early community endeavors. Added to this spirit of co-operation were a seriousness of purpose and a remarkable energy; all three were essential if the Believers were to solve the many problems confronting them.

VI

THE GOSPEL LOVE

IN THE YEARS BETWEEN 1816 AND 1836 THE
Shaker leaders, as well as many of their followers, became
more and more serious-minded in applying their religious theo-
ries to everyday living, and they set a high standard of
righteousness and industry for the backwoods community of
which they were a part. They were so entirely sincere in what
they believed, so dignified in their conduct, and so honest in
all their business transactions that "the world" came to admire
rather than to laugh at the religious enthusiasts.

One of the first ethical problems to be faced by the group
during these twenty years was that of slaveholding. Since the
days of its organization, the colony had maintained its Black
Family composed of the slaves owned by some of the individual
members. Needless to say, the ministry felt the ownership of
slaves to be in opposition to the humanitarian concepts of the
Shaker faith. The first public expression on the subject by
the leaders was at a meeting in July, 1816; but since the slave-
owners did not yet feel as the ministry did, a general argument
ensued.

It is interesting to note that some of the slaves were owned
by the society itself. It happened that when one of the owners
decided to leave the community, his four slaves expressed a
desire to remain at Shakertown; so the brethren agreed to pay
Judkins, the owner, two hundred dollars a year for four years.
In this way Sampson, Old Molly, Lucy, and Violet came to be

the property of the Shakers. Another slave whom they owned was Old Black Jacob, who, being too old and feeble to work, was taken out of slavery by the religionists for the sum of twelve dollars.

In general the slaves owned either by the South Union group as a whole or by the individual members were treated with consideration. There was, however, the case of "the obstinate yellow boy Mose," who was sent to the farm of a nearby non-Believer "to learn a little of slavery, or to get his haughty spirit reduced a fraction." Mose was soon brought back on the counsel of the elder who said he did not think the gospel could be put into the boy through the epidermis.

It was not until 1819 that a general freeing of the slaves became a reality, and it was not until the 1830's that the last blacks were emancipated. As each man was persuaded to give his slaves freedom, he was counseled to write a statement on parchment and to sign it. Then he was to have it counter-signed by the civil court clerk and have it recorded in the clerk's office. One such statement, drawn up in 1832 for forty-three-year-old Hannah Dickerrow, reads that Hannah is ". . . hereby . . . manumited, liberated and set free, and for ever hereafter to enjoy her freedom as though she had been born free, and is more over charged from the performance of any contract entered into during her servitude."

When all the Negroes had finally received their emancipation papers, Elder Youngs was glad; nevertheless, he felt somewhat dubious as to the result for he wrote: "All have been freed. So we may look for a stampede." Although this antici-pated rush did not occur, a number of the Black Family did leave to taste their new independence. One of the men left the colony after being thrilled by his first river boat ride. Going by river to New Orleans with some of the Shaker merchants, he quit his companions on the return trip at Nashville to take a steam boat job which would pay him fifteen dollars monthly. In answer to the men's admonition about leaving his religion,

Sampson is reported to have said, "Talk to me about Eternal Life! Why Jesus Christ never saw a steam boat."

Another to leave was Justinian, who flaunted his independence by walking out of a Sabbath meeting and getting into the stage "amidst the shouts of the Passengers" and probably amidst the audibly expressed regret of the Shakers. One morning not long afterward, however, Justinian was found in his old ox stable eager to resume his connection with the society.

According to one elder some of the slaves remaining at South Union showed "sauce and impertinence" to their former owners. Some slaves who "hitherto would jerk off their hat as quick as a monkey when spoken to & listen only to obey— when now, being kindly asked to saddle a horse would reply— 'No sah, tank God de time am come for ebry man to wait on heself.'"

Notwithstanding the consequent problems, the brethren were glad to be identified with the abolitionists, and they felt very keenly toward the people who continued to traffic in human lives. The numerous slave coffles were denounced in the journals. "Sept. 24, 1829 Negroes being driven south today— two and two chained together with a short chain to keep them from skedadelling. Drove of fine mules following after to the same profitable market!!! *Does God see this? Rather think he does.*" The leaders decided in 1836 that they would not hire, even as extra hands, the slaves owned by their neighbors. That the policy was not strictly adhered to can be seen in subsequent records. "Aug. 8, 1843 Paid Frederick Cox $16.00 for the hire of Granville 2 mos" and "Oct. 10, 1843 Paid Joshua Ham $46.65 for the hire of Prince 6 mos. and 15 days."

The intensified religious spirit which prompted definite action regarding the slave question stirred the colony to a concerted action in further warfare against "the beast and the whore." At the regular society meetings the leaders discussed many needed reforms and gave their followers a great deal of counsel. It was in February, 1817, that they discussed the impropriety on the part of the brethren and sisters "in making presents to each other secretly or openly out of the counsel of the Elders." They gave an order that no secret or private conversation was to be held between the sexes. Furthermore, there was to be no handshaking. "July, 1830   The ministry said the custom of the brethren to shake hands with the Sisters at any time whether their absence was long or short was to stop. We could, if we would, ask each other's welfare and make one another welcome home without the ceremony of shaking hands—" Much of this seems, however, to have been more the keeping of the letter than keeping of the law, and the common sense usually exhibited by the South Union members kept them from following these precepts to the extreme.

The leaders gave much advice on the subjects of landholding and debts to the world; and they made frequent talks at the family gatherings on selfishness, waste, and extravagance. The practical side of Shakerism was sounded at an 1819 service when an elder "*urged* that no more cattle, sheep nor hogs shall be permitted to run in the streets from henceforth forever." Also practical was the admonition given the members to improve the long winter evenings with work.

Much of the instruction given at the meetings had to do with good manners. The Believers were told that they "should walk softly through the halls and rooms of the Dwellings, and especially while in the house of worship. The doors must be closed gently and while speaking the voice should be mild and pleasant." In connection with this program of general improvement, the leaders insisted upon clean clothes at church services. Those wearing dirty clothes were dismissed publicly from the meeting. Thus did the leaders who had come from the East modify the roughness of the western frontiersmen.

It was still found expedient to remind the members that any money which came into their hands was to be given up immediately to their allotted order, and as late as 1827 the members were brought together at a call meeting to be admonished against selfish trading outside of the colony. Moreover, at appropriate times, the ministry read the business accounts of the general society, discussing the aggregate income and the steady reduction of the public debt.

On January 1, 1828, the Believers listened to a sermon concerning "the baleful effects of talebearing from one family to another; the necessity of keeping a proper separation from the world; and the pernicious consequences arising from the least indulgence beyond downright necessity of drinking whiskey and other ardent spirits." Possibly they thought the speaker was suggesting their New Year's resolutions to them. The leaders also pointed out that it was an impropriety to traffic in whiskey, especially with "the enemies of the cross." It was in 1823 that the Shaker Thomas Smith had put the first distillery in operation. From 1824 on, whiskey had been one of the Shaker products offered for sale.

Some months later a letter came from the leaders at the mother colony in New York containing an expression of the eastern views on drinking. "April 13—Sab.—1828—*Important Meeting*—This evening at 7 o'clock by appointment the society met—except Water Vliet (70 souls) Centre, North, East & East Section families about 225 present. Sang a hymn & all were seated—Eld—B. S. Youngs read a letter from New Lebanon from which it was learned that the Easterners had adopted the rule never to use ardent spirits unless advised by a physician. At the meeting the S. U. members adopted the plan—The pledge to which all raised the right hand certainly left no loopholes. That this gift is to every order & class of believers old & young—Old believers & young believers—*Ministry Elders—Deacons* Brethren & Sisters of every society— Every family, every individual everywhere—That ardent spirits by any name—Whiskey, Gin, Rum, Brandy, etc. are never more to be used by Believers—neither in the shops, nor in the fields, nor in Harvests, nor clearings, nor grubbings, nor House Raisings nor Corn Huskings—neither in hot weather nor cold weather, neither in the water nor out—neither wet nor dry at home nor abroad, under any kind of exercise nor any occasion. So let every soul that names the names of Christ & Mother depart from this iniquity now & immediately evermore Amen!"

Just after taking the all-inclusive pledge, the brethren spent some time doing road work and according to a journal item this was one time when there was "nary *Julip* nor *punch!* nor *Egg Nog!*" The July hay harvest was reported as having "more good hay than any previous year and all without a drop of 'how come you so'." The adoption of the pledge meant denial for the sisters as well, for they too had been known to stop their work long enough to have a drink of wine. "July 1, 1818 We (Molly and Mercy) went out to the flaxfield and gave all the sisters a drink of wine—lit our pipes and took a union smoke." It must be remembered that Molly and Mercy were two of the spiritual leaders at that time.

The temperance wave of 1828 which affected not only the Shakers but the entire country was responsible for the second Shaker restriction. The members were asked to refrain from the use of tobacco as well as alcohol. As one Shaker wrote, they were to use "their mouths for glad and heavenly songs instead of smoke."

By the decade of the thirties the society had established a regular schedule of meetings. Daily worship services were held first thing in the morning by the separate families in their respective rooms. As for the general meetings, there were four a week—three on Sunday and a singing one on Monday. In addition there were extra services such as those held in honor of the visiting leaders and the special yearly sacrifice, which was held each December. The last month was considered the proper time "For all to examine themselves & make a willing sacrifice of all their evil deeds by bringing them to the light by an honest confession & true repentance & a final forsaking & to set out anew to be more faithful & loving to each other."

The sacrifice meeting tended to overshadow the Believers' observance of the Christmas season.

At the church meetings, in addition to the sermon, the singing of hymns (both local and standard compositions), and the reading of letters of advice from the older societies, the leaders frequently reread Mother Ann's testimony for the edification of the listeners. In the spring of 1819 the testimony was given ten readings at successive meetings. After the readings it was customary for the audience to kneel and sing:

> Love is my treasure
> Love is my heaven
> I want to feel little I want to be low
> I want Mother's blessing wherever I go.

Sometimes the society meetings would include the business reports from the trustees or elders who had been away. Such was the case in January, 1831, when Elder Benjamin and William Ligier returned from legislative business in the Kentucky capital and Benjamin read his travel journal to those in the Center meeting. Good business was good religion.

Singing, dancing, letter reading, and business reports were often omitted entirely, and the service was devoted solely to a sermon. Perhaps the speaker's exhortation would be met by a manifestation so strong that "everybody operated with almighty power" although nothing was spoken aloud. The true Believers were critical of all the sermons they heard. They demanded to hear the direct, non-rhetorical discourses which emanated from the heart. Matthew Mecome found himself in ill repute because he "preached a good many dead discourses in the old heaven order." On one occasion when the Believers felt Mecome's spirit foreign to the gospel, they "broke into a powerful war—Silenced him and had a good meeting." It is no wonder that Mecome soon left for North Carolina.

Now and then the eldresses exercised their equal rights and exhorted as vehemently as the men. Eldress Molly was listened to with respect, and Elder Sister Susan Robinson was heard attentively when on a June Sabbath in 1830, she publicly exclaimed: "Oh, Spiritual Death! O Spiritual Death!! God is God of the living & not of the dead! Oh South Union why will ye die?" Much of Susan's talk was addressed to the young, urging them to be faithful and thus avert a sad doom.

The sermon might be given by some visiting layman. When the Shaker representatives had first come to Gasper in 1807, George Walls had invited them to speak at his house before they were granted permission to speak to the Gasper congregation. Walls, who had been greatly affected by the revival fires, had become known as the revival's great prophet. In 1829 this backwoods John the Baptist came to visit at South Union. Attired in coarse clothes and a long leather apron, he spoke to the Believers and pronounced some prophesies which the recorder said might come true, but they would have to wait and see. Another minister who came to visit was John Wesley Fortune, a young Methodist.

The public meetings to which the people of the world were admitted were always novel enough to attract large crowds from the surrounding territory. But not since the early days when the Ohio mob gathered to see if the Baptist Thompson would preach from the Shakers' stand had there been such a crowd at a Western Shaker village as assembled on May 18, 1834. Although no explanation is given for the extremely large gathering, the record contains the information that on that particular Sunday, 400 spectators came, 116 of them taking dinner at the tavern and some of them staying for supper and breakfast also.

The public meetings were held on dry Sundays only, and no one was allowed to come when it was wet and muddy. The Shakers themselves did not cross the village streets to the meetinghouse on rainy days but held family services instead. "Nov. 30 Enough rain falling to prevent our coming to the Meeting House. Attended at the Center & was cheered with

The Wash House, 1854. "Better brick or better walls are not to be found in the Green River Territory."

Building used as the dairy and the preservatory.

Interior of Center House.

the voice of angels." On a later occasion just as they "were about starting over to attend evening meeting a brisk shower commenced falling"; so they had "a singing meeting at home."

The outsiders who came to the public meetings at Shakertown were met by a Shaker host. After greeting them he would point first to one side of the church and then to the other and say, "Ladies. Gentlemen." At the left-hand door an eldress would direct the women and girls to their seats while at the right-hand door an elder would direct the men and boys. The Believers themselves observed the principle of separation by entering properly at the women's yard gate or at the men's.

When the first part of the service ended, the portable, backless seats would be quickly stacked in a corner so that the members would have room for their labors. Filled as they were with the gospel love, the Believers felt no restraint even in the presence of the public; they would sing their songs, "round after round, mid shaking, rejoicing, stamping and turning, the labors being carried on in three different ways—step-step, shuffle and common manner."

In one of the dances twelve of the Believers would go into the cleared floor space. At one end the women would stand, three facing three. At the other end, the men made a similar formation. The rest of the Shakers marched or danced with a swinging motion around those in the center, singing in a peculiar tone some such refrain as,

> Lowly, lowly, lowly, low
> Lowly, lowly, low.

or

> I will arise and break my bands
> And leave my sins behind.

At other times a selected choir sat in the middle of the room and sang for the marchers who circled them, waving their hands in unison with the doleful tune. Across their hands the men

placed folded handkerchiefs which they bounced up and down
as they hopped and skipped to the music. After each two lines
of the song, the company would halt, fold their hands across
their breasts, and wait for anyone who might feel urged to
dance by inspiration. Frequently it was some woman in the
choir who would feel inspired to whirl like a top, her full skirt
popping around her ankles. When she subsided, the solemn
march would continue as before with the singing of the next
two lines followed by another pause. At times no one danced
by inspiration.

Another dance order called for the formation of two circles.
The outer was led by the Church Family elders; the inner by
the elders of the Second or Junior family. In later years all the
leaders joined in one circle and left the formation of the other
to the children and the caretakers. Marching three abreast,
they executed the dance. The earliest exercises practiced at
South Union were those that had been witnessed by Elder
Archibald on a visit to New Lebanon.

It was in 1820 that the eastern ministry came on a visit and
helped the western society with its exercise. "Our Eastern visitors gave us kind instruction. We were rough and awkward,
stiff and careless, so they gave us sundry examples—in all exercises—especially were we at fault in the Holy Order or step
manner and stiff kneed in marching. It is to be hoped we can
put the lessons into practice. We are in the backwoods truly."
The neighboring Kentucky ministry of the Pleasant Hill society, formerly called Shawnee Run, came down in June, 1827,
to introduce some further changes in the marching exercises.

Since it was always customary for the several ministries to
exchange visits for the purpose of instruction and encouragement, South Union frequently entertained representatives
from other communities. Plans were always made to entertain
these guests in some special way. "Sept. 22, 1832 Visitors
from Pleasant Hill walked out to the top of our Knob and
enjoyed a season together and with our spy glass looked at

the lower world." Later when the ministry came from Union Village, there was again outdoor entertainment. "Went to flat rock to have a little picnic spree this afternoon. The company returned between one and two P.M. They were well suited. They played and jumped the ropes. Then partook of a little repast—then assembled together and sang, marched and danced. Then they had preaching." The following day the visitors were taken through a large nearby cave. "Our friends & a good company of Brn. and Sisters—Ministry also along, visited the cave—After exploring it, had a lovely meeting—sang & kneeled—& had a blessed season."

Love feasts and union smokes were usually arranged when there were visitors present. Just one year before the resolution was adopted to dispense with liquors, wine was served at the feast. "Oct. 1827 Love Feast: In the afternoon we met and sang. Partook of cakes and wine with Canterbury gospel kindred who had brought the cakes." Another group brought the host colony not cakes, but two wild geese and a barrel of fish.

Gifts of love were often exchanged between the colonies. It was in 1819 that Union Village made a river shipment of sixteen barrels of oil, salt, sugar, pork, and flax to their South Union kindred. One Christmas love tokens sent from the New Lebanon and Harvard Believers were lozenges and cloves, which were distributed by the deaconesses at the Christmas service.

Sometimes the Shakers had union meetings with the other societies without the actual presence of visitors. This practice was possible by prearrangement with members of other colonies who agreed to observe the union meeting at a specified hour. These meetings were generally those celebrating the Christmas Season. "Dec. 25, 1833 By invitation we had a union smoke with those of Union Village. Long stem pipes were supplied for all that could take a sniff. So for 15 or 20 minutes we were enveloped in clouds of smoke and chatted and sang and on the whole enjoyed our Union with our friends over the River immensely . . . Dec. 25, 1835 *Union Feast*—We also had a union feast with our good friends at New Lebanon & Water Vliet—taking the meridian & making allowances of longitudinal difference—We sat at meal the same time with them. Elder Benjamin wished we should take a glass of wine & we drank it with prayers for his health &c &c."

As early as 1814 the South Union ministry had begun making their own official visits to the Ohio and eastern colonies. They usually went by stage to Louisville and from there to Cincinnati by boat. In later years they traveled in their own carriage or went by rail. The Shaker who recorded one of Brother Benjamin's trips from New York found pleasure in the fact that the elder "came all the way home in a little buggy drawn by a red roan mare called Fox!"

All the early years of the society's history were years in which the young community was formulating its social and religious doctrines. This period of experimentation came to an end when the covenant was drawn up in October, 1830, by Benjamin Seth Youngs, Molly Goodrich, and Mercy Pickett. The compact, which was read aloud at the meetings several times before it was presented to the members for their final acceptance, was signed by all except thirty of the members, many of whom were minors. The covenant was accepted by the parent colony on August 29, 1835, and was certified by Seth Y. Wells and Rufus Bishop. Marked by logic and clarity, it set forth the Shaker organization as to those in authority, how they were to be elected and replaced, and what their separate duties were in the offices of elder, deacon, and trustee. It made clear the requirements for admission to the full church relation, giving specific information about the privileges and obligations of all the members. The tone of serious intent which pervades the entire document is to be noticed in the preamble as well:

"We the brethren and Sisters members of United Society of Believers called Shakers at South Union in county of Logan

& State of Kentucky, being for many years connected together as a religious and social community by virtue of our distinguished faith and mutual agreements, in order more fully to confirm our principles of government, increase our union, improve our social compact, protect our equal rights & privileges and secure to ourselves and posterity in the gospel, the blessings of peace and tranquillity, Do mutually agree to adopt the following articles of agreement, made, ordained, & declared by the proper authorities of the Church of our United Society in its senior departments as a summary of the principles, rules and regulations originally established in said church, and which we as members thereof agree to keep and maintain both in our collective and individual capacities, as a constitution and firm Covenant, which shall stand as a lawful testimony of the terms & conditions of our association, before all men and in all cases of question & law relating to the possession & improvement of our consecrated interest, property & estate, until the same be altered or amended by general consent and in union with the leading authorities in the institution."

Both the well-rounded organization of the young society and the satisfactory covenant reflect the strong leadership of the first ministry. That Elder Benjamin was an able and tireless leader is to be learned from a thumbnail sketch written by one of his contemporaries. "April 10—1818—He seems to be everywhere, sees and knows everything just how it is getting along—at Black Lick, Drakes Creek and at home." Five years later Benjamin was expending his energy, not only at Gasper, but at Union Village for the Shaker cause as a whole. "Oct. 4, 1823—Elder B. at Union Village helped McNemar revise and correct his *Testimony*." Such energetic leadership was productive of results; yet the time was not far distant when the "sceptre was to depart from Judah."

VII

THE BROAD ROAD

IT WOULD SEEM THAT A WRITTEN AND SIGNED covenant, an increase in the number of meetings held, an active and capable ministry, as well as a decided growth in spirit, would mean that the South Union community had become a Kentucky Utopia. But this was far from being true. Although there was a noticeable growth in many ways, the number of members had dropped almost forty per cent from its peak of 349 in 1827 to only 214 Believers in 1836.

It was inevitable that people would move away from the colony when the novelty of communal living lost its appeal. It was also an inescapable fact that some would lack the fortitude necessary to maintain the high standards of the newly adopted religious and social pact. Another explanation of the decrease in membership is to be found in the onward spread of the frontier. The people of the world had begun moving westward during the second decade of the century. "Oct. 15, 1816 Ho for Missouri! Multitudes of teams passing with families from the upper counties moving to the Missouri territory." By 1825 the movement was at its peak. "Oct. 28, 1825 Many movers all this month going to Missouri. Not many slaves along. Most are the poorer classes fleeing from Kentucky." A similar statement dated a month later evidences the continuous stream of the same classes. "Westward Ho! A great many movers with their white-covered wagons moving west. Mostly poor people—but few are slaves." The excitement of the passing parade began to affect the less zealous Shakers so that they too moved on to the new lands. "Nov., 1828 Esther Barnett off with Jas. McCord at last. The trustees paid her portion of $175.00 & off she goes to Missouri."

That this matter of members turning away remained an unsolved problem for the sect can be seen in Elder Eades' statement written in 1872. "We are still dying as we did in 1835 taking in all who apply, repeat and repeat at the experiment—but no sooner do they get to be full fed than at least 75% turn off!"

In their attempt to find a solution, the 1835 ministry planned extra meeting periods, which came to be known as Union meetings. When they were started in January, 1836, they were said to be the first such meetings ever held at the society. The plan was that on Sunday afternoon at five and on Tuesday and Friday evenings at seven the brethren and sisters who lived opposite one another were to meet together for singing and social conversations. It was hoped especially that the supervised social meetings would be a cure for the sometimes unruly conduct in the kitchens and work shops.

The meetings failed in their purpose, for both the disorder and the indifference seemed to spread. Now and then even the regular worship services had to be dismissed after the first song because of what was termed as "so much death." The same "death" was responsible for openly expressed dissatisfaction. Eliphaz, for one, wondered why the ministry would take John into the meetinghouse "unlearned as he is—when others had educated and prepared themselves for it." The answer was given when the elder wrote: "Meaning himself, no wonder at all." The meaning becomes even clearer in the news item of a later date which states that Eliphaz left for "the world" accompanied by Maria.

When the indifferent members "turned off", the Shaker journalists, under the terms of the covenant, had to make a written statement as to the "leavetaking." These accounts were examined at the end of the year by the ministry. Those entrusted with the keeping of the records were always staunch Believers, whose depth of conviction made them somewhat intolerant of the backsliders. Often the written accounts of the departures were marked with invective headings. These headings are clear indication that the journalists thought the ones leaving were refusing the higher plane of living in returning to "the world." There are such headings as "Backwards they go," or "Backed off the track," or perhaps just "Backing off." Other colorful variants are "Renegaded", "Wormed out", "Off the hinges", "Trotting fast", "Absconding", "Off to Babylon", or "Fleshed Off: Lucy M... with Carl M...." A fuller account of two others who "fleshed off" concerns the slave Justinian, who, though he had returned after his first excursion, was soon to leave again. "The mulatto Justinian C... took Lucinda S... with her copperas colored bastard and departed for other timber. They should have been driven from Eden on the first transgression." Since the Shakers did not believe in marriage for themselves, the expression "Fleshed Off" was applied not only to show disapproval such as in the case above, but also to show disapproval even of those members who might be leaving to take the civil marriage vows.

There was great excitement over a certain June wedding and its attendant circumstances. "*Elopement*: Wild Goose Chase—Robert Johns and Sally Whyte went off together to Davis Hardin's who took them over into Tennessee to be made one."

But the wedding party was followed by one of Sally's relatives who persuaded the couple to return home after the ceremony, "practically unharmed in the worse point of view." The story had a sequel. A few days later a mob of sixty men headed by Davis Hardin came "to rescue Robert and Sally from their imprisonment in Shakertown." This proved to be a futile attempt. Soon afterward both Robert and Sally made public confession of their "tramping expedition" and begged forgiveness, which was extended. This was the last fling of these two; the record states that they remained at the village and "died in the faith respected by all."

As the elders recorded the numerous departures, they often added their personal interpretation. "Benj. Goodhope and Polly Whyte went to Russelville and married. Poor Ben. He fled from his persecutors in Ohio to be caught napping in Kentucky." Another who, the elder felt, had been taken unaware was Andrew Barnett. It happened that soon after Barnett had been bitten by a spider, he left the colony because of his infatuation for Betsy Miller. The account had its note of tartness. "*Backsliding*—Andrew Barnett goes off in much trouble. Betsy Miller's bite is worse than the spider, Andrew." Such entries are numerous, each flavored by some acrid observation, such as: "Old Lucy McReynolds took her flight to the world—fat enough and mad enough. . . . Fanny Youngs took her flight. Had we not better take Paul's advice and not receive young widows? . . . Two youths chose the world with its filth. Those who *will be filthy—let them be filthy*." Twenty-six years later these same two youths—James and Zerilda—came back the parents of ten children. According to their own testimony, they had had a miserable life and desired reunion with the Believers.

Two others who left were Maria and Nudge. "Aug. 28—1824—Maria Small and Nudge Nudged off together—He came back after her clothes & goods the day before they were married & some mischievous Boy quoted the negro Song as apropos—

> 'Ole Mister koon you com to soon
> You ought not a come till tomorrow afternoon'

He would have had a legal right next day." There were still others whose departures called for invective remarks. "*Backtrack*—Ruby Martin—by the assistance of Hugh Mc-

Cutcheon—mean in Hugh B.... Ann T... left with her two children. Columbus Knowles goes with her. He is just at the green age to be a fool." Or as in the case of George, who left in 1834. "The woman Thou gavest me is the trouble with George."

At times the recorder told the story in the lively words of the backsliders themselves. When Viney left the community she announced in no uncertain terms that she "would burn in hell to a cracklen" before she would return. In spite of her "big talk," she came back. Another who came and went almost regularly explained that hell was hot but that he went there now and then to cool off. There was also poor James, who said, "... he would be willing to be burned up in a log heap, if that would be his salvation—but to get it in this slow way, he'll be D... if he can stand it. So goes off with himself." John admitted that the Shaker discipline was too rigorous. "Friday, October, 1834 *Backsliding:* John ... and Sarah ... leave to hunt a cabin in the woods. John says he wants to get into a cabin so he can throw the cobs of his roasting ears through the crack in the wall, and have no one to request him to clean them up!" As usual, the writer added his own bit of practical philosophy: "But get the ear first, John, they won't come without work." One who sought more ease was Henley. "February 1, 1822 *Backing off* Henley J... went to camp meeting yesterday and found as he thinks an easier way to get to heaven."

It was hard for the true Shakers to reconcile such evident weakness as shown by the backsliders with the philosophy of that time embodying the innate goodness of man. Not only were some men weak, thought the Shakers, but some displayed very bad manners in being ungrateful. Two such cases were those of Jeptha and James. "Jeptha W... who came in rags some time since, now well dressed, takes his leave without a thank you for medicine or clothing—so the world wags," and "James J... leaves today for his old nest—looks up every old horse shoe that once was his—good enough he will need them all."

When the "Winter Shakers" left and took away property and money in proportion to what they brought, the amount was always recorded with meticulous accuracy "*Going the Broad Road:* Houston Shannon left. Given one horse valued at $60.00 and $45.00 in cash." In addition to the minute journal account, the Shaker trustees had the further protection of the signed statements from the departees themselves, stating they had received the full amount of their property.

Although a large number of the members were leaving and the population was showing a decided drop in the 1830's, there were still many new people who were making confession and signing agreements. Some of the new converts were second generation immigrants who were beginning to appear in the Kentucky settlements. During the years 1819 to 1821, confessions were made by Nahum, a Jew; two Frenchmen, Louis and Chevalier D. St. Ledger; and Carolus Perry, a German. A little later William Edwards came to the society, a Welshman who became the village cooper; Henry Lindeman a Dutchman; and John Snyder, who was hired as the blacksmith for $400.

Many of the newcomers asked to come into the Church relation. "Oct. 22, 1829—*Dedication & Signing* Agreements —23 Individuals put their names down today 6 making dedication of themselves & their all—property worth some 12,000 dollars—the Others signed agreements not to have anything for their '*work*' labor or service past, present & to come . . . Earnest souls!" Among those who came and made confession were several craftsmen. "Aug. 11, 1823 *Confession*—Charles Hirnigh to Robt. Houston—He is a tanner by trade & from New York. . . . Aug. 12, 1823—*Confession* Henry Forman to Robt. Houston—He is a plough maker by trade from Virginia. . . . Sat. Aug. 30—*Confession*—Joseph Smith, the wool carder."

During the 1820's and 1830's many were readmitted to the Shaker life. Of these applicants only a few proved to be stable in character. Too many were like William M. . . . who had joined first at Union Village and later at Pleasant Hill before coming to seek admission at South Union. When his admission was granted, the elder remarked pointedly that he hoped William would let "the third time be charm."

Recorded along with all the accounts of those who "hoved up" and those who "turned off," are some leavetakings of a different kind. These were the departures made in answer to death's summons. During the first twenty years of the colony's busy life, the journals contain few references to the deaths of members; but in the decade of the 1830's the hard, busy days began to take their toll, and the deaths of many of the older members were recorded. One of the most remarkable things about the Shaker colonies is the longevity of the members. Evidently the Shakers were very conscious of this and expected nothing else. When Mother Lucy Wright, head of the New Lebanon colony, died in her sixty-second year, the news of her death was recorded in the South Union journal, followed by the question: "Why so short lived?" Again, when Sister Sarah Robinson died at the age of seventy-two, the recorder wrote, "too soon Sarah." A twentieth-century Shaker who knew long life was Emma J. Neal of New Lebanon who died in December, 1943, at the age of ninety-seven.

The general good health of the Shakers is attested to by the low death rate during the cold plague of 1814 to 1815 and by their seeming immunity to the Asiatic cholera epidemics of 1832 to 1833 and 1835. During the time the cholera epidemic raged along the rivers, the Shaker merchants were often on boats where passengers were dying of the malady. Yet the brethren remained "confident and unconcerned for themselves because they did not believe the Shakers would be attacked by it." Strangely enough, only one of them ever died of the disease. Jesse McCombs, who was never strong, contracted the malady and died in St. Louis in November, 1834. Perhaps the Shaker merchants may have escaped the cholera because they were more prudent in their eating than was the average boatman.

The epidemic also came close to those who remained at the colony, for the neighboring town of Russellville was greatly affected. Many people left the town to stay in the country or to live in tents outside the town. The Bowling Green *Gazette* for September 1 carried an acount of the Russellville disaster, reporting the death rate as being a "dozen a day." The number dead up to that time had been sixty whites and forty-three blacks. When the Shakers were called upon to house many refugees, the women spent much of their time making soups and giving medical care. The only death at Shakertown during the epidemic was that of a young New York man who came in on the stage.

Some few yards south of the principal part of the village was the burial ground, where the young New Yorker was buried in the row reserved for strangers. The members were buried "males and females side by side just as they decease, but the different orders... in different rows." The graves were always marked with simple, hand-lettered stones. The regular funeral service consisted of hymns and talks which were made by those "who spoke to the purpose and to the satisfaction of the hearers."

The accounts of the deaths occurring at South Union are couched in the euphemistic phraseology of the times. It was December 23, 1832, when "Isabella Paisley finished her course in time 35 minutes after 5 P.M. in the 85th year of her age, full of years and full of honor." And on July 27, 1833, there died in his seventy-eighth year Charles Eades, "who had fought through the Revolutionary War for liberty of Body and gained it, and then fought equally brave for liberty of Soul, and gained that also." Other such euphemisms were "breathed her last inspiration in time", "shuffled off his mortal coil", "passed over beyond the vail of time", and "took her flight to a better world." The accounts frequently carried an expressed benediction such as "Sister Frances passed out to her long home . . . Peace to her ashes."

On December 9, 1935, it was written sorrowfully that "Eldress Molly Goodrich is no more in body on earth. She left the body this morning 12 minutes after 12 o'clock in the 56th year of her age, having been born in Hancock Township, Berkshire County, Massachusetts." The eldress who so long had helped to direct the activities at South Union was deeply mourned. "*Funeral* — The Society attending—commenced this evening. At 3 o'clock, in consequence of the advancing decomposition of the corpse—& continued until the day was pretty well spent—so much so, that by the time the burial was completed the sun was sinking below the horizon—The meeting was appropriate to the occasion— a great deal of feeling, love, sorrow, gratitude, and respect were manifested by the body at large. It seemed that Elder Benjamin could not say enough in her praise—She had been to him as a guardian Angel & Eldress Mercy was also mentioned with feelings of gratitude and respect but now that both of them were gone—the former to heaven above, the latter to her heavenly home at New Lebanon—Eld. Benjamin seemed to feel like a father left with a house full of motherless children—There were several effusions composed for the occasion all alike meritorious."

Only one of the songs honoring Molly was sung; the others were read, probably because the texts were not yet adapted to the tunes. When the elder had spoken and the hymns had been read or sung, all passed by the casket to have their last look at their beloved eldress. Several exclaimed aloud in sorrow. "Sister Sally Whyte was impressed to exclaim—'O ye sons, protect the daughters! lead them not into carnality nor forbidden paths. Do, Do I entreat you, protect her motherless daughters!!' This was said with much emphasis & feeling with a flood of tears—it seemed that Mother Molly inspired her— She repeated that the daughters now, more especially needed the protection of the sons—seeing their Mother was gone— The gift was heartily responded to by the assembled multitude.—Elder Sister Susan Robinson took the opportunity to express her thankfulness for Eldress Molly's help in time of need—the same reiterated by many voices." After the funeral Eldress Molly's temporal things were divided according to her request that each person in the colony should have a love token.

The society members had hardly adjusted themselves to the loss of their favorite eldress when others of the pioneer organizers began to return to the East. In the summer of 1833 the emissary Issachar Bates, who had spent considerable time at South Union, left the western territory. Two years later South Union's other Eldress Molly—Mercy Picket—left after having given "twenty-five years of service without blemish."

By 1836 there was evidence in the daily chronicle that the relation between the veteran easterners and their young western charges had become strained. The story tells itself in the pages of the journal. "Jan. 1, 1836—214 souls. Elder Benjamin very weakly and troubled in mind. . . . Jan. Sab. 10. *Meeting.* Elder Benjamin administered strong reproof to such as said 'We are all coming to nothing—and praying at the same time it might be so'—poor, pitiful, rotten hearted souls & cowardly—pretty strong, Father. . . . May 15. It seems there is some stir about all the Eastern Believers returning home as they are mostly now gone from Ohio & Ky. Save Eld. Benj. & Eldress Anne Cole. There is at this time a pretty strong feeling hereabouts that Elder Benjamin's gift at South Union (omission in journal). He is almost alone with no Eastern Sister nor brother to keep him company. He no doubt feels that the usual respect and obedience hitherto yielded is giving place to more or less independence and insubordination & it is more than likely he will soon follow the others who have already gone. This cold feeling towards our head is doubtless wrong, but it is a query, whether there is a possibility of altering it for the better." By June the elder seems to have been winding up his South Union affairs. "June 2—Trip Elder Benjamin set off by the Stage today to Nashville—His object is to get a large clock which he had imported from England either finished off or changed for another."

On the ninth the elder returned, having been detained in "getting some books bound." At a society meeting a few days later, "Elder Benj. attended & among other things gave strict orders concerning Brn. & boys running to *Quigleys Store* at the Cross Roads—that no one was to go to that Store but the Trustee Eli McLean or by his order—doubtful if this will be attended to. . . . July 1, 1836. *Breakfast Lecture.* As soon as we had finished eating our breakfast this morning Eld. Benjamin came in & proceeded to give us a sound castigation, for the violation of our agreement entered into on the 31st of last December, in which we solemnly agreed to hire no more slave labor on our premises—But it seems they are brought in, in utter & total disregard of the general agreement & that without a word of request on the subject . . . Now he desired that every slave should be immediately dismissed—even if the whole months wages had to be given to their masters as the result. In other words—slaves were not necessary—2nd, it had not been done in union—'but the sceptre had departed from Judah'—Our good Elder could not enforce his command."

When the elder left South Union a few weeks later, he was given a "suitable leavetaking" and was accompanied as far as "Bowling Green and over Big Barren River by Eldress Malinda, Sister Sarah and Harvey." Going with him as far as Louisville were McLean, Shannon, and Johns. Trustee McLean gave Benjamin $563.00 as expense money in addition to his steamboat passage to Cincinnati. After leaving South Union, both Elder Benjamin and Eldress Molly lived at their eastern home for approximately twenty years before death came to each at the age of eighty-two.

As the older members left South Union and the younger members began to take over the duties of leadership, the colony tended to review its first thirty years of life. The reviewers found that the Gospel Love which had been preached and practiced by the serious-minded ministry had been forsaken by some but that it had been accepted wholeheartedly by others. They also realized that, on one hand, the years had been marked by turmoil and change, with the population showing a drop after its 1827 peak; but, on the other hand, there had been a deepening of spirit on the part of those who really believed. Furthermore, the true Shakers were glad that the religious tenets which included economic policies were now fully stabilized and written into a covenant. In general they felt that the immature community had attained its full stature as a United Society of Believers.

VIII

TO LEAVEN THEIR WORK

D URING THE YEARS FROM 1816 TO 1836 THE
South Union society not only effected its full religious
organization but also established numerous industries, formu-
lated its economic policies, and greatly increased its land
holdings. In 1817 alone the society contracted for twelve
hundred acres at seven thousand dollars, some of the land
costing only four dollars. The very next year land values
began a pronounced rise; the trustees, who had held the average
of all their holdings to $6.25, had to pay $20.00 an acre for
a desirable tract. Not long afterwards they sold sixteen acres
from their own rich Black Lick fields at $25.00, land for
which they had paid an average of $8.00 only five years before.
The elder who recorded the sale stated with charming simplicity, "Good sale."

There had been a society agreement in 1816 not to go into
debt for anything except bread and water, salt and medicine.
Yet when there was land to be bought and sufficient cash, or
even the initial payment, was lacking, the sympathetic leaders
allowed the trustees to assume large debts, as well as to borrow
money from a Bowling Green bank. Perhaps they reasoned
that since land was essential they were not violating the agreement too much. They continued, however, to speak in the
church services against going into debt and to regret the
necessity for borrowing money. "Wed. Fbr. 17-1819—*Society
Meeting*—In this meeting (½ p. 7 p.m.) positive counsel

given to no more *Go in debt*—not for the value of a cent, unless by the trustees themselves, in counsel."

Twice during the period of expansion the colony's financial strain was relieved by "gifts" from the older colonies. One gift of two thousand came from Union Village; another was received from the parent colony. Although the sums received were referred to as gifts, they were actually loans which were later repaid.

In 1824 and 1825 the trustees felt they were particularly justified in buying land for which they could not pay in full because town lots were being laid off on the lands east and west of them; and, according to rumor, taverns were to be put up. In order to avoid the perpetual annoyance of such neighbors, the brethren concluded that it would be better to have the annoyance of debt. In buying "Rowdy Town," they learned how the economic principle of "unearned increment" works, for they were forced to pay twice what the land was intrinsically worth just because it lay next their own well-cared-for farm land. Payment was to be made in specie or in its value in Commonwealth paper which was then at a discount of 45 per cent. By 1826 the trustees had increased the society holdings to approximately six thousand very fertile acres. The land, in scattered tracts, was watered by Gasper River and by three creeks—Clear Fork, Black Lick, and Drakes.

In all their land expansion program the trustees, with an innate sense of land values, made only one bad purchase. This was the Warren County mill seat known as Mill Point, located on Drakes Creek some sixteen miles from the village. Here the brethren expected to erect a second flour mill and a third saw mill to serve the people who could not easily come to South Union, thereby increasing the income for the society. But two months after they acquired the property a jury appointed by the court examined and condemned the "mill seat." Feeling that the judgment was unfair, the Shakers immediately contracted for 169 more acres, and a month later they bought an additional 400 for "7s-6d per acre." In all, the Drakes Creek property, bought in four separate tracts, included 1,141 acres. The usual down payment was $200. Once at least it was paid "down in horses."

The trustees fought the condemnation further by appealing to a higher court. Samuel Whyte, who went to the state capital in June, 1818, with a petition signed by twelve hundred of the neighbors, brought home the good news that the decision favored the society. So construction began anew.

In order to be "on the job" a number moved from South Union to the Mill Point. "Apr. 14—1818—*Ho! For Drakes Creek*—a proper big move—Three sisters go to cook. Two wagon loads of furniture & provision—Also Saml. Shannon & Black Matt. John Rankin goes to begin the orchard." By May thirty men were living and working at the new property. Eldress Molly was pleased that the men regularly made the long trip home for the Sunday services. "Sat. June 6, 1818— *Home to Meeting*—About 20 of the Brethren return home to attend meetings Sabbath—& all go back Mondays—This feels very agreeable to me to see the Brethren this interested in their spiritual welfare—Molly. . . . Sab. 13—*Note John Rankin Senior* comes every Saturday on foot to attend meetings from Drakes Creek, some times others with him—this is the way to prosper—Molly." Ten years later the loyal John was still making the trip back to South Union. "June 15—1828—Aged John Rankin walked home from Mill Point today. He is now in his 71st year! and this walk not less than 16 miles. He has for a long time been assisting at the saw mill." Appended to the account is the comment written much later by Elder Eades. "I must improve my time well. I shall not live to walk 16 miles in my 71st year."

Christmas was the time for a general homecoming. "Dec. 25—1818—*Christmas* Meeting at 10 a.m. All here from Drakes Creek. I spoke & read—Had a joyful and powerful meeting, all seemed happy & thankful—indeed were so." One of those returning for the holidays said Merry Christmas "with a nice parcel of fish."

After much work had been done on the dam and the mills, the laborers realized that the land was so cavernous that in dry weather the water would disappear into the great sinks on the hill above the mill, go under the bluff, and come out below the mill. This, of course, meant a loss of power. Over a period of two years the greatest effort was made to fill the sinks. The journal entry for August 23, 1820, sounded a note of discouragement. "Work on the Sinks of Drakes Creek has been prosecuted—Doing only present good." Matters grew more hopeless. The project grew more expensive. The brethren, unaccustomed to financial reverses and failure, appealed to their neighbors for help. They circulated a written statement designed to convince outsiders that the mill would be a great "Public Utility" which would contribute to the wealth and improvement of the county. It pointed out that the Shakers would incur a very heavy expense since by law they were compelled to keep open the navigation of the stream. That would mean opening a canal round their dam or constructing slopes and locks in such a manner as to admit the safe and easy passage of boats and water craft. Since this expense would be additional to the sum required to erect the necessary mill works, the society would need considerable help from the good citizens nearby. Whether the neighborhood was unresponsive or whether the Shakers decided against the subscription plan is unknown; the fact remains that the list shows only three signers who promised to pay the small total of $12.00. At last the Shakers admitted that the purchase was an unfortunate one. Fourteen years later they were willing to sell the mill and all the land at a loss of $22,500. This was one of the two greatest losses, aside from war losses, that the South Union Shakers ever experienced. The second did not occur until 1870 when the Bowling Green bank failed because its cashier T. C. Calvert stole a large sum to cover his cotton speculations. The $60,000 loss was in deposits and in lumps of gold which the trustees had placed in the bank vault. Eventually part of the loss was restored to the society.

Minor losses were suffered from time to time, such as the 1829 Christmas poisoning by strychnine of twelve horses. Many of the chickens died too—after "having picked around where the Dr. made a post mortem." Angered by the whole matter someone wrote:

> Who did commit this horrid crime
> Can any mortal tell?!—
> Who has the will, or who the power
> To keep them out of H——!!!!

In spite of the financial setbacks at Drakes Creek, the trustees went ahead with the society's enlargement program. Not only was the farm acreage increased but the village came to have many new buildings. The earliest buildings had been the log dwellings belonging to the first Logan County converts. To these had been added frame buildings such as the 1810 schoolhouse and the meetinghouse. Gradually all the first buildings, except the schoolhouse, were replaced by brick ones, all designed on the principles of simplicity, endurance, and utilitarianism.

Among the first to be replaced was the meetinghouse, the location being changed from the north side of the main road to the south. Next came a brick home for the East Family. At its completion the society held a celebration. It was a simple ceremony but one that called for agility on the part of the forty-one-year-old Eldress Molly who was asked to climb to the top and lay the last brick in the roof peak.

After the East House was finished, the workmen began at once to dig the foundation cellar of the great Center House, the outside of which was completed in 1824. Ten years later the large North House was finished. According to the Shaker custom, the date cut into the long stone slab over the front entrance of each house was the year when the outside work was finished, not the date when the work of evacuation started. Many years were required for the completion of the large buildings because most of the materials were prepared by the members themselves. The bricks were burned at the village, the nails were cut, the lumber dressed, and the stone was hauled from the nearby quarries. At Drakes Creek the workmen prepared sixty thousand black oak shingles for the Center House. The women helped with the building program in various ways. Under supervision of David Smith, the boss painter, two of them painted the "venetian blinds" for the Center House, the chosen color being verdigris green.

It was not until May, 1833, eleven years after the large central building was begun that the men and women who belonged to the First Family moved to their new home and became known as the Center House Family. Here they found their appointed places and arranged their furniture. New handmade bedsteads were already in the rooms, and in some of the rooms there were built-in drawers and cabinets. The furniture which they moved from their old quarters consisted of "bureaus, chests, boxes, and chairs." Around the walls of each room a little below the top level of the doors ran a strip of wood filled with wooden pegs. This arrangement was the usual one in Shaker buildings everywhere. Such orderly rows of pegs meant that articles not in use were to be placed on the pegs. The long hallways were artistically broken up by a series of arched doorways. Near the front of the building two graceful stairways, one for the men and one for the women, connected the four floors. A large brass clock was put in the lower hall, and a good wooden clock was placed in the upstairs hall between the elders' rooms. Elder Benjamin, who had come from a Connecticut family of clockmakers, lovingly cared for the clocks as long as he was at South Union. The elder's grandfather Ben Youngs and his uncle Benjamin Youngs both had been well-known clockmakers. The uncle, who was also a silversmith, had operated shops in Windsor, Connecticut, and in Schenectady, New York, before joining the Watervliet, New York, Shakers in 1806.

The moving day for the Center Family was so filled with activity that the noon meal was overlooked; but at four o'clock in the afternoon a supper was prepared, and the ministry attended to observe the Lord's Supper with the family in their new home. At this service a song of dedication was sung. The third stanza of the hymn emphasized the character requirements of the people who were to live in the great new building.

> Lo! the Building is prepared
> God has spared us to see
> For the righteous it is reared
> Honest Souls who will be free
> Zealous, living interested
> In all good they find to do
> Of old self & pride divested
> Careful neat & decent too.

The Shakers continued with this large building program until the middle of the century. Not only did they build the very large dwelling houses known as the Center House, the East House, the West House, and the North House, but they also constructed a new home for the ministry and a large frame building which they called the office. On the building program also were specially planned shops for the carpenter, the blacksmith, the doctor, and the wheelwright. In addition, the village boasted of a buzz saw house, a chair shop, a brick shop, a bark house, an ice house, a stone shop, a wash house, a milk house, a preservatory, and a carriage house. Connected with the construction was other related work such as preparing lime and brick kilns, sinking vats for the tanning operations, and digging wells and cellars for the fruit and vegetables.

Although this large program required much time, the Shakers did not neglect the general improvement of their property.

The meetinghouse yard, newly leveled and sown in bluegrass, was soon enclosed by a paling fence which contained two gates —one for the women and one for the men. Connecting the many family houses were stone walks, the width of which did not allow the Believers to walk two and two.

Throughout the village grounds many trees, both useful and ornamental ones, were planted. In the summer and fall carefully tended flower beds added color. A sun dial, which proved very interesting to visitors, was set in the office yard. The property limits were marked with corner stones bearing the initials of the original land owners—John Rankin, Jess McComb and others. Into the new buildings went handmade furniture, all of which was simple and practical in design. In building furniture as well as houses, the Shakers made a very real contribution to American culture by their consistent choice of good materials and good lines.

So strenuous were their industrial and agricultural programs that the Kentucky Shakers soon came to understand the good sense of mixing fun and the spirit of competition along with the steady work program; consequently, they often met together to accomplish a piece of work, making of it a social occasion. Such activity was commonly labeled a *Frolick* or a *Bee.* The sisters had many spinning frolics when there would be "music in the wheels." Favorites with the men were the numerous grubbing bees, chopping frolics, logrollings, and cornhuskings. Quite often the bees were held at night, after a long day which had already been filled with hard work. "March, 1828 Night Frolick: Fifty men gathered about dark for the purpose of gathering and burning brush. Sight was beautiful. We burned the brush clean off of 2½ acres before nine and returned home."

One of the principal social bees was that of cornhusking, in which the Shakers followed the usual custom of the neighborhoods everywhere in the corn territory. The huskings were ordinarily arranged for moonlight nights. When the company

gathered, two captains were appointed to choose sides alternately from the company present. The sides being ready, a
signal was given and the huskers began on the "long ridge of
corn." Much cheering, laughing, and talking filled the air;
and in the days before the alcohol pledge was signed, the jollity
would increase as the bottle was handed around. At other times
the whiskey was measured out to the worker once or twice
during the husking "to warm them and keep up the spirits"
until the job was done. After that everybody gathered to hear
the announcement of the winners and to eat the roast pig and
to drink coffee or sassafras tea.

The Shakers always had a large amount of corn to husk
because, in addition to the corn raised by themselves, the trustees bought the surplus crops from their neighbors. However,
much of the husking was done without the accompanying fun
derived from a gala social gathering. On such occasions the
men, already tired from a full day's work, went alone to a
neighboring farm and husked as many as one hundred barrels
of corn which had been bought. The Shaker men never
dreamed of a forty-hour week!

It was a common practice to hold a bee in honor of someone
or some event. Eldress Molly's fiftieth birthday was such an
occasion. After the special dinner and union feast held at the
Center House, the sisters honored Molly with a "spinning
frolick" and spun 120 runs and wove 40 yards. It was the
women again who decided it would be proper to clean the
meetinghouse yard in remembrance of Elder Benjamin, who
was visiting the New Lebanon colony. Sixty sisters "turned
out and made a proper big bee," working all day. A few weeks
later as the time of the leader's return drew nearer, the women
felt that the road should be repaired. Since it was July, the
men could not stop their farm tasks for the road work; therefore, the sisters, hating to have "mud holes and shattered fences
stare the elder in the face first thing on his return," undertook
the road work themselves. All the able-bodied women turned

out for the task. They were aided by one of the boys, who helped with "one old horse, a cart, and a few tools." Appended to the journal account is the succinct remark that "the women worked hard and did little."

Besides the large group of activities there were competitive races for two or three workers. No doubt the contests served a double purpose: they were found to speed the work and to satisfy the desire for fun. One such race was held between J. R. Eades and J. Whyte, who were shoemakers. Eades commenced at 5 A.M. and finished six good pairs of shoes by 7:30 P.M. Whyte, who started ten minutes late, did not finish his six pairs until 9 P.M.; so Eades was declared the winner "by neck and shoulders."

Harvey Eades and Milton Robinson, both of them in their early twenties, engaged in a race while plaiting straw for the hats made for sale. The race, which started at three o'clock in the morning, lasted until nine o'clock that night. Only one hour of the entire time was taken for meals; during the sixteen hours of actual work Eades plaited 120 yards of straw and Robinson plaited 114 yards. But the winner remarked that the race was a draw because "Milton's was as much better as mine was longer." This was considered a real day's work, for it was thought that if a man braided two hundred yards in a month along with his other tasks he had done remarkably well.

The Shakers enjoyed outdoor meals, and they found many excuses for arranging them. When the men were working on the new road north to their big timber tract, the women prepared a dinner and took it down to the creek bend where it was spread on a temporarily constructed table eighty feet long. Sixty-six people sat down at once to partake of the bountiful meal.

A combination picnic and hazel nut hunt was held in September, 1833, when a large party went southeast beyond Pone Springs to gather the nuts. After having a glorious time, they returned to South Union, the two dearbornes being used to convey both the hazel nuts and several of the weakly sisters.

Pleasure trips made through the surrounding countryside were known as "rideouts." A picnic lunch was often taken along. "A group went out on a spree or picnic to have a little recreation. They went as far as the head of Muddy this side of Russelville (8 miles) and returned home safely after sundown." After riding over to visit with the Black Lick or Watervliet Family, one group "... baked their cake, fried their chicken, and made coffee in Jefferson's shanty, and then ate two meals out under a shade tree."

Further proof that the Shakers believed the cliché about all work and no play is to be found in a number of stories preserved in the society chronicles. As the Center House neared completion, the plasterers worked hard every day, even "bending the Sabbath." In late November after weeks of such high-speed work, the three principal plasterers "took off a day" for recreation and "chose the gun and the Chase." Armed and equipped they betook themselves to the forest and returned about sunset with three wild turkeys and a basket full of squirrels—"Jemina Rice added a chicken or two and on Friday morning we all enjoyed their recreation with Jemina's kindness."

Even stump speaking was offered as relief to steady manual labor. "Apr. 22—1831—*Finished Shearing the Sheep*—& by a bargain with the shearers for a stump speech—H. L. Eades agreed to speak one hour at the close—so Eld. Benj. says '*Harvey stump spoke it.*'"

The children living at the colony, all of whom had their assigned tasks, knew that the completion of their tasks was often the signal for some planned recreation. "June 3, 1818. *Fishing.* Sandy & all the little boys go to Drakes Creek fishing & for a little out pic-nic. Return the 5th. ... April, 1837 Casendana and her flock of little girls went out to the Cave for recreation and amusement after having been confined some weeks platting."

The men and women very seldom worked at the same tasks, but there was an exchange of aid if it was needed. Some of the men always turned the wash mill for the sisters. If the men were caught in the fields by a drenching rain, the women would get a hot drink ready—perhaps a ginger stew. Now and then in the rush of harvest days they all went to the fields together to save the crop. Once when many of the Shakers and Shaker-esses were out pulling the flax, "the muses got into J. R. Eades," and he began to compose and sing. The beginning lines of his spontaneous work song ran as follows:

There is a sweet union that's strong like a chain
'Tis felt in the flax field and in saving the grain.

Everything about the work routine was orderly. A plan was evolved in 1831 by which the sisters were to blow three blasts on the trumpet precisely fifteen minutes before meals. All the men were to quit then and come to the house to be ready for the meal and the union meeting which was held daily by each family in its respective meeting room.

Even though the work program was a part of the saintly living, it was the custom for the Shakers to observe Sunday as a day of rest. At times, however, they found it expedient to get the ox out of the ditch. The word choice of the following headings indicates the recorded activities to have been de-partures from the regular custom. "July 14, 1822 *Temporal Sabbath:* Brethren turn out today to save and stack their hay. No meetings in consequence.... July 21, 1822 *Trading Sunday:* As soon as Publick Meeting was over, Jas. McCord and others start on horse back to Mill Point on horsetrading busi-ness.... June, Sabbath 28, 1829 *Bending the Sabbath—* Twenty-seven young brethren bound and handstacked twenty acres of wheat today—right good worship!"

When such work kept the men from attending services, the women took charge. Often on moonlight nights, the women had to hold the regular evening service, for on such nights special liberty was given for the brethren to "chore around" in the dooryards until nine o'clock, thus taking advantage of the moonlight to put the fences in good repair.

The general impression today seems to be that the Shaker villages were always quiet places where the members worked undisturbed by anything which could be labelled excitement. This is far from being the truth, for the house journals and individual diaries are filled with unusual and exciting events: unexpected gifts; journeys to nearby towns, with sometimes an accident enroute; suicides; robberies, particularly during the Civil War; and fires.

The journals contain a wide variety of happenings. "October 12, 1819 Over the dam! Yoke of oxen and cart swept over the mill dam at Drakes Creek! Killed of course."

One who deliberately went over the dam was James Gorin. "Suicide: —Hired youth deliberately got into the canoe said farewell & purposely steered over the Dam. the reckless youths carcass was not found for 4 or 5 days afterward." Less disastrous was the accident in which young Robert Paisley found himself being swept over the dam. "He quickly took his seat in the skiff and trusted luck—It went over safely & kept right side up." Another who was involved in an accident was subject to Father Benjamin's criticism. "May 2, 1822 Nelson Miller got his leg broken by tilting a cart and I hope he will be a better boy so that he may not get his neck broken. B."

Each day had its bit of excitement. "Aug. 12, 1824 Tonight three horses were stolen.... Dec. 2, 1827 Party of 8 Indians camped here.... Nov., 1827 Johnathan Douglas is here trying to get Sister Sally McComb to elope with him, but she is true blue and will not be persuaded to forsake the cross.... July 11, 1828 A mullato baby was left on the shop steps. ...August 4, 1828 The foundling was taken to Russelville and delivered up to the court. . . . Jan. 15, 1830 John Seth Meigs hanged himself by the neck with two or three kerchiefs in an old vacated frame house. He was buried 'Sans ceremonies.' "

Chief among the social events were the visits made by many leaders of national importance. South Union was a convenient stopping place for anyone who was traveling between Louisville and Nashville. The hospitality and good food caused many a traveler, even national leaders, to plan to reach Shakertown around meal time. "June 17, 1819 *President Monroe* and party and Gen'l Jackson and family dine here today. . . . Sept. 15, 1829 *Extra Visit*—The Hon. Henry Clay, John J. Crittenden and company took dinner at our tavern today— about forty at table. . . . Sept. 24, 1829 *The two great statesmen* returned here this evening and a splendid supper was prepared. A number of Brethren as on the former occasion ate with them. They were presented with a fine hat on their visit."

Then there was the time ex-Governor Sam Houston visited the colony. "Sabbath, June 15, 1834 *Ex-Governor Sam Houston* of Tennessee is here on a visit and attended meeting today. J. R. Eades addressed the world." Another person of distinction who visited South Union was the veteran leader and author from Ohio. "Aug. 5—1830. *Arrival*—Eld. Eleazar Wright alias R. McNemar arrived unexpectedly—walked from Bowling Green—saddlebags on his arms."

Numerous other visitors, who gave the Believers much to talk about for weeks, came during these years. There was the man who came pretending to be deaf and dumb. After being admitted, he remained several weeks before it was discovered that he was a thief and that his affliction was feigned.

Another who attracted attention was the young Texas Ranger John Frierson who introduced himself as a lawyer and minister but who "proved to be a real scamp . . . fluent in words but plum dead in spirit." Frierson was asked to leave after he had forged a free pass for a Negro in the community.

There was also the eastern merchant who came with his darky waiter. During the night, the merchant died. When the darky was told of his master's death, he remarked sadly that "Man may 'pint, but God will disappint."

In August, 1827, a circus and animal show came to Shakertown. Elder Benjamin considered it: "A disgraceful caravan of nonsense—exhibited under the shade trees near the office at South Union today. Believers mostly attended. Circus Riders and Shame!" Three years before the arrival of the caravan, there had been an elephant exhibition: "Aug. 2. The great elephant Bettie was showed here today—& tonight 3 horses were stolen."

Nature provided the South Union Society with some of the daily excitement. It was on February 20, 1820, that the wild pigeons came over in such large numbers that large trees were badly broken under the weight of the birds when they roosted. "*Pigeons*—Clouds of wild pigeons flying North to South seemingly a mile in width and as far as the eye could see through the falling snow. Query? Where could they come from?"

The Shakers made a habit of trying to domesticate wild fowls, when they could be caught. "February 1, 1821 *Wild Geese*—Caught—They alight and are fed at our pond with those that are tame—until we can drive them under a shed in the fence corner. When the wild one is caught and the first joint of one wing taken off, so he remains." Quails were even put into coops in the hope that the birds might be domesticated. Who can be surprised at the phenomenal success of the religio-socialists when they were so assiduous in taking advantage of every opportunity?

Less welcome outdoor visitants were the locusts and the army worms. "May 28, 1821 *Locusts* The Fourteen or seventeen year Locusts made the welkin ring with their eternal song— Pharaoh!" In May, 1824, the army worms appeared in the wheat fields of the Shaker farms. In order to combat the worms, which were "playing Destruction," the religious farmers pulled ropes over the fields. The elder thought that this fighting the worms might be better termed frightening the worms, but even so, he did not think the worms were very badly scared.

Any mark of community progress was considered important enough for a day's entry in the journal. "Jan. 2, 1823 *Wooden Shoes* introduced. John McCombs has a pair. . . . Sept. 1823 1st new carriage made here—a good two horse carriage for the ministry. . . . May 22, 1826 First Post Office established at South Union. David Smith today received the appointment of Post Master for the office now designated South Union Post Office. The appointment was made by the Post Master General in the first of April last. . . . May 18, 1829 Union Village, Ohio, sent a cooking stove as a present. This day is famous as having the first cooking stove set in our kitchen—Farewell to pots and skillets and frying pans. . . . April 22, 1830 Mail stage first time this year. . . . April, 1833 Hair mattress—made by Sister Malinda for Eldress Molly. The first made at South Union. . . . May 9, 1833 A large stone sink was placed in the Centre House Kitchen. . . . Nov. 1, 1833 Arrived the Franklin stoves for new house."

Or the day's happening which caught attention might be an astronomical wonder. . . . "July 12, 1819 A large comet appears about 5 degrees West of north. . . . Feb. 12, 1831 An eclipse of the sun. Moon in centre left a golden ring suspended in the heavens. . . . Nov. 12, 1833 Falling stars: This morning the whole heavens as far as the eye could see was filled with meteors or shooting stars. It seemed like millions of stars falling to earth. Beautiful."

Weather conditions were always recorded, because the weather was important to the agricultural community. Sometimes the weather was at such extreme temperature as to become not the ordinary, but the extraordinary news item for the day. On February 7, 1823, for example, the temperature had been sixteen degrees below zero, but the record for February 15, 1831, was far worse for the Kentuckians.

At sunset	zero
At 7 o'clock	8 below
At 8 o'clock	20 "
At 10 "	22 "
At 12 "	25 "

"Then," says the journalist, "it began to rise and I returned to my couch." January 26, 1832, was recorded as a day having a temperature of eighteen degrees below zero. "Old people say it equals the cold Friday of 1805, and the strange feature of the cold weather here has been that it has been moderate in the north." On February 8 three years later, it was seventeen degrees below; mice and rats froze, and the society's cat died of cold.

After the strenuous days of building and land expansion during which the Shakers had learned to leaven their hard work with play, they began to look forward to enlarging their several industries and to adding new ones. It was in the subsequent large-scaled program of business enterprises that the backwoods men and women began to evolve and practice the "economic virtue" which closely paralleled that of the Puritans in the seventeenth century.

IX

THE ONE THING NEEDFUL

FROM THE VERY EARLIEST DAYS OF THEIR organization, the Shakers considered the economic phase of their life of paramount importance. While directing the activities of the first struggling Shaker community at Nishayuna, Mother Ann had spent much of her time and energy emphasizing the principles of industry and economy; and these principles became so deeply embedded in the religious thinking of the Shakers everywhere that industry, honesty, and frugality came to be as greatly stressed as prayer and humbleness.

Believing earnestly in the practical virtues of spiritual living, the South Union Shakers came to speak of money as "the one thing needful." It is through a peculiar twist in Shaker thought that Christ's expression used in commending Mary's desire for spiritual things as opposed to Martha's concern for the welfare of their guest should be thus applied to the gain of material things. Yet, the Shakers believed so firmly in economic success that "the one thing needful" came to represent, not the spiritual virtues, but money. It must be remembered, however, that their gain of money was the natural result of constant, honest endeavor. In following this economic virtue as part of their religious creed, the Believers were exceptionally zealous in carrying on manifold enterprises, in raising all possible crops, and in finding good markets for all their products. Careful buying, also, accounted for the growing bank account. In the early years of the colony's life, the leaders often sought the advice of the trustees elsewhere. This is evidenced in Brother Urban's trip to Watervliet, New York, to get advice as to where he might find "the desired articles on the cheapest terms." As the economic life progressed, there was a surplus of supplies for sale. Not only were things sold or exchanged nearby; but, as time went on, the colony sold on the markets as far away as New Orleans, Louisiana, and shipped as far as Galveston, Texas.

In building the industrial life of the colony, the leaders throughout the years showed great resourcefulness in learning everything new. Whatever they found practical, they adopted. In all their trades, they strove for perfection in craftsmanship. In fact, soon after the society's products began to go on the markets, the Shaker name as a trade name became a guarantee of the highest quality. Frequently, men skilled at certain trades not yet mastered by the South Union Shakers were brought in to teach the brethren. Such was the case when Charles Davis, book binder, came from Nashville, Tennessee, getting $10.00 per week and travel expenses as pay for "learning Brother Hervey to bind books." When the brethren first engaged in the straw hat industry, there was a hired hatter working at the North House with Samuel Eades. Sometimes one of the brethren went elsewhere to learn a trade. In March, 1813, James Rankin went to the other Kentucky colony, Pleasant Hill, to learn the tanner's trade. Several months later two of the men left South Union for a short time to learn something about a cotton factory. The cotton industry was never very large, but by 1822 the community did have a cotton gin which could care for two hundred pounds of cotton per hour.

By the early 1830's the silk industry at South Union was large enough to supply silk kerchiefs for all the men and women. The sisters cared for a great many worms, picked the silk balls, and reeled the silk. By Civil War days, the industry furnished some income. The crop was measured in terms of cocoons and pounds, with 805 cocoons making a pound.

Other duties for the sisterhood were gathering dried beans, gathering corn cobs to burn, raking leaves to put on the strawberry vines, cleaning the meetinghouse, helping the men in the rush harvest times, and, of course, doing the usual tasks. That the women were responsible in their work, as well as diligent, is seen from the following statement: "The sisters went to Canaan for to glean what beans were there but not having a load they brought home chips." The accumulated funds derived from the women's work were often allocated to some part of the improvement program; for example, the stone walk running from the office to the meetinghouse was made possible by the women's gift of $108.65.

As the years passed, the Shakers became very efficient in the numerous trades. The earliest Shakertown industries, shoemaking and the sawmill business, continued to thrive. By 1814 a woolshearing machine had been brought from Union Village, Ohio, and the Shakers were prepared also for dyeing their materials, having gone to Nashville to get the fuller's plates and dye kettles. However, the women continued to use the native sumac berries for coloring their wool black.

The fulling mill enjoyed a large business on its opening day in the fall of 1815. The enterprising Shakers had printed handbills struck on the presses of the *Weekly Messenger* at Russellville, advertising the fulling mill as a "Publick Utility." The advertisement was designed to attract customers from all western Kentucky and Tennessee in order that the slender community coffers might be filled.

Exemplifying the manner in which all the enterprises were pushed, the handbill announcing operation of the fulling mill carried explicit directions. The cloth would be received at the Kentucky stores of Amos Edwards, Russellville; A. Graham, Bowling Green; and S. H. Curd, Hopkinsville; and at the Tennessee stores of Faulk Shaifer, Gallatin; and J. Tifford,

Nashville. The customers could rely on the "utmost punctuality, neatness, and dispatch." In sending the cloth to the mill, the prospective patrons were to fasten to each piece written directions stating the owner's name, the county in which he lived, the date, the number of yards in the piece, and "What is wished to be done with it." Also, no cloth was to be sent or called for on the first day of the week. Sheets of further instructions were to be had by calling at the stores listed in the advertisement.

The additional instruction sheets contained minutely stated directions outlined in eight points with several *N.B.*'s added for greater clearness. Reading the sheet, the prospective customer found express directions as to what to do from the time he was to wash his sheep in a clean pond or creek, through the second step of corraling the animal in a clean pasture for seven days, down to the final step of sending the cloth to the mill where it would be fulled and dressed. If the customer followed the directions and the clothiers did their duty, the customer would "be satisfied with his work and the fuller's work too." The method outlined was said to be according to "the methods practiced by some of the first manufacturers of woolen cloths in the Northern States; and it is hoped they may prove acceptable and beneficial to all those who feel interested in their domestic improvements, so necessary and useful." This is the fashion in which the South Union industrialists advertized in September, 1815.

A grist mill was soon in operation, and a blacksmith shop took care not only of the society needs but also accommodated those of their neighbors. It was in 1819 that the colonists paid $85.00 for a bark mill. Two years later they swapped three horses for a $400.00 carding machine. Not long after this, they added to the Shaker machines an herb press, needed for preparing the herbs for sale; a hominy beater, attached to the counter wheel of the mill; and a hand printing press to be used in printing the seed envelopes. In 1823 the Shakers began the operation of a distillery; but five years later when they became prohibitionists it was closed.

From the beginning both the agricultural and industrial programs had been organized by the South Union trustees with the view of not only meeting the society needs but also of having sufficient surplus for sale. By the early 1820's the Shaker production was such that the trustees began to organize trading expeditions. These peddling trips took the merchants over a large part of the South, for the greatest amount of income was to be had by selling the surplus on the distant, as well as the local, markets. The merchants went occasionally on foot, sometimes by horse and buggy or wagon, but most frequently by boat down the rivers. As early as 1824, when the colony was still young, the merchants were going overland as far as the Tennessee capital with flour, brooms, and straw hats. The next year the first seed-peddling trip was made. The long river trips to New Orleans began some sixty miles away on the Cumberland at Clarksville, Tennessee, or on Red River, a Cumberland tributary, which was nearer. If the boat had been built at Shakertown, it was hauled overland with the merchandise to Red River. More often ox teams hauled the products to Clarksville, where they were loaded onto a flatboat which the trustees had bought from some individual or firm.

Guiding the flatboat slowly down the river to the port city, the merchants in charge would pull in at all the villages and towns along both banks of the Cumberland, Ohio, and Mississippi rivers. Arriving finally in New Orleans, they would buy the needed supplies, sell the boat, and secure passage by steamboat back to Nashville, Tennessee. Here they would be met by the South Union drivers with teams to haul the supplies back to the village.

The meticulous bookkeeping reports of all the peddling trips are evidence of the patience, honesty, and shrewdness of the men entrusted both with the wide sale of their products and with the purchase of the supplies at the faraway markets.

The success of the sales varied, but usually the results of the trips were highly satisfactory.

One of the earliest river trips was made in November, 1824, by John Meigs, who was accompanied by a hired hand named Small and a hired captain named Bratton. It was not long the custom to hire a captain because the Shakers soon came to be expert rivermen who manned their own boats and thus saved a hundred dollars a trip. Meigs' boat, 15 x 60 in the clear, had for its cargo 250 hogs, 100 sheep, and 2 barrels of kraut. In December two years later the Shaker river traders had garden seeds, brooms, onions, baskets, books, and gauging rods for sale from their "little Batteau." In March they returned with $500, which was a small amount in comparison with the financial return of later trips.

In 1832 the South Union merchants made two long trips: one by horse and buggy through Alabama netted $1700; the other, by water to New Orleans, added $2,502.25 to the exchequer. In February of the next year the amount of the sales on the New Orleans trip reached $4,113, and the following year it yielded $2,720 in cash and $768.83 in groceries and supplies. In 1836 Eli McLean, with little John Truitt for company, made a forty-eight-day trip to Georgia, traveling in a two-horse carriage and returning with $150. The river or "coasting trip" of the same year was much more profitable, for the merchants returned with $4,000 in cash and a large supply of groceries which they had purchased on the New Orleans market.

All of the early trips were fraught with danger because the merchants were traveling first through very rough frontier, then along the river with its many rough characters, and later through war territory with all its attendant dangers. Yet they were extremely fortunate in that they met with almost no foul play and were highly respected wherever they went. The *Memphis Appeal* gave an account of Brother Solomon when he visited the city to buy hides: ". . . his dignified appearance, his plain style of apparel, his very friendly and peculiar manner of address seem to have made quite a sensation in the city."

The merchants themselves spoke of their good fortune in not being robbed, especially during the Civil War period. Nancy, whose personal diary covered the first three years of the war, stated that the merchants were not molested in any way by guerillas, robbers, rebels, or federal soldiers. "For this," she wrote, "we are thankful to an all wise Providence."

Just before the war drew to a close, some of the merchants were robbed, but it appears that they were victims of some jealous neighbors. "Feb. 2, 1865—Joseph Averett started South with seeds—Guerillas stopped Joseph 30 miles from home—robbed him of his change, best horse, blanket, & shawl—and left the young Brother in a pickle. . . . Mch. 5—1865. Eld. William Ware returning from seed trip with $150.00 was robbed within 30 miles of home. Had previously sent $500 by express."

Although the merchants did not meet with much foul play, they did, nevertheless, suffer from the hardships of travel in a rough country. Many of the journeys were made in the rigorous winter months.

Whenever the merchants returned from their journeys, they were accorded a hearty welcome. Several of the occasional songs composed for the homecoming seedmen were written by Sally Eades, who believed firmly that God watched over those who put their hands to the work of marketing the wares.

> Praise the Lord, the God of Heaven
> Who has blest them on their way
> And may love so freely given
> Feed and clothe us day by day.

In another song Sally spoke highly of the traders.

> We feel them a treasure at home or abroad
> They are of our Mother the Children of God.

The South Union products that brought in the most regular revenue were the packaged seeds, brooms, flour, and the straw hats which sold for two dollars per dozen for both men and women. Of these regular articles, the garden-seed sales formed the largest part of the total amount although the packages sold for only seven cents each. The Shaker seed business had begun in 1790 at Watervliet, New York, when the gardener Joseph Turner had offered the surplus seeds for sale. Thirty-five years later the South Union trustees were conducting their seed business as it is carried on today by commercial firms, the seedmen bringing the new seeds, collecting for what was sold during the year before, and taking up what was left on the storekeeper's hands. Because the South Union gardeners were extremely careful in keeping up the pure quality of their seeds, they gained a wide reputation, and their seeds were always very much in demand. As early as 1836 the colony was importing York cabbage seed from Dods, Scotland, to further improve the quality of their own, and they also ordered seeds from Prince and Sons, Flushing, New York. The Shakers knew full well how the farmers and gardeners felt toward a seed merchant who sold seeds that refused to sprout, and they knew, as fully, how the same men would be quick to buy again from the merchant whose seeds were all they were said to be.

The seed papers were all packaged and boxed in the fall before the trips were started in late November and December. The journalists took a peculiar pleasure in recording that all the packages were ready. In the fall of 1831 the gardeners had ready seventy-five boxes containing 32,290 packages with a monetary value of more than two thousand dollars. The next year 50,273 papers were ready for the market. What a tribute to Shaker patience and ingenuity to have, as one of their many sources of income, several thousand dollars worth of seed from the society's gardens and fields.

It was the exercise of such business shrewdness that made it possible for the Shakers to go through the panic of 1837 without any severe reverses; whereas, such well-established firms as Louisville's Lemon and Son, the third oldest jewelers' and silversmiths' establishment in the United States, failed to weather the panic of those years and went under temporarily in 1842. The steady success was true, not only of the Kentucky Shaker communities, but also of those in the East. When Horace Greeley wrote his *Recollections of a Busy Life,* he commented upon this phenomenal success of the Shakers by saying: "... the fact stares us in the face that, while hundreds of banks and factories, and thousands of mercantile concerns, managed by shrewd, strong men, have gone into bankruptcy and perished, the Shaker Communities established more than sixty years ago, upon a basis of little property and less worldly wisdom, are living and prosperous today."

Although most of the income on the trips was derived from the sale of seed, brooms, hats, and flour, the merchants had other articles among their wares. There were herbs—penny royal and stramonium, called Jamestown or "Jimson" weed—coverlets, carpeting, jeans, tow linen, half bushel baskets, barrels, casks, gauging rods, rules, and books on Shaker theology and practices, such as the revised *Testimony.*

For sale on the nearby markets were fresh garden products, fresh fruits, cider, cheese, and bread. Some fourteen thousand hills of sweet potatoes were set as early as 1823 to provide a sale surplus. It was from the constant local marketing of all surplus supplies that much of the accumulated wealth came. The house journals are filled with many references such as "the sisters cut two barrels of greens and sent them along with the load of sweet potatoes to Bowling Green." Sometimes there was pure exchange. "Exchanged sage for medicine," or, "We traded cider and apples for a bushel of pecans." Then there was the time they "Exchanged potatoes for fresh fish."

Fruits and vegetables were stored in the large cellars and offered on the late winter markets when prices were higher. The January record gives the account of the Shakers' having parsnips, carrots, turnip greens, and potatoes ready for the Nashville markets. Marketing the products was not without its difficulties. There was the time a shipment destined for Nashville reached Bowling Green, but could not be sent on to Tennessee because of a washout on the railroad. When the brother in charge discovered that his cargo was still in Bowling Green, he learned too that part of the vegetables had frozen and that the potatoes and eggs were likely to freeze. Not to be utterly defeated, "he stirred around and sold the vegetables and got what he could for them."

Even though the Shaker products, particularly the seeds, were much in demand, the merchants did not find all the sales easy. In Jefferson Shannon's river diary one gets an insight into the many problems. "We landed at Randolph late in the evening and remained there until Thursday 12 o'clock. The reason why we remained at this place was the men with whom the garden seed were left with last year were not at home, and stayed until one of them got home, with the expectation of receiving the proceeds for the seed left last year, but in this we were disappointed. We received nothing but fair promises that the money would be sure on our return home from New Orleans."

Again Shannon wrote of being discouraged. "We called at some of the houses where they got seed from us last winter and found that they had sold but few of them and had the balance on hand. This was quite discouraging as we had expected to find sale for a great many garden seed in this place."

These experiences of Jefferson Shannon were similar to those of all the society merchants; yet through persistent effort and shrewdness the Kentucky seed merchants came home each time with profit. Only once in the business history of the South Union colony is there a record of a merchant who failed in his obligation to the colony. When Elder Brother Benjamin K. returned in December, 1835, he reported only seven hundred dollars in sales which "should have been more." Suspicions were deepened when he prepared immediately to leave with Nancy C—. Yet the Shakers, true to their custom, gave the departing couple their part, which in this case consisted of a horse, fifty dollars in cash, two beds and bedding, two bureaus, clothes, one ox, and "some other trifles." The brother broke down with sorrow at leaving, but "the harlot had him bound by bands unbreakable." As for Nancy, "she kept a bold front entirely undaunted with a nerve that never trembled, nor eye that winced. All her feelings crystalized to zero."

The honest peddlers never failed to recognize a good market. When the Civil War days came, they sold bread, pies, and cakes, as well as barrels of cider at the nearby camps. "Reuben went with bread, pies, etc., for the soldiers. He went around their camp and peddled out his load and came home on Saturday evening with eleven dollars and two pounds of coffee. One poor soldier offered to give his shoes for some bread." As the years passed, the Shaker bread came to be a popular item in all stores of the neighboring towns. During the last decade of the nineteenth century, the income from the bread sales was at its height.

Each Shaker colony carried on many industries, but they all specialized in one or two things. For example, the Mount Lebanon parent colony became widely known for its chairmaking industry; whereas the South Union colony became as well-known for its packaged garden seeds and its preserves. By the time the demand for the Shaker preserves was the heaviest, the river traffic had given way to that of the railroad; therefore, the preserves were not peddled after the fashion of the earlier products, but were shipped by freight.

The preserving of the fruit was a tremendous task for the women who had to fit the work in with all their other tasks. "Gathered and made 320 jars of strawberry preserves today besides doing up the washing," or, "Sisters made 100 jars of preserves today and sorted and washed wool." Even the Shaker women objected to the tediousness of canning. Appended to an entry stating that 417 jars of strawberry preserves had been made one week is the statement: "A slow business to gather small berries and nip both ends." Another cause for complaint might well have been the heat. Standing over the large preservatory stoves stirring the boiling contents of the large kettles, the women must have found the work exhausting during the hot summer days.

The fruit season lasted from the time of the early May cherries to that of the late fall apples. At the time of the apple harvest, the men were enlisted to help with the fruit. ". . . a two horse load of apples. Tonight the Brethren pared & cut them for drying." Perhaps Cyrus and Logan thought theirs was a better task, for they "went to Potters with a big wagon load of apples to make brandy." Apples were used not only for brandy and dried fruit, but also for apple butter and cider. One gets some idea of the large apple crops when he learns that on a certain fall day in 1831, 111 barrels of cider were made. The villagers kept an ample supply of the apple products for themselves. In the fall of 1835 the Center Family alone put away for their winter use sixty barrels of cider, one hundred bushels of dried apples, and one hundred gallons of apple butter.

Offered for sale along with the preserves were the choice Shaker wines made from elderberries, grapes, and other fruits. Available also was blackberry cordial. The sisters were so expert in their winemaking that they were often asked by their neighbors to make wine on the shares or for a set price. "Today several went to Newton McCutcheons to see his grapes, he wants our people to make them into wine for him." Customers for the Shaker preserves and wines either ordered by mail or came and made their selections. "Our principal merchant from New Orleans, accompanied by his lady, paid us a visit—out on excursion: Ordered 100 cases of preserves, 50 to be shipped immediately."

Problems arose frequently in connection with the fruit shipments. There was the time when six boxes of preserves were shipped to Clarksville, Tennessee, and upon arrival three of them were found to be filled with stones. "In this day, what is it some people can't be mean enough to do?" exclaimed the recorder.

The ample stores of fruits and vegetables kept in the Shaker cellars were used in preparing company meals. These meals were meant to be another source of income but the Shakers, being as hospitable as they were thrifty, often served meals free to special visitors. Even when there was a charge for the meals, it was a nominal sum. Once, however, the sisters were so tired of cooking that they decided to ask a crowd of Clarksville, Tennessee, people a dollar a plate. Eldress Nancy, who tells of this occasion in her Civil War diary, seemed both delighted and surprised when the company "never grunted but paid it in full." During the war the Shakers fed many of the soldiers in both armies. Sometimes they received money, but other times they got only receipts for the meals. One time when they believed they had been given worthless receipts, the substantial meal had consisted of light bread, warm hoe cakes, fried ham, pork, cold fresh mutton, fried potatoes, stewed peaches, blackberries, and coffee. Not only did they offer meals to transients, but they sometimes kept regular boarders. Shakertown was an ideal place to spend a summer vacation or to live if one had no other home. Many people came to board with the Believers while considering whether or not they would accept the faith. One of the boarders, named Colonel David Vinton, was found dead one July day on his cot. The economically-minded recorder wrote that the colonel had just paid twenty dollars of the ninety he owed. One wonders whether the business-like brethren found a way to collect the remainder of the debt.

Throughout the years of the colony's existence, the members sought "the one thing needful" from many sources. Of course farming was never neglected as corn, oats, wheat, flax, rye, and hemp were all grown in the earliest days of the community's organization.

Much attention was given also to the raising of poultry, hogs, fine cattle, sheep, and horses. The raising of cattle had been one of the early ventures. By 1822 the Shakers had purchased Comet, their first fine Durham bull. A few weeks after Comet had been brought to the Shaker farm, he was "found dead—by drinking water from the little house." His successor, Orion, cost the trustees one thousand dollars. For the hundred remaining years of the colony's existence, the herd at South Union was recognized as being "top notch." The herd was kept up through the importation of thoroughbred sires from abroad as well as by purchase of good cattle from the bluegrass section of Kentucky. The journal pages of the 1830's are filled with live stock transactions: "Sold cattle in Tennessee for $1800. . . . Jesse Rankin and Geo. Waddle to Nashville to see some fine cattle lately imported from Ireland—bought a heifer. . . . Hooper took Orion to this bank of Green River, Met Br. Stephen Manise of Pleasant Hill & exchanged the bull for Dunn Duff Pleasant Hill's bull."

Even the feminine diarist Nancy was not averse to discussing the importance of breeding, for she recorded the trip made by two of the brethren ". . . to purchase a couple of young animals of the Bovine kine to improve or rather to keep our stock from running down for want of a cross."

It seems appropriate that today when the principal part of the Shaker farm is in the hands of one individual that fine cattle still crop in the fertile pastures and attract the attention of the passers-by on Highway 68.

The colony did not raise thoroughbred horses, but they did keep horses for their own needs and some for trade. As early as 1813 several of the men went to Vincennes, Indiana, to sell horses. Two years later some went to Mississippi. All of these sales brought money into the treasury at a time when cash was badly needed. In 1838 horses were still a source of income, for it was then that "Eli returned home from the Western district of Tennessee bringing with him part of his horses having a poor business toward selling—on account of the distracted state of the country in reduction to matters of finance."

Before the trains replaced the stage coaches, the South Union Shakers were getting five hundred dollars a year as pay for caring for eight stage horses.

Sheep and hogs were also raised. In 1836, as a gesture of friendly encouragement, the New Lebanon colony sent three Bakewell sheep, and Union Village, Ohio, presented the Kentuckians with three pigs. The large number of hogs which were raised at South Union were used chiefly for slaughtering. The hardy western Shakers not only fed their hired hands pork, but they ate it themselves, a practice not followed by the easterners. One frequently finds statements in the house journals such as, "Killed this season 8,617 lbs. of pork," or "Killed 8,803 lbs. of hogs—40 hogs."

There was really no end to the versatility of the South Union economists. One of the odd sources of income was from the sale of hand-made coffins to their neighbors. These sales ran exceptionally high during the times of the cholera scourge.

The cholera epidemics resulted in still another source of income for the Shakers in that they were asked to care for numerous children who lost one parent or both. One young Tennessee father, who lost his wife and was left with three small children ages five, three, and two, brought them to the society. He agreed to pay all expenses and the school tuition if the Shakers would take his children.

Even in the days before and after the prevalent diseases, the large school order, sometimes called Watervliet, was partially made up of children whose parents had brought them to the Shakers for an education. Indenture papers were drawn up for all children who came on such terms. The Shaker astuteness is much in evidence in the wording of the papers by which means they fully protected themselves. For instance, there is a paper which was signed in 1823 by Winston Harvey of Hopkins County. The paper stated that Harvey was giving up his two young daughters, Nancy and Mary, to the care of the Shakers, who were to take good care of them, furnishing them with good wholesome boarding, lodging, and apparel suitable to the age of the children and to the order of the society. The children were to remain at South Union until reaching their lawful age. The passage which most clearly shows the wariness of the Shakers has to do with the children's education: "... and also to learn them to read and write—provided they or either of them retain capacity to receive such learning."

A number of complications must have arisen from keeping the children of any non-Believer. The following letter evinces that something was amiss:

"Carthage No 23 1833

"Friend Eli

"Your letter by the boy with the Cow is recd. I am truely sorry you think I have exceeded the Bounds of your limited time for the removal of Mary. But let me here assure you it was not a disposition to abuse your kindness that has kept me from having her away before now but wishing to procure a place where she could live comfortably which I have now done —And shall therefore have her removed very soon.

"I had a letter from her a few days since in which she mentions that some persons from this county had been over there and told some of your people that I was deceiving you that I had no intention of sending for her and I am only sorry if it caused you any uneasiness I am truely gratefull for the Kind attention she has received ever since she has been with you and would be very sorry if you should think I would willingly impose on your good feelings when I saw you I could not tell precisely what times it would be when I could be ready and preferred her staying with you during the time she had to be absent, but told her to stay no longer than it was agreeable to all, altho I ask no favors but those I am willing to pay for yet I am gratefull when they are extended in a friendly manner.

"You will please say to any of your people who may be under a wrong impression from listening to tatlers that I have no disposition to deceive them everything I do I do it openly without regard to the good opinion of the public which I detest. With due Respect your obl. servt.

"Rich. McConnell"

To examine the business records kept at South Union for a period of more than a century is to understand how the socio-religious ideals of the Shaker sect found immediate and lasting expression in a vigorous program. As one follows the growth of the many enterprises which in turn measure the financial growth of the colony, he comes to feel the sense of romantic adventure which the Shakers enjoyed as they worked to make their communal dream come true. Mirrored also are those Shaker traits of dignity and honesty, capability and shrewdness which were practiced by a people who considered their work program an important and integral part of their religion.

X

DOWN THE RIVER

THE SIXTH OF OCTOBER IN 1831 WAS A DAY
of considerable activity at South Union for that was the
day when two of the Shaker merchants, Jefferson Shannon
and Jess McCombs, accompanied by John McLean and the
black man Sampson Anderson, were to start on an ambitious
peddling journey that would take them by wagon to Clarksville, Tennessee, and by flatboat from there to New Orleans,
Louisiana, a distance of 1,225 miles. The remarkable record
kept by Shannon of this journey is more than a Shaker business chronicle; it is a well-written chapter in the great American river epic.

When the men left Shakertown, their allotment of garden
seeds, jeans, coverlets, linsey, straw hats, sage, thyme, apples,
and cider required four wagons with teams of two to five horses
to transport them and their goods to the Cumberland River at
Clarksville. Although the wagons were heavily loaded, the merchants made steady progress, driving twenty-one to twenty-six
miles each day. Lorenzo Martin, traveling in the village dear-
borne, accompanied them as far as the river.

Arriving in Clarksville, the company made camp, bought a
flatboat, and began preparation for sailing on Tuesday, October 11. The boat, thirty feet long by thirteen feet wide, had
a planked-up bow with a fireplace in the center and bedsteads
arranged on each side.

Exhibiting their usual traits of orderliness and efficiency, the Shakers hung a door and put shutters on the boat windows before calling everything ready. When the trip was under way, the diligent merchants stopped at all the points along the river banks to call on their old customers and to solicit new trade. One of the first stops in Tennessee was at Palmyra, a small town situated on a high bluff on the south banks of the Cumberland. Arriving there between sunset and dark, the men sold the inhabitants $1.25 worth of articles, but they bought a skiff for $3.00 which Shannon said in a regretful tone made "more outgo than income."

While traveling, the men found it a very simple matter to provide themselves with a variety of fresh game. Wild turkeys, squirrels, and quail were to be had with little effort, the Cumberland shores in Kentucky and Tennessee yielding the most game. The men had provided themselves with fishing hooks and lines and the first night's haul was a catfish "near three feet long." On another night as they floated along, they saw a large buck swimming in the river. Recognizing this as a chance to secure venison, they quickly landed the boat and got ready to fire when the buck came near enough. In recording the event Shannon wrote: "I took the rifle and Jesse the shot gun, both intending to fire at the same time, but unfortunately Jesse's gun missed firing. My gun went off but done no execution. He made for the shore, we followed him a piece and while we were looking for him, there came another smaller one and put into the river below us. There happened to be a man fishing on the opposite shore that made him swim back again and as he approached the shore, I discharged my gun and killed him."

One of the early stops was at Yeatman Woods and Company's steam establishment, where Shannon was extremely interested in all mechanical devices and was delighted by the variety of machinery and industries. Here he saw in operation a combined rolling mill, refinery, saw mill, and nail factory. He was immensely pleased at such economic planning. The overseer, Morris Belknap, and the mill hands bought $35.00 worth of jeans and garden seeds. In return, the Shakers gave the mill some business by buying one hundred feet of thin plank needed to line the cracks in their boat.

An indication of the high regard accorded the Shaker honesty and reliability is noted in the fact that when the merchants left the ironworks the next morning at daylight, little Mary Belknap was on board as their guest. Mary, who had been visiting at the mill, wanted to go to her home in Dover, Tennessee. Upon reaching Dover about noon, the merchants rested a few minutes from their labors of tying up the boat before accompanying their little passenger up to her house where they were "kindly received by her mother, who returned her thanks for the care and delivery of her daughter Mary."

Following the crooked Cumberland, the men were soon back in Kentucky, where their first call was Canton, a little town then consisting of two stores, one tavern, one grocery, and a blacksmith shop. When they arrived next in Eddyville, they were interested in seeing two large tobacco warehouses and two potteries. Arriving in Smithland, Kentucky, ten days after they had left the Tennessee town of Clarksville, the merchants went to the post office and received a letter and some garden seed advertisements sent from South Union.

Soon after leaving Smithland, the merchants came to the Ohio River and made their first stop in "a flourishing little town" called Paducah. Continuing from Paducah to Memphis they pulled into both banks many times. They stopped at "New America," Illinois, and Columbus, Kentucky. They visited at Indian Charley's, the Widow Lumford's, and at free Negro Bob Love's. They halted a little while at the house of an old man who had formerly been a member of the Shaker society at Old Enfield, Connecticut. Another night was spent cabled up at the home of Kinney who lived in the Chickasaw nation with his Indian squaw wife and their six children.

After leaving Helena, Arkansas, the merchants put off down

to Islands Number 42, 43, 44, and 45, commonly called Paddy's Hen and Chickens. Shannon wrote: "We run to the left of the Old Hen and two Chickens and to the right of one of the Chickens and landed at Memphis."

The Shakers were always skillful boatmen. One account which emphasizes not only their nautical skill but also their dignity and decorum is related by Shannon. While they were going down the river a companion boat ran on a sand bar. Being quite close, the Shakers pulled to the left, and their oars rubbed the gravel for a distance. When the other boat finally got out in the main current, the men, thinking the Shakers were stuck, called out, "Hurrah for Shaker Town! Come on, Brother." But the Shakers were not to be baited. Shannon reported that "We made no reply, but minded our own business, made the chute to the left of the island (which is much nearer) and got a long way ahead of them, and when we got to the lower end of the chute, we could hear them calling for a long ways behind us."

In those days democracy flourished along the river. The keelboatmen knew no class distinctions, but rather they composed a boisterous brotherhood in which each man was for himself—and for his brother riverman if the latter was in trouble. The Shakers joined in with the river brotherhood and were happy to lend aid to any who needed it. Once, they lost an entire day's travel while aiding some stranded boatmen. After spending long hours tugging at the ropes, both of the merchants suffered from badly blistered hands. The Shakers knew that it was dangerous to answer all the cries for help, for the river thieves often posed as stranded boatmen.

Shannon and McCombs exemplified the strong character of the men and women who made up the South Union colony. They were not retiring religionists who lived apart from life itself. Instead, they were keenly aware of all that went on along the river, for the economic policies to which they subscribed demanded that they be alert to all that was new in business everywhere. Shannon was especially interested in all the boats that were passing up and down. He always noticed where the boats stopped and what they carried. In fact, he was quite disturbed one day because a steamboat going down "run so far from us that we could not ascertain its name."

As his boat moved slowly down the Father of Waters, the diarist Shannon kept his finger on the commercial pulse of the United States. His journal is replete with the names of all the boats on the river. He saw the steamboats *Lafourche*, *Carlton*, *Tippecanoe*, *Jim Crow*, and the *Tally-Ho*. He watched the government snagboat *Helipolis* as it moved along, ridding the Mississippi of its snags. One day the *Phoenix* and the *Powhatan* passed going down and the *Constitution* and the *Watchman* going up. On another day there was a great deal of passing to be recorded. "While we were at the wood yard, the steamboat *Huntsman* called in and wooded. Several boats passed . . . the *Charleston* at the little chain going up, the *Favorite* going down, and the *Cumberland* going up, the *Mobile Amazon* going down, and the *Huntsville* bound for New Orleans."

Shannon usually managed to discover what the boats were carrying. The steamboat *Argus*, from Louisville bound for New Orleans, had on board a good many cabin passengers and horses. The *Forester* from Florence ran over to Giver's Point and loaded in salt from some flatboats; whereas the little *Kitty Clover* "called in for passengers but got none." The steamer *Atlantic* on her way up made the biggest waves Shannon had seen since he had been on the river. When Mark Twain was Bixby's pilot some twenty-five years later, there was still a steamer called the *Atlantic* that was known for establishing record runs.

Moving along toward New Orleans, the Shakers had many experiences which were novel to them. One day they saw a large boat sink with her cargo of flour, whiskey, sheep, horned cattle, and horses. On another day they witnessed a whipping of a man who had stolen a skiff. It was the first time Shannon had ever seen such an exhibition, and he hoped that he would never witness another.

Still another kind of excitement, which the Shakers shared with other honest travelers, was learning of the large circulation of counterfeit money. The brethren first realized that they must be careful in exchanging their money when they learned that some passengers from off the steamer *Delaware* had passed such money. When these passengers went ashore at the different landings, they would visit the taverns and stores and would call for something to drink, a handkerchief, a pair of socks, or some trifling article and would present a bogus ten-dollar bill. Receiving the change in good money, all of the criminals would gain eighty-five or ninety dollars at a place. Shannon reported that it was hard to detect the counterfeit bills since the notes were only a little shorter than the genuine ones and the paper was fully as good. Yet, upon close inspection it could be seen that they did not have quite the same regularity of design in "the dates in the wheels."

The Shakers sometimes found the river itself to be their chief concern. One night the roughness of the water made landing very bad. In fact, at the first attempt they failed because "the water run so powerful swift." Finding it necessary to have help, they called to attract the attention of some shore dwellers. Hearing the call for help, a boy came down with a torch of fire to light the bank. Thus aided by a light, McCombs plunged out into mud over his boot tops and checked the boat with the cables. It was thought expedient for someone to stay up all night to keep other rafts or driftwood from running against the boat. Evidently Shannon was chosen, for the next day he wrote in his diary, "The wind blew pretty hard the greater part of the night, and upon the whole it was the most gloomy disagreeable night that we have experienced."

A few days later when they prepared to leave a landing, two grand jurors, named Sulcer and Lofland, asked permission to ride a few miles down the river. The request was granted, and when the boat was just above the cutoff at Bunche's Bend, another man, a land speculator named Lewis, applied for the privilege of riding with them until he could get a steamboat going to New Orleans. So with their three passengers, the Shakers came to the difficult chute at the bend. The chute was something over a mile in length, but if it could be made, it meant the saving of twenty-two miles. The self-invited guests were enlisted as helpers. McCombs and Sampson manned one of the sweep oars; McLean and Lofland the other; Sulcer and Shannon took the steering oar. In this manner the boat went through the chute "handsomely" in four or five minutes, and everyone was "very proud."

The trip was being made at the time when the government was moving the Choctaw Indians up the Arkansas River. The steamer *Walter Scott* passed up one day with 1,165 Indians on board. Later they saw the *Walter Scott* again as she lay in port receiving another load of Indians. The boat's name was a direct compliment to the great English romanticist, as was the name of a cotton boat, *The Lady of The Lake.* A second boat being used for transportation of the Choctaws was the appropriately named *Reindeer.* Accompanying her was a keelboat, filled with the overflow of Indians and their possessions.

By the time the men reached Bass's landing, the December weather had turned very cold. The ground was covered with ice and snow. While they were at the landing, they saw many of the Choctaws pass with packs on their backs. Shannon felt concern for the "creatures trudging about through the streets barefooted." With the group was a little old squaw who looked as though she might be eighty or a hundred years old, but it was she who had much the largest pack—a big basket filled with various articles. Shannon reported that it looked as if it might weigh "upwards of a hundred pounds."

Arriving finally at the stopping place of their passenger Sulcer, the merchants received an invitation from him to walk up to his house and "set awhile." This they did, staying until after supper. When time came to leave, the old man, his wife, and their two daughters walked down to the boat and bought some garden seed. Trust the Shakers to look out for their mercantile interests.

The merchants not only found trading opportunities along the river banks, but they often walked or rode some distance in from the river. They hired horses and rode to Port Gibson, Arkansas. Returning to the river, they hired a wagoner for "four bits" to go to Port Gibson with the seed which they had engaged.

Now and then one of the men would get off and walk down the river bank ahead of the boat. As Shannon says, "I left the boat and walked down the river three-fourths of a mile to Lowery's. Sold him thirty yards of carpeting at 62½¢ per yard."

The Shakers, always mindful of getting the "one thing needful," solicited the trade of individuals as well as that of the country merchants. The accounts are filled with such statements as "We sold garden seed pretty well today," or "Sold 1 coverlet, some jeans, and a few seeds," or perhaps, "Sold some penny royal." The sales in Vicksburg, Mississippi, consisted of $5.00 worth of garden seed, $75 worth of hats, and $25 worth of herbs. The merchants' bookkeeping was complicated by the fact that they had to keep separate accounts of the products which they sold for the different families. "Sold thirty hats belonging to the East House," and ". . . a little over $200. $30. of it belonged to the sisters."

The morning of December 6 was a rather exciting one for Shannon and McCombs. As they moved down the river, they began to notice a continuous crossing and recrossing of canoes. Inquiring into the matter, they discovered that the night before two young Mississippi men from Clinton, named Allen and Phillips, had been at a ball where they had disagreed about what particular tune should be played. The disagreement quickly became a bitter quarrel, and in turn, the quarrel resulted in a duel challenge from Phillips to Allen. At sunrise Allen sent word that he would accept the challenge, which had come to him at three o'clock in the morning, and that he would meet Phillips the next morning at eight o'clock on the opposite side of the river from Vicksburg. The duel was to be fought with old-fashioned muskets loaded with buckshot, and the duelists would exchange shots ten paces apart. Allen got his second, crossed the river, and spent the night in Vicksburg.

Acquaintances of the two young hotbloods began crossing and recrossing the river in an attempt to bring about an understanding. Just as the Shakers had come upon the scene, the friendship had been restored. Hearing the story, Shannon expressed his opinion that this was a much more satisfactory way to end the quarrel.

While the Shakers were in Vicksburg, the *Creole* came up from New Orleans and stopped there. The merchants were pleased to see two of their Kentucky neighbors who had "come passengers on the Creole." Since these men were soon to go through South Union, McCombs gave them his letter written to John Eades.

The weather remained very cold. On Thursday there was a heavy sleet, and Sunday Jefferson wrote: "The sleet is still lying bountifully on the ground. The timber is very much broken to pieces with it. I do not recollect ever to have seen as much broken in Kentucky as it is here in Louisiana and Mississippi."

When the merchants got up the next Sunday morning in Natchez, they discovered that the ice was running rapidly in the river. Because it was the first time in the memory of the oldest inhabitant that ice had come that far down, the people flocked to the river in large companies, not able to believe the presence of ice until they saw it.

More exciting to Shannon than the ice was the steamboat *Planet* that came into the Natchez Port with "a band of music on board, which they played handsomely a while before landing." Still another event which excited him was the tragic ending of the steamboat *Stranger*, which burst her boilers, killing the pilot and three other persons. This was the seventh steamboat to be lost since the Shakers had been on the river. Six of these they had seen running.

Before leaving Natchez the Shakers "met with a man by the name of Little that was in the habit of making our plastering cisterns." They also saw their neighbors Edmonson Harrell and Austin Kelley, who were enjoying the free use of the Mississippi given them in the treaty of Ghent.

Preparing to leave Natchez, the men exchanged their Mississippi money for United States and Louisiana currency. Then they went up "on the hill" to the post office and found that a letter had been advertised for some time. Shannon paid for it and read its gratifying contents immediately. They had received only one other letter since leaving home, and they had been very much disappointed upon not receiving mail when they first arrived.

Soon after they arrived in Fort Adams, the Shakers lost their dog. After several hours of diligent search, they left without him. If the loss of the dog had lowered their spirits any, they were to have them raised soon; for as they passed along down Point Coupe to Bayou Sara, several three-gun salutes were fired for them as Kentuckians.

In honor of Christmas Day, the Shakers pulled into the river bank, landed, washed, shaved, and put on some clean clothes. Then they walked up to St. Francisville, which was a mile from the river. But since it was both Sunday and Christmas, they were able to do but little business with Hoyer and Fisher.

The next town on their itinerary was Baton Rouge, situated on the east bluff thirty or forty feet above the high water mark. Here were some government barracks, which the Shakers learned were the most commodious of any government barracks. The village of 1500, they thought, was "tolerably compact" with many neat houses. They admired the wide streets which were clean and in nice order. Perhaps they thought somewhat wistfully of their own well-kept village back in Kentucky.

McCombs and Shannon, acting in accord with their usual desire to learn everything, went to visit the barracks. There they were welcomed and escorted through by one of the soldiers "who was well acquainted with the Believers at New Lebanon and Pittsfield." While at the barracks the two Kentuckians witnessed, most likely for the first time for them, a deer hunt that was in the nature of a sporting game. A large number of hounds were released in the government park to chase the deer, which soon eluded its pursuers by plunging into a pond where it could outdo the twenty or thirty dogs. The soldiers then made a running noose on the end of a long rope. A Spanish butcher, among the number, threw the rope around the animal's neck and drew it to the shore. The moment the deer was dragged ashore, the dogs all sprang on it and made it "bleat most pitifully." Then the chase was repeated. Each time the deer escaped, it was brought back by the officers of the garrison until they tired of the sport for the day.

A short time after leaving Baton Rouge the Shakers tied up at Bayou Lafourche. While there they walked some distance inland to visit a sugar house. They inspected the sugar-making process and discussed it in terms of their own limited sugar making at tree-tapping time. It is highly probable that the men were considering the possibility of growing sugar cane in Kentucky, for it was not many years later that the Kentuckians began cultivating a variety of cane from which they could make their own molasses.

New Year's Day was spent in floating down the river and in arranging their pecuniary affairs preparatory to getting to New Orleans. The port city was the destination of almost everybody in those days. Shannon and McCombs were arriving in New Orleans five years behind a visit of Abe Lincoln. Ten years before, Audubon had visited the city and had found it to be a noisy place with the mingled sounds of ringing church bells, knocking billiard balls, and firing guns. Arriving in the city, Shannon wrote that he and McCombs "fixed up a little and put off for the post office," where they were glad to find two letters.

The boatmen first landed up the river out of the wharfage duty zone, but they concluded later to move down opposite the city and pay wharfage because the place where they landed was filthy and dirty and a great many accidents "were daily or rather nightly" happening to those who walked to and from the city. Soon after the boat was moved to the wharf, a man named Manning offered the Shakers twenty dollars for it, at the same time offering to let them use it for living quarters as long as they wished. But when Manning learned that the Shakers had not yet been solicited for the wharfage, he asked if he might move it out of the zone again. They agreed; but unfortunately, Manning did not move the boat far enough, and the wharf master came to collect the money. The brethren explained that the boat no longer belonged to them and that he needed to see the new owner, Manning. But when Manning was asked for the duty, he went back on his bargain. Even though they had discommoded themselves in allowing the boat to be moved, the merchants still had to pay the eight dollars. Determined to get full value for the money spent, the frugal Shakers moved the boat again to the principal part of the wharf. At last they were settled enough to walk about and view the curiosities of the city.

The day turned out to be a gala occasion in New Orleans, for the citizens were celebrating the Battle of 1815 with a parade of the militia on the "publick square," and all the troops belonging to the city were on parade in front of the Catholic Church. After the cannon firing ceased, the crowd repaired to the church, where the priest delivered a "speech adapted to the occasion in French." The sermon was followed with several more rounds of firing the cannon and small arms.

During the days they spent in New Orleans, the men busied

themselves going from place to place buying the necessary supplies at the best prices. Not only did they go "to a good many houses" looking for such commodities as sugar, coffee, and Roman cement, but they "looked in several Jewelers Stores for a Sett of Silver Spoons" which one of their South Union neighbors had asked them to buy for him. A set was finally purchased at the store of Claudius Rendon for twenty-four dollars.

As soon as the Shakers could complete their sales and make their purchases, they took passage home on the steamboat *Kentuckian* bound for Louisville. On the day of their departure they were quite busy collecting all their freight. By sunset they had it all aboard. As Shannon wrote later, they "had about the most fatigueing day" of their entire journey.

Included in their forty-three purchases were such things as:

4414	lbs.	of	sugar @ 6.5¢	per lb.		
542	"	"	" @ 6.25¢	"	"	
1511	"	"	coffee @ 15¢	"	"	
1	bbl.	"	molasses 37 gal. @ .26			
1	"	"	N. O. rum 33 gal. @ .37½			
4	bbls.	"	mackerel			
3	bxs.	"	codfish			
1	bbl.	"	tanners oil			
1	bx.	"	pine apple cheese			
½	bbl.	"	copperas			
4	gals.	"	Holland gin			
48	lbs.	"	Catty's tea			
4	gals.	"	Jamaica rum			
4	"	"	Maderai wine			
8	lbs.	"	sperm candles			
1	bbl.	"	Roman cement			
43	lbs.	"	ligum vitae			
76	x		Spanish hides			

The total cost of supplies was $996.30; the trip's expenses had been $159.25. The total sales had amounted to $2,-590.54¼, with the sale of garden seeds at 7¢ per package accounting for $1,773.41 of the total. The $1400 profit had been deposited at the New Orleans Office of Discount and Deposit so that "the one thing needful" could be taken home safely in the form of a check.

The return trip held much of interest for the men. Living as they did in the orderly atmosphere of their religious community, they naturally found much that was exciting and even dangerous. They would not have agreed with Mike Fink's statement of ten years before that the river was getting too civilized. Crooks and fourflushers were still so numerous that all the cabin passengers had to be mustered on deck at one time in order to determine who had and who had not paid the fare. Deck passengers who usually worked out the price of their passage were not included in the roundup.

Many were the stories to be related by the merchants when they finally arrived at home—stories of robbery and deception. Soon after the *Kentuckian* left New Orleans, a robbery was reported by a young passenger by the name of Garrison. He informed the captain that someone had ripped open his watch pocket and had robbed him of sixty-five dollars in United States paper. Although the captain posted a reward of twenty dollars, for the return of the money, the reward was never claimed.

There was also the story of the deck passenger who gave his shirt to a black man to wash. After he had given the shirt to the Negro, the owner remembered having tied a ten-dollar bill in the corner of the tail. Hurrying to the servant he asked for the money; but the Negro denied having found the bill. The Negro's owner was summoned. He threatened him; but it took Captain Buckner's stronger threat of the "cat and nine tails" to frighten the darky into confessing that he had found the money and had showed it to a man named Reynolds, who had said the bill was counterfeit and had thus persuaded the Negro to sell it to him for three dollars. The search was renewed, this time for Reynolds, who was found at length "with his clothes bundled up (in a very unsuitable place!)". Confronted by the captain, Reynolds admitted his guilt and said he was willing to refund the money but that the bill was no longer in his possession. This acknowledgment involved a cabin passenger who, when found with the bill, returned it to the original owner. The captain put Reynolds and his accomplice, "who looked very much like a swindling cutthroat" off at the next stop, Madrid, twelve miles below their destination.

At Madrid, time was taken to fill the wheels of the boat with new buckets. The passengers felt assured that, after getting rid of the trifling men and having the buckets replaced, they would have a good night's rest. Little did they know what lay ahead; for very soon after the trip was resumed, the boat ran into thick ice and, after battering along for two or three hours, was forced to a stop. The ice continued beating against the boat so constantly that at last the captain ordered the boat moved across the river where it would be somewhat out of the strong current. The next morning they got under way again.

On that day a dog fight furnished the quota of excitement. A cabin passenger named Ewing urged his dog to attack the dog belonging to the deck passenger Robert Little. Infuriated, Little shoved Ewing into the icy river. When he had been pulled from the river, Ewing went for his loaded gun. The harassed captain, who heard the brawl, came in time to interfere and to shoot off the gun.

Just before the boat reached Smithland, Kentucky, the *Kentuckian* got into a race with the *Farmer*. The race was good fun, although it was spoiled a little for the *Kentuckian's* crew when their boat ran so close to some flatboats that one was wrecked. But the accident was not allowed to stop the race. Instead, the captain shouted to the owner of the flatboat to make out his account for damages and he would settle with him on the return trip.

As the race continued, the *Kentuckian's* wood supply gave out. Not so easily discouraged, the crew began a search for old barrels and boxes. They made use also of "bacon rhines or anything they could get a holt of." Even though a race was in progress, neither boat failed "to put in" at the places of call. The speed with which the separate crews could load and unload only increased the sport of the race. In Smithland Shannon and McCombs had to transfer to a boat going to Nashville. They were both sorry not to be "in on the finish of the race."

It took some time for the 13,152 pounds of Shaker provisions to be unloaded, but the brethren made certain that it was all properly done. Then while one stood guard, the other went to rent a house near the landing so they could move their things in out of the rain and wait for the Nashville boat. The men moved in the light goods by themselves, and after dark they moved the rest in by the help of a hired dray and driver. Supper was secured from a grocer for "two bits." As soon as he ate "a check," McCombs made himself as comfortable as he could on the floor of a cold house. Before Shannon retired, he went to Wells and Barner's and "wrote a few lines to Eli." As he stood at the desk before the fire writing, the weather was so extremely cold that the ink froze in his pen. This twenty-sixth day of January, 1832, he recorded as having wind from the north with the mercury eight to ten degrees below zero.

With the river so full of ice, very few boats were running. While they waited for their boat, the Shakers paid a picayune for each stick of fire wood they used. After a few days a boat came up the Cumberland from Nashville, but the captain tied in at Smithland when he heard the Ohio was filled with ice. The stranded people bargained with him to turn back to Nashville. He agreed to do so for three hundred dollars. The Shakers took passage on the boat and accepted their part of the fee. After the boat had traveled some distance, however, the captain demanded an extra twenty-five dollars. The astute Shakers refused to pay their part of the extra fare, telling him to put them off, if he liked, for they would be nearer home

at Dover, Tennessee, than they would be at Nashville. The ire
which the unjust demand provoked was sufficient to force the
captain to proceed according to his original bargain. No doubt
the majority of the passengers agreed with Shannon that "the
captain was obstinate; he was not of the right stuff but rather
of the good natured, easy, good for nothing class." As the boat
moved down the Cumberland toward Nashville, the Shakers
observed again the abundant wild life along the banks. Near
Dover they discovered a deer standing in the water; also, they
saw many turkeys and a good many ducks.

At last they arrived at Nashville "about dark on January
31" and were met by two of the South Union members who
had been waiting some days with teams. After the usual salu-
tations and general inquiries about friends and matters at
home, all the men went to a tavern to spend the night. The
next day they loaded their freight, attended to some business,
and left Nashville. Spending the night on the road, the group
started again the next morning at five o'clock and traveled
until nearly ten o'clock before they stopped to eat breakfast
and to feed the horses. By half past eleven they were on their
way again. Shannon wrote in his diary that they might have
given the horses some more time to eat and rest if they had not
been in such a hurry themselves to get home.

After having been gone from South Union since October 6,
the men arrived home between sunset and dark, February 2.
At the office they received a hearty welcome and a good hot
meal. Then they went to the Ministry's House to make a report
of their long peddling trip. When the report had been given,
they were escorted to the Center House where all the brethren
and sisters had gathered to do them honor. The two travel-weary
men found themselves placed in front of the meeting. "The
Brethren and Sisters then united and sung us a very handsome
little welcome hymn, which was prepared for the occasion after
which thanks were returned on our part. Indeed it was impossible for us not to have felt deeply sensible of this manifesta-

tion of their kindness. It has been my happy lot, to have long been connected and raised with the most of those present, and have felt myself much indebted for the frequent manifestations of their kindness, but this scene imposed greater obligations than all the rest. Obligations which never can be repaid but from the overflowing of a grateful heart . . . After meeting was over and I had spent some time with the Brethren asking and answering questions concerning matters and things generally, Eli and I returned home to the office . . . and retired to rest at a late hour."

Thus came to a close a long and successful business trip, only one of the many made frequently by the Shaker merchants during the time when river travel was the most expedient way of getting goods to the market.

XI

A BODY CAN DREAM ALMOST ANYTHING

FROM THE EARLIEST DAYS OF SHAKERISM all true Believers have been mystics. Just as Ann Lee acted in accordance with a vision and left England to establish the new faith in America, so her followers have felt themselves led and instructed by divine revelation. There was, however, a period of seven years (1837-1844) when the Shakers, especially the eastern societies, were almost overwhelmed by an influx from the spirit world. So stirred were they emotionally by these manifestations that they were swept into accepting as true some testimony and publications which were afterwards discredited.

The middle of the nineteenth century in both America and England was a period remarkable for a series of spirit manifestations, a time when the whole spiritual world seemed displayed. It was the Shakers who first received the notable visitation. After ten years, seven of which had been marked by a close and continuous relationship, the spirits announced that they were leaving the Shakers temporarily to visit the people of the world. The next year newspapers all over America carried the news of the Rochester rappings, an event which is said to have ushered in modern spiritualism.

In the world, as well as among the Shakers, those who found themselves in tune with the spirits began to speak in unknown tongues; to receive visits from people of many lands, especially

Indians; and to have their revelation confirmed by dreams, visions, and extraordinary manifestations.

Among the Shakers the epoch of renewed spiritualism was announced first to their youth. Acting as a "prelude to the extraordinary work" was a vision experienced on the twentieth of December, 1835, by the twelve-year-old Emily Pearcifield of South Union. After the vision had passed, Emily described for the ministry "her sights and travels with minuteness, much simplicity and . . . accuracy . . . having seen Jesus— Mother Ann and all the 1st fathers and mothers." It was thought, wrote the journalist, that Eldress Molly, who had just died, had taken "possession of the child's spirit and conducted it to the blest abode of our parents in the bright spirit world."

In 1837 the Watervliet society underwent a remarkable religious revival. It was during that summer when a young teenager in the society, Ann Maria Goff, was the first in any eastern society to become aware of the pronounced spiritual operations. The following summer some of the little girls at North Union, Ohio, began involuntary exercises: ". . . going with great speed across the room, back and forth, with great velocity—nor could they stop, nor be stopped by any human agency. Suddenly prostrated on the floor—with their eyes closed, muscles strained, joints stiff, they were taken up & laid on the bed—Held conversations with their guardian spirits—would sing heavenly, melodious songs—motioning gracefully with their hands—Sometimes appeared to be flying, or swimming. They were taken to the cities of the redeemed and to the mansions of the blessed."

It was not long before the old as well as the young began receiving spiritual messages and inspirational songs. Those who received messages were expected to reveal them for the benefit of all; those who received songs were asked to write them down. It has been estimated that between one and two thousand songs were produced and learned.

The most elaborate message received during the period was

delivered by a holy angel to the New Lebanon brother Philemon Stewart on May 4, 1842, "between the hours of six and
seven." Al' sign te' re Jah' do, the prophesying angel, had
been commissioned for the task by the Lord of Hosts in the
presence of the other mighty angels and all the seraphs.
When he left on his mission, "the Angel of Mercy went before,
and the Angel of Power followed after, with a red robe; whose
eyes were like flames of fire." Arriving at New Lebanon, the
angel addressed himself to the chosen Philemon: "Arise, O
thou little one, and appear before the Lord, on the Holy
Mount; and as thou goest, kneel seven times, and bow low,
seven times to earth; for the Lord hath words for thee to write;
and thou shalt kneel, or sit low, by the side of His Holy Fountain, and the words shall be revealed unto thee, in flames of
fire."

The inspired Philemon said afterward: "I kneeled, and
bowed the number of times required and as I reached the foot
of the hill, whereon the Fountain is placed, language cannot
describe the sensations of my soul; and the noise as of a mighty
rushing wind, or as of distant thunder, did roar throughout
the hill. But as I approached the Fountain, and seated myself
low, to write, all became calm; and an inexpressible feeling,
as of a consuming fire within, filled my mortal frame, and prepared me to write the following communication."

Philemon was told that he was to spend six hours each day
in the appointed place writing what the angel would read from
the roll. At times he would be required to "leave writing the
Roll and write the word which was sent forth for immediate
application in Zion." Although Philemon had only an ordinary
education from a common school in the society, he recorded the
angelic message in a style comparable to that of the King James
version. Characterized by high imagination and daring, the
book was composed of two parts. Part I contained the angelic
message which was God's estimate of his own creation as seen
in 1843 and his warning that people should humble themselves

and keep the commands of the blessed Son "either in his first or second coming." Woven into the proclamation was a defense of Shaker theology. Part II was made up of testimonies from various Believers of the time who expressed their faith in the divine origin of the Roll. The revelation, said to have been given in "the last days," and the testimonies were published by the Canterbury press in 1843. Though only a few copies are now in existence, *The Holy, Sacred, and Divine Roll and Book, from the Lord God of Heaven to the Inhabitants of the Earth* was one of the most unusual books published in nineteenth-century America. In order to spread the Shaker teachings five hundred copies were sent gratuitously to the leaders and rulers of all nations. Only the King of Sweden acknowledged the gift.

In the book there was specific command that each society should prepare a frame and place it in the meetinghouse yard. From the frame there was to be hung a copy of "the short roll . . . that all such of the children of men, as may pass this street . . . may read and understand the same. . . ." "But touch it not, saith the Lord of hosts; for I have placed four of my holy angels to guard my sacred word." Further warning was issued: "But unto such as make light . . . saying within their own hearts; *These are the Words of Mortals and not of God;* I will surely visit them, in my own time and season, with sore destruction and desolating judgments, till mountains sink and valleys rise, and kingdoms into pieces rend."

In 1849 there was published a second book of Holy and Eternal Wisdom, which had been written at Watervliet, "through the instrumentality of a female"—Paulina Bates, who was "an illiterate writer." Paulina's book, edited at New Lebanon and published at Canterbury, was another work which was not to be imagined as "cunningly devised fables or the inventions of man or woman."

Whatever was the truth concerning the two unique publications, it was not long before the eastern leaders suppressed both books. Even though the high pitch of their spiritualism may have led the Shakers into accepting some false revelations, there were after all many other Americans who were also greatly affected by the spiritual upheaval of the time. Keeping the Shakers company were the emotional Millerites who were expecting Jesus to come to earth momentarily on an azure or refulgent cloud and to announce the end of time. There were also the throngs of people who had been caught up in the excitement of the contemporary religious revival; the prominent men and women who were discussing the Rochester rappings and were attending seances; and the more dignified and intellectual transcendentalists.

That the manifestations of this period did not seem as strange to the nineteenth-century Shaker as they do to the twentieth-century reader is learned from the straightforward, factual style in which the South Union journalists set down all of the spiritual manifestations noted at their own western village. "April 20, 1838 About this time involuntary exercise begins to be extensive among the young Believers, having been more or less among them since about the 1st Inst. . . . Apr. 29 A good deal of jerking & involuntary exercise in public meeting. . . . June 7, 1838—*Trances*—This evening at the gathering order Two Sisters were carried away in a trance to the world of Spirits—To wit—Olive Jenkins & Patsy Roe."

If a spiritual message had been received, it too was accepted at face value and recorded without any elaboration. "Last night Elder Hervey heard a voice say with emphasis, Save your parents! Save your parents!! Save your parents!!! Last night Eldress Betsey heard a voice which said, God will do for you what you cannot do for yourselves. A girl under the control of foreign spiritual power was wrought upon to exclaim, Wo! Wo! to this generation the rising generation—Wo! to the wood land and to the forest trees! Wo! Wo! to the world if they turn not to God!!"

From 1837 to 1844 when the manifestations were most noticeable throughout all of the eighteen Shaker societies, the easterners closed their public meetings to the world. According to Elder Frederick Evans of New Lebanon, the step was necessary "in consequence of the then unprepared state of the world, to which the whole of the manifestations would have been as unadulterated foolishness or as unexplicable mysteries." When the heightened spiritualism first became evident at South Union in the spring and summer of 1838, the Kentuckians did not consider it necessary to close their meetings as did the easterners, nor did they ever refuse admittance to the world because of the unusual spiritual exercises.

The westerners soon became aware of the miraculous events which were occurring everywhere. Such happenings were recorded by the local scribes along with those in their own society. From a nearby town came a story which took on added interest when viewed in the light of the gathering events of that time. "Dec. 7, 1843—*Prophetic*—a pious negro, named Stephen, who was the Servant of the clerk of the court, came into Elkton, Ky. under the operation of invisible power & spoke in the street about two hours—Among others things said—I came not in the name of Stephen—but in the name of the *Mighty God of Israel*—You believe me not, but let any one of you put your hand on me to prevent my mission & you shall be convinced this Government is a government of strife confusion & gloom but that which shall succeed will be a government of Universal Emancipation." Stephen was not the only spokesman who emphasized the coming strife, confusion, and gloom. A letter from the Mount Lebanon colony brought news of a similar prophecy "given by inspiration in their church meeting" on March 18, 1857. The prophecy, which was said to have been very "long and heavily enforced," was condensed and written into the South Union records. "The time is near at hand when no man will be safe at home nor abroad; & it shall be one continual scene of confusion and uproar throughout the land—And to ye strong ones of the South, I do say, Ye who make merchandise of the souls of your Brethren, & spill the blood of poor captives for your aggrandizement—Beware of me, for my hand is against you."

Although stories of happenings elsewhere were made a part of the official South Union records, the writers indicated that they considered some of these events rather startling. Others they thought were questionable. "Aug. 20, 1841—Strange, if true—we see it stated by the Papers that on this day a small shower of blood or rather flesh and blood, fell on the farm of one E. M. Chandlers, near Lebanon, Wilson Co., Tenn!!! Hoax in all probability.... Sept. 7, 1841—We see by the Papers that another phenomenon similar to the one in Tennessee has taken place in Kensington, Massachusetts. This is said to have reddened in a measure the face of the Earth by a shower of blood for 2 miles in circumference."

By 1844 all the Shaker societies had followed an inspirational order to set aside a small secluded plot of ground located on the highest point of their land. This plot, generally known as the "chosen Square," was dedicated as a place where the members could go to commune with the voice and receive the great outpouring of the spiritual. For a ten-year period the societies were expected to hold two formal meetings a year—one in the spring, one in the fall—at the outdoor sanctuary.

The South Union square seems to have been one of the first, being set aside as early as 1836. Each society had a particular name for its holy plot, the one at South Union being known as the Holy Ground. It was a plot three-quarters of an acre in size and was located "on an eminence or top of a rising slope, South of the Grave yard, or burying ground." It had been selected "by an inspired instrumentality as a place for occasional worship by the assembled Society ... at such times as the leading authority sees fit to assemble the Society there." The meetings usually lasted from two to three hours. Both the meetings and the meeting place always remained a mystery to the neighboring world.

Although the wave of spiritualism reached its crest nationally in the 1840's, the more numerous references to revelations at South Union are to be found later in the Civil War records. Undoubtedly the general war disturbance, felt more keenly by the Kentucky Shakers than by their northern kindred, increased the many outward expressions of mysticism, such as trances and prophetic inspirations. Many of the dreams and revelations are to be found in the war diary kept by Eldress Nancy. All the experiences of her co-religionists Nancy recorded at length, but in telling her own mystic communications she never elaborated. Instead, she stated only the simple facts: where she was at the time the Voice spoke and what it said. "May, 1863 Early this morning before the bell rang to rise from slumbers; The spirit seemed to say your rough places shall be made smooth & your weak places will be made strong. . . . Oct. 1st Thursday, 1863 Just as I was trying to doze off to sleep, a voice seemed to say. The wicked will prosper, but this ungovernable people will yet do wickedly. . . . Aug. 1864 A little while after 3 o'clock this morning I seemed to hear a voice say distinctly I've been to see Lincoln, and you may depend he give me a real dressing. It may do some good, for he is a man of God and a prophet. This spirit seemed in a degree humbled or subdued."

The Voice which Nancy heard so frequently became the subject of one of her many poems written by inspiration.

THE VOICE OF HOLY WISDOM

My home is on the mountains
My home is in the breeze
'Tis also in the fountains
And in the towering trees
My home is in the heavens
My home is on the earth
I scatter seeds of leaven
Throughout the haunts of mirth.

My home is on the desert
My home is in the sand
I'm seen in all creation
I give the Lord's command
My home is in the forest
My home is in the glen
I should be reckoned foremost
Among the sons of men.

My home is in the waters
My home is on the land
Among the sons and daughters
And on the rocky strand
My home is on the Ocean
Yea with the ships at sea
I give to each their portion
Whatever it may be.

My home is here in Zion
I've marked the chosen few
Who do my word rely on—
They will my will to do—
Yea with the speed of lightning
I move from pole to pole
I am a living substance
To every honest soul.

Inspiration by Eldress Nancy E. M.
April 18, 1861

Nancy's hymn was only one of the many which were said to come by inspiration from the spirit world, being communicated either by the supernatural Voice itself or by the voice of some departed Believer.

The spirits of departed Believers came with messages as well as with songs. Nancy reported receiving a message from Mercy Dunn. "Mch., 1863 The weather is cloudy and spitting snow at intervals all day. I was reclining in a passive quiet position when the spirit of Mercy Dunn and another shadowy spirit at a little distance behind Mercy asked the question Q. What does it take to make a sound believer? Ans. Mercy D ... answered, One that dont flinch at crosses or trouble, but bears a sound good cross." References such as this appear as late as 1872.

A month before Nancy's visit from Mercy, the villagers had been discussing a strange phenomenon reported by Brother Urban, who had been aroused by the spirit of Samuel Shannon telling him there were robbers about the place. Having received Shannon's warning, Urban hurried outside, but as far as he could tell things seemed to be as usual. The next morning, however, the men learned that the guerrillas had set that particular night for stealing every horse in Shakertown. That their barns had been visited since feeding time of the night before was evidenced by the many corn cobs scattered over the barn lot, which was ordinarily neat and clean. Supposition was that Urban had appeared in time to frighten away the robbers before they had been able to accomplish their purpose.

Often the dying, as well as the dead, indicated in some way that they had connection with things spiritual. About an hour and a half before Robert Houston "breathed his last," he asked those who were attending him what the trumpet was sounding for. Since no one else heard the sound but himself, he was told that it must be "the Angels sounding the trumpet to summon him home to his blest abode." It was also not unusual for the dead to make themselves known at their own funeral. In December, 1845, John Lacy "left the tabernacle of clay." On the day of his burial, he appeared and expressed his thankfulness through inspiration to all "the brethren and sisters for their care and attention during helpless old age."

On the same night when Urban had received the out-of-the-ordinary warning, Angeline, the caretaker at the little girls' house, had been frightened by a rapping on the tables, bedsteads, and the floor, and by the inexplicable scattering of articles over the room, such as books, shoes, stockings, sticks of wood, chips, cobs, pillows, and bed covers. The strange happenings had gone on until four o'clock in the morning. During the time some of the little girls "seemed to go into the trance state;" at other times they were stiffened with spasms. The following day the ministry went down to investigate. Eldresses Betsey and Nancy remained over night; yet next day they had nothing more extraordinary to report than that they had seen the table move.

Some weeks later the eldresses had occasion to wonder whether or not they too were being signaled. In her diary Nancy wrote: "Today about half after one o'clock we had a loud and significant rap near the cupboard which startled Eldress Betsey and I for we could see nothing which caused it. It sounded somewhat like a percussion cap bursting." The rappings came again in February of 1864. It was then that Elder John H. was aroused four times in one night by an audible rap, and "at the last one of the four he heard a clear voice say '*At each end.*' "

Many of the recorded revelations are of considerable length. On January 22, 1863, the following dream was reported by one of the brethren. "I saw as it were the spirit of this war represented in the form of two enormous curley headed antagonistic animals of the Bovine kind. The one that represented the Federal was of reddish brown color, with straight, sharp-trimmed horns, plump, sleek-bodied . . . and stood more erect. The one which represented the Rebel was of dark motley pied, with a mixture of yellow, black, white, or greyish color. Its horns were crooked, its body was of a rawboned, gaunt looking appearance but very active." The rest of the account describes vividly the struggle which the brother thought the Rebel would win until the Federal made a fresh lunge, driving one horn into the Rebel's vitals. "This," he said, "was the death blow and I awoke."

This particular dream seems to have been a mixture of sev-

Center House, 1824.

Rear view of Center House.

A. L. Eads.

eral things: a reversal of the dream Joseph interpreted, the truth about the Yankees and the rebels in 1863, and the fact that the South Union colony owned a large herd of fine cattle.

Lucetta Buchanan also experienced a revelation which she told to her co-laborers. Emphasizing the lesson she received from the dream, she said: "I dreamed last night that I was in the ministry's shop lot on the North side. There was a fence running East and West about half way between the shop and street fence; wherein were enclosed three beautiful well formed fruit trees they were full of ripe fruit which was of a clear transparent whiteness about the size of our Binford peaches, but they were not peaches. I was not able to determine what kind of fruit it was. It was unlike anything I had ever before seen. Elder John appeared to be engaged viewing them; It seemed they were his own. I however took the liberty to pull some of the fruit and was eating it, when I turned my face toward the shop and saw the sisters Eldress Betsey and Eldress Nancy standing near the window and I thought to myself how I wish they had some of this good fruit, It is so good, and extremely delightful to the taste. I noticed Elder John maintained a very solemn countenance and an entire silence, which I wondered at. He appeared to be engaged in taking care of the fruit which he stored away in a mansion which stood near the north East corner of the shop above the Earth in the air, on which I am unable to describe. He gave me a significant look, and then walked to his place as much as to say, behold, this is the fruit of my labors. I seemed to understand this by impression, for he never spoke a word. I looked at it with admiration and obtained an Idea that it was what he had laid up for his own use; A reward for his faithful labors while here in time. There seemed to be such a large quantity I thought I would have been glad of a share in it, but he did not offer any to me, and he appeared so solemn, I had not the courage to ask him for it. With this impression I awoke."

Almost a month later another young sister, Theressa Williams, had what Eldress Nancy termed "a very correct vision." On Monday morning, the ninth of March, just as the morning bell rang, Theressa dreamed that Brother Robert had died suddenly on the Sabbath day and that the funeral service was held on Monday. A large audience was present, and many were overcome with weeping as Elder Robinson spoke of the departed's good qualifications—his kindness and his accommodating and peace-loving disposition. Waking from her dream, Theressa felt glad to find it not true. Later in the morning Robert came into the washhouse where Theressa was attending the wash mill; so she told him her dream. He smiled and said, "O yea, a body can dream almost anything." What Theressa and Robert did not know was that he would actually die on the following Sabbath day and that his funeral service would be held on Monday afternoon at two o'clock.

The diary kept during 1863 and 1864 by Eldress Nancy relates many prophetic inspirations as to war victories. Maria Price seems to have had the closest communion with the spirits, for it is Maria who is most often quoted. "Sab. 12th *Maria Price* has had another interview with the spirits they told her that the Federals had taken Port Hudson. said they had three successive & successful battles and they gave her another song of victory. . . . Thurs. 16 The trains have come down from Louisville today with the mails once more. It is confirmed that Port Hudson is taken." The entry for the next day was a more detailed account of the same story. No doubt, the newspaper story had stimulated Nancy's questioning Maria more closely. "Fri. 17th On the tenth of July Maria P. & Lucinda B. were impressed that Port Hudson was taken by the Federals, and to Maria a song of victory was given which runs thus:

> Port Hudson is taken with her arms and ammunition
> Port Hudson is taken by the Federal army
> I hear the martial music playing around
> The fifes & the drums are beating to the sound.

Maria not being well posted asked the spirit who was conversing with her if it was Fort Hudson or Port Hudson the spirit spelled it P-O-R-T. she asked how it was that we could get the news before it came in the papers. The answer was we have a spiritual Telegraph—& we sometimes attend the battle grounds and take the spirits to their proper places. Lucinda and Maria were both impressed that Vincent Powers was killed in one of the battles, and they both thought they saw him on the tenth and eleventh in our halls. Lucinda is impressed that Charleston, S. C. is taken by the Federals."

The spiritual war communiques continued. "Sab. 19 While at breakfast Table this morning the spirit spoke within Maria saying, ://: Richmond is taken ://: And to Lucinda it was said Chattanooga is taken://: Now time has come to determine the truth of these statements. . . . July, Wed. 8th, 1863 We received an extra *hand bill* today giving information that Pemberton surrenderd Vicksburg to Grant & the Federal forces on the 4th of July & captured 2400 rebels. Just about 10 o'clock P.M. Maria Price's hand was suddenly raised with the arm in full stretch—She asked mentally what is it? And the ans. was Vicksburg is taken . . . She asked when was it taken, & the answer was on the fourth of July, then she asked how was it taken . . . The ans. was by unconditional surrender . . . Then the spirit sung a song of victory, which she learned. So if the little hand bill is correct she has had a very correct vision."

One of the most elaborate visions reported at South Union was the one which came to Eleanor Meigs on April 24, 1864. To read Eleanor's narrative is to learn that she was familiar with the Holy Scriptures, especially with the prophetic utterances of Ezekiel, Isaiah, and Amos. Said Eleanor: "I heard my name called loudly and hurriedly, I awoke from sleep and the clock struck twelve (12) very soon after this I appeared to be traveling with my guide who took me on to Washington City & into the White House. I saw a number of Soldiers, my guide who was a brother spoke to them in a loud and commanding voice—told them to be wide awake. He then told me that there are ten times as many soldiers around the City of Richmond as there are here (around the City of Washington) I marveled at this and began to look again. I looked around and saw a line which came down thro' the middle of the House. He said what do you see? I answered I dont know; It looks like a line extending down through the house but I can see neither end of it. He took hold of my arm and said in a very impressive manner *A plumb line a plumb line*, by which both parties of this political strife will be tried and judged. Inasmuch as they have strayed from it, they will be scourged and all will have to suffer in proportion. After the scourge has passed over they can then stand unitedly together. And when they can stand together and have confidence in the Almighty power of God; then they will be in a condition to administer the Laws of the constitution in justice and equity. Then seven Grey Eagles came and placed themselves in a circle with their faces to the center. they straightened themselves up and looked so tall as so many men; Their feathers and wings lay so close to their bodies; and they stood so closely united together they looked as smooth and round as a Barrel; their eyes were sharp and keen & they appeared to be looking in every direction. Those Eagles stood in the Center of the White House in the City of Washington. Suddenly I found myself at home.

Elder Lorenzo dreamed about two of the seed merchants, a dream indirectly influenced by the existing war conditions. When Elder Hervey and Jackson did not return from their peddling trip at the time they were expected, Lorenzo had a dream in which he thought himself to be in the meetinghouse. He dreamed that it was at the close of the service when the Shakers were standing in the ranks waiting for him to dismiss them. As he stepped forward to pronounce the benediction, he noticed Elder Hervey on his knees "at the foot of the alley." Wondering whether it were a spirit or whether it were really

Elder Hervey, Lorenzo spoke to him, asking what had become of Jackson. According to the dream conversation, the boat on which the two men had been traveling had sprung a leak. Elder Hervey had secured passage home on a gunboat, but Jackson had stayed behind to oversee getting the freight transferred to another boat. Lorenzo awoke, however, before getting complete details of the trip.

When Hervey and Jackson actually did reach home, thirteen days later than they had planned, Lorenzo was not surprised to hear that the merchants' trip had been filled with difficulties. For one thing, the boat had been so crowded with soldiers that there were no state rooms available. Being forced to take deck passage, Hervey had become quite hoarse from the long exposure to the cold night air.

The various spiritual revelations were frequently centered around the popular object lesson. Such was the allegory told by the visitor "Friend Peebles" when he visited the sisters' shop in the late spring of 1871. Peebles said a bright angel, wearing a golden girdle, appeared to him in a wheat field, where the grain was beautiful, green, and vigorous. When the angel said the wheat would speak to him, he thought it was wonderful; and while he was wondering how that could be, the wheat commenced speaking.

"I shall not remain wheat, for I have a higher mission. I am to be made into bread which will be put on the table for guests." Presently the reapers came and cut the wheat. "It hurts," said the grain.

"Ah," answered the spirit, "it can not be any other way. You must pass through this process, if you would be fit for a higher purpose." As Peebles had watched, the grain was taken to the thrasher and torn and scattered in every direction. Then it was fanned and made clean.

Again the wheat complained, "It is bad. How it hurts!" And for the second time the bright spirit pointed out that there was no other way to become fit for a higher station. Then came the milling process which caused the wheat to cry out in torture again, "How it hurts! What bad treatment!"

"But remember," replied the spirit, "progression can not be made without the grinding process."

Stirred into dough, kneaded, and put into the oven, the grain cried out from its fiery furnace more piteously than before, "O this is awful! It is perfectly terrible and there is no way of escape."

"There is no other way to obtain the high mission for which you are destined," spoke the spirit soothingly.

When Peebles had finished relating his revelation to the women, he expressed his desire to hear some singing. So the sisters sang "a number of beautiful songs—among these was one he selected as his choice—it commenced—God is infinitely able—to sustain the weak & feeble." At the close of the impromptu meeting the sisters danced and bestowed on the visitor their love and blessing. Peebles, who united in the dance and "gathered freely" of the love, was soon to accompany the eastern leader, Elder Frederick W. Evans, on a speaking tour of England.

Four years later when Peebles again visited South Union, the Believers gathered in their new Music Hall to listen to "the great lecturer on Spiritualism." The lecture seems to have been more of a travelogue than a discussion of spiritualism. "December 10—Lecture—Br. J. M. Peebles lectured for 1½ hrs. yesterday as calculated & also today, again. He took us all around thy little globe. Among the different nations—On the wall were hung the pictures with different kinds of costumes—told us of their habits & religions—and then at 1 o'clock attended a Shaker meeting in the Meeting Room & seemed the freest & simplest Shaker in the crowd. He has entertained & instructed us in the worlds affairs—left on the train for Memphis."

During one of their infrequent war trips, a small group of South Union members became acquainted with a spirit medium who was also traveling by boat from Cincinnati to Louisville. Just as the Shakers had arrived at the Cincinnati wharf, their carriage had overturned, and one of the group, Sister Olive Jenkins, had suffered a dislocated wrist. Soon after boarding the boat, Olive began to receive the sympathetic attention of the medium, whose "help and comfort" were appreciated by the entire group. No doubt conversation between the two centered around their spiritual experiences, for Olive had been one of the first, as well as one of the few, members of her society to be carried away in a trance.

It was in the decade of the 1870's that spiritualists began coming to South Union seeking admission to the society. "Feb., 1872 Admitted Spiritualists—Fannie Brown and her children. . . . May 17, 1872—Spiritualists admitted—Caroline Loving from N.Y. State."

It is probable that the presence of the newcomers stimulated the spiritual experiences of the South Union members, for one of the most mystical revelations to come to any member of the colony came that same year to Elder Hervey. "Just as we finished our dinner today Bro. Hervey arose and stated that when about to make ready to come to the house, he saw a beautiful bright star light on his hat—it was brighter than anything he ever saw and directly his hat was covered all over and he was surrounded with lights. The spirits wanted him to tell it at the dinner table and he thought someone present could tell him what they were. Br. Solomon said they were the good spirits, who had come to comfort and bless him for his obedience."

From twelve-year-old Emily's visionary trip to the bright world in 1835 to Brother Hervey's experience with extraordinary lights in 1872, the South Union society records give evidence that the members shared in the spiritualism prevalent throughout America. That the South Union Believers did not become extreme enthusiasts was probably because of their abundance of common sense, a declining state of religious fervor among their members, and the great distance between South Union and the Mother Society. No doubt the distance tempered the encouragement which seems to have been given deliberately by the eastern ministry for all Believers to throw themselves into the current spiritual revival. It is true that the Kentucky religionists proclaimed their dreams, recorded their inspirational songs, and acted in accordance with frequent inspiration; yet they did so with considerable restraint, displaying a feet-on-the-ground attitude about the whole matter. Not only were they skeptical of certain happenings reported from other sections, but they showed little interest in their copy of *The Holy Roll*, though they did obey the command to post the sacred roll in the meetinghouse yard.

Even though their interest in spiritualism may have been less than that of most Shakers, it is not surprising, during the nineteenth century when the air was highly charged with religious fervor and visions were general, when many Americans of all classes were inquiring into spiritualism, that the practical-minded westerners joined the spiritual-minded easterners in an attempt to recapture the inspiration known to Mother Ann and to the other early leaders.

XII

ORDERED LIVING

THE MOST NORMAL YEARS THAT THE SOUTH Union Believers ever experienced were those of the 1840's and 1850's preceded as they were by a financial panic and followed by a second panic and a war. The organization days, marked by hardship, persecution, and disappointment, had passed. The large building program was nearing completion. The cleared land was yielding good crops, and the extensive industrial program was returning satisfactory profits. Upon retirement of the first ministry to the East, a new and younger ministry had assumed the responsibility. The society membership, which had leveled off to an average of 232, was accepted more than ever before by "the world" as part of the county and state life.

During this period the land transactions were not for the sake of enlargement of their holdings, but for the sake of owning a single body of land rather than several scattered tracts. As a result, much of the large Drakes Creek tract, which lay sixteen miles from the village and which had not been sold with the mill point, was now offered for sale in sections, some of it bringing only $2.75 per acre. As the Shakers sold their distant tracts, they reinvested the sale price in farm land which bordered their immediate South Union property. In 1846 the brethren bought a tract adjoining them on the southwest; four years later they obtained a second piece of land southwest of them when the James Proctor farm was sold at public auction. A secret bidder bought the land for the society at $14.80 per acre after the Shakers themselves had stopped bidding at $12.00. The Trustees had learned that there were still a few neighbors who liked to make them pay high prices. "The neighbors," they gloated, "were somewhat enraged when they found we had got it by strategy." The farm, later known as Grassland, proved to be a better paying investment in farm products than in neighborhood friendliness.

The new ministry continued all the economic undertakings of the first leaders, making only the changes that resulted from the general Shaker practice of adopting whatever they believed would improve the speed and efficiency of the workmen. In keeping with this policy three improved spinning wheels, made to order, were purchased at $100.00 each and installed. In 1855, only a short time after sewing machines were put on the market, several were purchased and placed in the women's workrooms, while in the same year the men were pleased with the appearance of new corn shellers in their barns.

It was in July, 1850, that glistening new lightning rods appeared on the tops of the sturdy houses. Each rod had cost the trustees only fifteen cents, but since the points were one dollar each, the total expenditure for the rods was boosted to $81.00. That the Believers had confidence in the new scientific device is attested to by the fact that the mill and the North House were similarly equipped a few months later.

Although the main building program had been finished during the first part of the century, the enterprising men and women found much that was yet to be done. It was decided in February, 1841, that a new trustees' building was needed nearer the dwelling of the First Order. A site was selected south of the public road and west of the meetinghouse. Sashes, panel doors, and venetian window blinds were ordered from New Orleans. Nails and glass were brought in from Pittsburgh by Jefferson Shannon, who made the trip by horseback. The trustees explained that this new policy of ordering and buying materials as opposed to construction on the premises was to avoid having too many hirelings about.

A substantial frame building was finished in August of the following year. Until gutted by fire in the 1920's, it stood, surrounded by a neat lawn, flower gardens, and a white picket fence. Before the group moved into the new building in October a water shed, a woodhouse, and a post office were added; and four years later a "darkies dining room" was built onto the south end. Because the building always served as the village tavern, someone had to occupy the front room in order "to notice strangers." Samuel Robinson was the first to be appointed as tavern keeper. It was also Samuel's duty to attend to the post office.

Two other large houses were constructed. The three-story wash house, located a short distance to the northwest of the Center House, was begun in 1839. A new home for the East Family, built of the bricks from their own kilns, was finished a few years later.

Many small buildings were also added to the village premises: a hennery at the Second Order, a slaughter house, a new stone shop, a garden house, a tan house, a barn, a woodhouse for the ministry, a small brick house in which to steam the cow feed, an additional ice house, a smoke house, a corn crib, and a horse stable, built with a driveway "running across the building for the convenience of moving forage."

Through their extensive building program the Shaker men gained valuable experience and became such skilled craftsmen that they were often sought as supervisors of large work projects outside their own village. Such was the case when R. T. Mallory was asked to take charge of laying from one to three million bricks for the second Kentucky lunatic asylum being built in 1849 at Hopkinsville.

The general work program set forth by the trustees included much besides the construction work. Sale of the Black Lick timber necessitated the clearing of many new acres, some of which were turned into meadowlands. The rough hillsides surrounding the village were replanted in peach, apple, and pear orchards.

As in the earlier years, the work of clearing the land was often lightened by some form of entertainment. "Feb. 5, 1851 *Bee*—a general turn out of all hands working at the clearing on the Knob. Sisters go to cook or prepare dinner and supper. Fence all done by noon. . . . May 1, 1860 40 Brethren cleared off the Knob north of the village & 50 sisters came out raked up the leaves & put them around the trees & we all ate supper there."

In addition to the setting of fruit orchards, the 1844 tree-planting program included the setting of five hundred white walnut trees in the bend of the creek and the planting of a row of sugar trees connecting the East and the Center buildings. Pine trees brought from Clifty, Todd County, were planted in the Holy Ground.

The society farmers gave their hearty support to the policy of constant improvement. In the summer of 1857 they experimented with a new Chinese sugar cane. "We have concluded," wrote the journalist, "to try the sorgho & see if we cannot obtain molasses at least, better & cheaper than that we usually get South from Louisiana cane."

Three years earlier they had been concerned over the appearance of a new grass. "*Sedge Grass*—a poor hard stemmed grass, has for a few years past been overrunning the whole Southern Country—Made its appearance about the year 1835—was pretty strong in 1840—& now seems the enemy of all other grasses & is too powerful for them. We suppose it was brought in movers wagons from South Carolina—by some called Broom Sedge—it is considered a curse to the country."

The Shakers' reputation as good agriculturists went far beyond their immediate vicinity. "June 30—1846 Visitants from Nashville. One Fanning who keeps an agricultural school near Nashville came with 90 students to see our place. They encamped at the head of the creek."

The reputation accorded the Shakers as model farmers rested upon their ready acceptance of all the latest inventions that were practicable, their experimentation with the new crops, and their habit of keeping up the quality of their poultry and livestock. They had learned very early how much more profitable pure bred stock was than the common. Each required approximately the same feed and care; yet the purebred could be sold for much greater returns.

During the 1850's the trustees were caught up in the new enthusiasm for purebred chickens. "Mch. 5, 1854 *Hen Mania* There has of late been some new large & fine fowls imported into the U.S. & they are now becoming the rage of the whole country—We have got into the trade & occasionally sell to a decided pecuniary profit. . . . Mch. 23, 1854—go to Russelville with load of Shanghai chickens to sell. . . . Sept. 1854— Merchants went to Gallatin to sell chickens at the fair. . . . Oct. 30, 1856 Ellis goes out again with a load of chickens to sell—The world seems agog for Roosters."

Being progressive industrially as well as agriculturally, the Shakers were constantly beginning new trades. It was in the spring of 1838 that they began for the first time to make bonnets of palm leaf, a trade which they had learned from their gospel friends at New Lebanon.

Since the New Lebanon brethren were proficient also in the art of chairmaking, they were probably responsible for the Kentucky Shakers' beginning the home manufacture of chairs on the "blessed New Years day" of 1849. Ten years earlier the South Union trustees had bought some chairs in Nashville. It was a satisfaction to the members when they could make, rather than buy, the chairs needed to replace the dining room benches. At South Union chairs were never constructed as an article of trade.

As for the trading interests, the merchants continued their

seed and handicraft sales trips throughout the southern territory, but during the years immediately following the financial
panic, the sales were considerably lower. It was January,
1839, when the merchants came back with $1500, "having done
a safe, but not quite so profitable business as the year or so
past, owing mainly, to the general pressure of the times in
the South, and the derangement of the currency."

By 1857 sales were again high, and during the first three
months of the year the income from the peddling trips was
$7,685. The Kentucky Believers seemed to have fared better
during the years following the panic than did their Ohio neighbors; in 1846 the South Union colony sent a $1000 gift to
relieve the distress at another Ohio colony, Watervliet, followed by a larger loan of $5000 six years later.

The former policy of direct sales by the merchants was
being affected by the changes in transportation. More and
more, the boxes of seed papers and preserves were sent by
freight to Alabama, Texas, and to other states, where the
products were sold on commission. Sometimes the shipment was
made in compliance with a direct order from a merchant; at
other times a supply of seeds or canned goods would be sent
to a merchant with the understanding that he was to sell what
he could and what remained at the end of a certain time could
be returned to the original shippers.

A principle of modern business which was practiced early
by the Shakers was that of giving exclusive rights to only
one merchant in a certain territory. When James Stow of
Montgomery, Alabama, placed a large seed order in June,
1847, he wrote: "I think that the understanding between us
was that if I would take 5000 papers that you would not sell
to any other persons in this section of the country and relying
upon that I have ordered between 5 & 6000 papers."

The November shipment for 1856 was 6,090 pounds of preserves; shipment for the same month two years later was 500
boxes containing 6000 jars of preserves. The fall shipments

followed busy summers of canning and preserving when the cellar shelves received rows of blackberry, cherry, peach, pear, and strawberry preserves, as well as glasses of grape and apple jelly. Seven hundred jars of canned peaches were prepared in one September day, which was a real feat in the days when all the work had to be done by hand. From such ample stores, boxes of Shaker goods were filled, hauled to Bowling Green, and shipped South.

Another sales plan which was put into effect during the 1840's was one by which the merchants went by steamboat down the river to be met at certain landing points by wagoners who would load the produce and drive back into the country to sell on a commission basis. The merchants had extended their river territory by beginning their trips on the Barren River at Bowling Green and on the Green River at Bellars Landing. When the Kentucky legislature launched its improvement program of the navigable streams, Barren and Green rivers had received first attention. By 1836 the state had spent $215,000 on its river system.

The completion in 1860 of the Memphis branch of the Louisville and Nashville railroad eliminated the necessity of the Shakers' hauling their products to the river; now they could be shipped directly to Bowling Green or Nashville. The society members had gladly welcomed the engineers who came in June, 1853, "with their instruments for the purpose of locating the contemplated railroad."

That the new transportation facilities would require taxes was evident to the elder who wrote: "A barbacue was held at Black Lick to harangue the people in reference to being taxed to make the railroad from Bowling Green to Memphis." The combination barbecue and speaking was successful in that the tax plan was accepted and construction of the road began immediately. The tracks, which ran quite close to the back of the East House, went southwest of the village proper, separating the graveyard from the Holy Ground and from

the southern part of the farm. The foresighted brethren furnished materials and constructed a depot on their own land,
three-fourths of a mile southwest of the village. By agreement
with the railroad company the Shakers were to have control
of the depot unless the company desired possession, under
which plan they would have to assume all the costs.

Soon after the construction of the depot, a store and a hotel
were added, and the railroad stop became a business center.
To distinguish this new center from the village itself, the
people in the nearby locality began to speak of the railroad
group as South Union and of the village as Shakertown.

The first passenger car came through South Union in August, 1860; a month later the first complete passenger train
pulled into the depot. From then on, the Shakers took advantage of the new and convenient transportation, making
frequent trips "on the cars." Sometimes they went to the neighboring towns of Auburn and Bowling Green; at other times
they made out-of-state journeys to the East and South. An
earlier train trip taken by some society members had been
recorded in the house journal with a tone of disapproval.
"*Pleasure Excursion* Sept. 5, 1859—17 Brethren and Sisters
went to Bowling Green there took the Cars for the City of
Nashville, Tennessee. Returned the same evening or rather
night—having paid dearly enough for 'their whistle.' "

Of course the convenience and novelty of the train service
increased the number of visitors to the society. There are
numerous accounts such as: "Twenty more persons by the
train today—quite a clever company from Daysville—they
were sensible as clever—they brought their dinners with them.
They were mostly young under the guidance of Dr. Bailey. . . .
Thirty more came by the train from Russelville today—did not
bring their dinners with them—a heavy tax on our sisters—
Like the fable of the frogs—'What is sport to them is death
to us.' "

Sunday was a popular day for visiting Shakertown, espe-

The home of the Ministry, 1846; the Meetinghouse, 1819, with separate gates and doors for men and women; and the Office, 1841.

Tavern across from the depot.

The last of the five stores built on the same site
near the Louisville-Nashville depot.

Row of maples set during the Civil War.

cially from early April to late August when the Believers held public meeting at eleven A.M., followed by the closed church meetings at two P.M. "Sunday June 6, 1841 Great gathering. An uncommon multitude of people of all grades & shades came here not today but last Sabbath expecting to see something great as it was what they call Whit Sunday—the most of whom if not all went away disappointed. the multitude was so great that we were deprived of even a formal worship—they were variously estimated at from 1000-1600! . . . May 1, 1849 Disappointment—a very large concourse of the world's people gathered here with the expectation of seeing us march to the Holy Ground and worship there—but as we had made no such appointment—nor arrangement—They were doomed to disappointment—people must learn by what they suffer— . . . May 1, 1850—a good many people gathering about to see what is going on among the Shakers."

From 1830 to 1845 the Shaker society had been depleted by many backsliding members, but the following period of fifteen years seems to have been one of deeper religious feeling with a more stable membership. During those days there were nearly two women to every one Shaker brother, and it is a matter of record that the women were faithful, industrious, and generous, and in every way as worthy as the brethren.

Besides the regular worship services on the Sabbath, there were special religious observances of Mother Ann's birthday, Thanksgiving Day, and the Yearly Sacrifice held in December. Thanksgiving seems to have been observed not so much for its religious significance but was observed rather in compliance with the proclamation sent out by the governor of the state. It was in 1846 that the Thanksgiving service, at which Brother Urban read the Holy Saviour's prayer, was followed immediately by the felling of two large forest trees.

The improved spirituality noted at South Union after 1845 had not affected people in general if the two following accounts can be taken as an indication. "Jan. 22, 1847 Preaching Tour

—Elder J. R. Eades Starts for Duck Creek Tennessee—on a preaching expedition—Rather a *Duck Chase* for these times. . . . February, 1848—Preaching tour—J. R. Eades, Eldress Polly Rankin, and Elder Brother S. Shannon went to Richard Chambers near Dixon Springs in Tennessee. There Eades sang a hymn & Preached. They visited Frances Manchester & offered her another home. She did not accept. They came on home having effected nothing visibly."

Encouragement in religious matters had to be sought elsewhere. Perhaps the greatest satisfaction came through the continued exchange of visits between the ministries of the different societies. The coming of the railroad had facilitated the visiting. It was in 1854 that the South Union ministry, composed of Elder John Rankin, Brother Urban Jones, Eldress Betsy Smith, and Sister Nancy E. Moore, made an extended visit. The trip, which lasted from July 23 to September 10, included visits to the ministries at White Water and Union Village, Ohio; at Watervliet and Mount Lebanon, New York; and at Shirley and Harvard, Massachusetts.

The day-by-day account of the journey reveals that the group traveled by carriage, by river and lake boats, and by train. An exact account was kept of all expenses: fares, the bridge and pike tolls, and the tavern charges. Travel facilities were described in detail. The lake steamer was reported as being 336 feet long, 70 feet wide, and having a burden of 2000 tons. The reporter found Croton Junction, New York, to be a busy place where six railroads met. The passenger trains connected every day with a daily average aggregate of three thousand passengers. There was a corresponding number of freight trains. The rather routine report is enlivened by the Kentuckian's interest in all that he saw. His keen interest in the nation's transportation system was shared by his economy-minded traveling companions. Their first duty was the spiritual welfare of their charges, but they made the most of this opportunity to become thoroughly acquainted with all possible ways of sending supplies to market and getting merchandise home.

The ministry traveled by carriage to Louisville where they "shipped aboard the good steamboat City of Wheeling" for Cincinnati. Arriving in the Ohio town at sunrise, they "got carriage and horse on shore . . . drove up to the Walnut Street House." There they refreshed themselves and waited until time to take the cars to White Water. Reaching their destination at four in the afternoon, they found "the good brethren and sisters in good health & were made welcome in their lovely habitation."

After three days at White Water and six days at Union Village, where they visited their former Elder Hervey Eades, the ministry took the cars at Middletown, "passing through Dayton and Springfield to Tiffin and Sandusky." An eighteen hour lake trip brought them to Buffalo, where they again took the cars, this time for Niagara, Rochester, and Albany. At Niagara the travelers saw some Indian squaws and "bought some little curiosities from them to shew our sisters when we reached home." The final stage of the journey to Watervliet was made by omnibus at the cost of seven dollars.

While on their eastern trip the Kentuckians kept busy inspecting the buildings, the industries, and the schools of the older colonies. The Botanical Gardens at Harvard proved to be of unusual interest, especially when they learned that the gardens brought the Harvard Society eight thousand dollars annually. Inquiring into the spiritual affairs at Harvard, the visitors learned that their hosts held meetings which sometimes ran as long as fourteen days with only four hours per night for sleep.

Not only at Harvard, but at all the societies, the Kentuckians joined in the worship services, noticing always the order of the service. Later they discussed which practices were uniformly observed and which were peculiar to a certain society. All observations were carefully noted in the written account. "The order was on entering the Meeting House to bow—after taking their places in flaring rows we bowed four times—Then sung a hymn. Then Elder Amos spoke a few words. Elder Brother Daniel Crossman stepped out & read a farewell to us. It was then sung. They then labored two songs in the square order or what we call step & shuffle, then one step song—Then marched three songs—then a quick song, but don't turn & are longer about it. . . . Elder brother raised a shout of welcome to the good spirits who might attend meeting with us, all raising our hands unitedly saying welcome, welcome. The brethren did not try to march so precise as we, but their labor seemed to be to give spring to their step & down. The young brethren in a special manner marched as if they had springs to their knees and joints. Their singing was loud & strong & abounded with life. . . . When the Elders spoke in behalf of the people, The brethren & sisters spoke after them & repeated the sentence unitedly, they being careful not to give a longer sentence than all could remember to speak at once. This we found to be the common practice wherever we have been."

According to the true Shaker custom, the visitors were the recipients of many welcome and farewell songs. The scholars at Holy Mount, i.e. Mount Lebanon, composed some verses and sang them to the departing guests, asking that the greetings be relayed to the Kentucky scholars.

> Our kind and affectionate love we now send
> With joy we will roll it for each little friend.
> This token of love we send for the hand
> Of children residing in the Western land,
>
> Tell them in obedience we're bearing the cross
> To refine & redeem us from nature's deep loss.
> Tell them too, that sweet sweet flowers do bloom in our way
> We'll pick some & send them so cheering & gay

They're emblems of Heaven on which they may feast
A present from their little friends in the East.
A token of union, sweet roses of love
Such as angels do gather in heaven above.

In gospel affection we give these to you
With a promise that we will be faithful and true
Tell our dear little sisters we love them all best
And hear ends the message we send to the West.

Not only were the Kentuckians honored with special musical compositions, but as they went from colony to colony they were presented with gifts. Usually the gifts were the products for which the colony was best known. "They gave us a changeable pinner a piece—A nice little brush broom & a white pocket handkerchief—checked neckerchiefs a little bodkin a piece, green pinner, feather brush. ... They gave us a present of changeable cloth for trousers for our brethren & a pinner a piece for our sisters, & flannel for 2 undershirts & shirting for 2 shirts & 2 pocket handkerchiefs & pure gospel love in abundance."

Other gifts which the Kentuckians tucked into their luggage were fine cotton thread for darning, "nice candies of different kinds," cologne bottles "filled with cologne of their own manufacture," and palm leaf table mats which were made for the New York City market.

One of the most pleasant experiences of the eastern journey was the renewal of their relationship with the older ministry who had retired from active leadership in the West and were now living at New Lebanon. The day the visitors spent with Elder Benjamin must have passed far too rapidly because there were so many things to tell Benjamin and so much to ask him. Realizing that this was probably the last time he would ever see any of his former charges, the venerable elder divided some of his possessions among his visitors and asked that they be carried to South Union. "He had several journals which had been written here before he left us, which he said belonged to South Union. He had a good mackinaw blanket some Jackets & a worsted coat & a first rate trunk with his initials on it. He gave Sister Nancy his little writing box with some of his penholders and ink stand & a little box of wipers, a card of pens, & a razer, & a rule, & a pencil, All these things he wished us to take home with us & another little trunk filled with the Journals & many little accts of matters & things pertaining. to his journeys in the West. He gave us his parting blessing and greatly desired the prosperity of South Union."

Benjamin was correct in his belief that he was having a last visit with South Union friends. Early the next spring he died at the age of eighty-two.

When the ministry returned to Kentucky in September, they had many interesting details to report to those who had stayed at home. Unless the Believers were appointed to the ministry or to the positions of trustee & merchant, which appointment would give them opportunity for long business journeys, they spent most of their days in the village working in the shops, kitchens, and gardens, as well as in the barns and fields. While they worked, they probably found vicarious pleasure in reviewing the numerous reports made by the traveled members. At other times the workmen discussed the many local happenings. Sympathetic comments were made about Eli McLean who was scalded by the bursting of a steam boiler when he was returning home in December, 1845, on the Mississippi steamer *Denison*. Eli was again an object of concern the next December when he was knocked senseless by the fall of the sweep pole which was used for dipping the hogs in a scalding tub.

On a certain November day there was much speculation regarding a newly born foundling who had been discovered at the front door of the East House. Little Peter, as he was named, was sent to the county infirmary where he soon died.

Considerable comment was excited at the return of Urban Jones from New Orleans in January, 1843. Accompanying Urban were eighteen orphan boys who were to be bound to the society by the proprietors of an asylum. The boys, ranging in age from eight to thirteen, were placed under the care of Augustus Couchou and Reuben Wise. Among the new arrivals were Eugene and Achille L'Hotte, Joseph Fulzenberger, William Isole, John Rozer, Vallry Casson, and others. Of this number several became Shakers and remained for many years at the village.

Another topic for lively conversations was the return of coffee and "store tea" to the Shaker dining tables in January, 1856, after having been discontinued thirteen years earlier. It had been at the time when spiritualism and religious excitement were at the peak in the East, that orders had been sent out from New Lebanon abolishing the use of tea and coffee as well as re-emphasizing the restrictions on pork, tobacco, and strong drink. Other meats and beverages were limited "according to age and infirmity" of the user. The Kentuckians, who did not adhere too closely to the eastern restrictions, had been using a substitute drink made from redroot leaves gathered in the woods. Such being the case, they welcomed the return of the hitherto banned drinks—real coffee and tea.

Frequently daily conversations evolved around sickness in the community. During September, 1841, there was "an uncommon share of sickness—mostly conjestive chills." No deaths occurred among the Shakers, but throughout the surrounding country, deaths were frequent. The following March, thirty Believers had bilious pleurisy. Three of the aged died before the epidemic abated. When cholera swept the countryside for the third time, in August, 1850, there was discussion regarding the 380 deaths reported in Nashville and conjecture as to whether the dreaded plague would strike Shakertown.

Whenever a member attempted some new or unusual cure for his illness, he knew that both his disease and the remedy would be discussed thoroughly in the kitchens and the barns. Perhaps one of the most discussed cases was that of John Broadbent who came to the village in December, 1853, to take his daughter Eliza with him to Cincinnati that they might try the new and popular water cure.

Another who left the village and the resident physician in her search for health was Volumnia Miller who first went to Hopkinsville to consult a homeopathic doctor. Three years later she was taken to Tennessee to be examined by Dr. Simpson, a cancer specialist who pronounced her case hopeless. Accompanying Volumnia on her unprofitable trip was Lucy Shannon, who was to become the society physician at the death of her father, Doctor Samuel Shannon.

Samuel Robinson, who died from an enlarged liver, had been sufficiently interested in modern medical science to have left papers which stated that he desired to have his body opened to see "if anything could be learned or information gained by the operation."

Robinson's scientific attitude stemmed from the general Shaker desire for knowledge. Their respect for learning had caused them to include a schoolhouse among the first group of buildings constructed. From 1810 regular sessions had been held. The colony's educational system first included the boys' school which usually began in December and was dismissed three months later for spring work, and a school for the girls which began in March, as well as in October, for short sessions. From the beginning a joint evening school was held for all the families during the winter months.

During the decade of the 1850's the school commissioners came "to organize a school in accordance with the later school laws." Examining Jess Rankin, they awarded him a certificate as a teacher for the district.

Composition and speeches on any interesting and edifying subject composed the main subjects for study at the adult school; whereas, assignments for the regular school were made in the Comby speller and the Pike arithmetic. Orders of school supplies included slates and Webster's dictionaries. The teachers could get material for current event programs by reading the newspapers which were subscribed for at the village. As early as 1829 there were subscriptions to the *National Banner*, the *Nashville Whig*, and the weekly *Louisville Journal*. The usual annual rates were ten dollars for a daily paper and three dollars for a weekly.

A subject which early caught the attention of some of the Shakers was shorthand. During 1839 the daily accounts for February 24, August 4, and August 7 were all written in what was then called stenographic sound hand.

Through correspondence and visits the Shaker leaders everywhere had been able to bring about a greater uniformity in all their affairs—industrial, religious, and educational. By 1830 the desire for standardization had been applied to clothes also. The first uniform dress was designed for wearing to the church service. "What to wear" was settled by the New York heads; "when to wear" was determined by the weather at each separate colony. "Mch. 12, 1863 *New caps for sisters*—New forms for sisters' caps lately sent from New Lebanon. . . . July 15, 1866 Uniform dress circular—printed at & issued from Holy Mount—was read in Church Meeting at 6 o'clock & was well received. . . . May 8, 1864 This is the day we commence to wear our light striped gowns to Church Meeting."

The Shaker clothes, both for men and women, were simple in design and inconspicuous in color. The chief characteristic of the costume was the kerchief. At South Union, where silk worms were raised "with tolerable success," the members could afford to wear silk kerchiefs, some of which were "changeable." "Jan. 6, 1832 *Silk Domestic:* The sisters appeared dressed in their homemade silk kerchiefs the first time at South Union. . . . Jan. 1, 1833 The sisters gave each of the brethren a New Year's gift or silk neck kerchief—made from the cocoon by their own hands."

It was hoped by the elder who recorded the above that the brethren would not soon forget the sisters' kindness and that their love for the sisters would outlast the kerchiefs. The women deserved the appreciation; for in addition to making kerchiefs, they had the task of sewing for the men and children as well as for themselves. "May 1—'37—The Nankeen Trousers cut for making. June 16—'37—Sisters Gingham Gowns prepared for the needle. Jan. 21—Commenced today to cut coats for the Junior Order. Sat. 24, Jan.—Little trip—Sewing Sisters who have been making coats for Brethren—All ride out to Canaan take with them Bro. Geo. Rankins coat."

References to the women's needlework are numerous in the house journals. There are comments as to how they had "nearly completed a summer vest around for the brethren," or how the eldresses had spent a day at the North Family "getting their gowns fit on," or even that Eldress Betsy had finished Elder Hervey's wig which "he put on and wore to supper."

The material needed for the clothing came not only from the South Union sheep and silk worms by way of the dye vats and looms, but also from the faraway markets. It was in May, 1841, that Jefferson Shannon went to Pittsburgh "to buy Brownish Drab Cloth for uniform meeting coats for the Brethren." Later some of the Shaker ⋆trustees went to Louisville where "they purchased dark grounded goods sufficient to make the sisters all a dress, also a new style of woolen fabric denominated Empress goods."

The custom of wearing uniform clothes at the church services extended beyond the Civil War period. In the later years there seems to have been more variety of material. "Sept. 25 —1867—*Mozambique*—Pronounced mozambieek—Dresses— The good sisters are now engaged in making their fine uniform mozambique dresses—Rather dull chance for the 'Ulan dance' in those dresses!"

Sometime later the elder wrote bluntly that the mozambique looked well but there was too much fear of shaking it.

In the spring of 1871 the sisters received two dresses—one lawn and one print.

The brethren too found pleasure in having suits fashioned from new material. One wonders whether new cloth was responsible for their changing into summer uniforms earlier one season than the women. "Sab. 7 June, 1868—The sisterhood contemplated turning out in their uniform dresses today— should the weather continue favorable—The Brethren have been clad for two Sabbaths past in their uniform meeting dress —of Parker Mix—selected by Parker—minister at Canterbury —All wool 90% Indigo blue—rest white."

In 1849, while Hervey Eades was still living in Ohio, he published *The Tailor's Division System*, which answered the demand for "a system of designs for cutting out various articles of men's uniform dress." The large unpaged folio contained a number of plates accompanied by explanatory text.

Mrs. Finch, the English woman who visited the States during the middle of the nineteenth century, wrote a book of travels in which she devoted more pages to the Shakers than she did to the natural wonders of Mammoth Cave and Niagara Falls. In describing the Shaker dress, she wrote that the men, wearing their broad-brimmed straw hats and dark trousers, some with waistcoats and some without, looked like respectable farmers dressed in a comfortable but not unbecoming costume. As for the women's dress Mrs. Finch was not so complimentary: ". . . the dress of the women . . . is certainly the most ingenious device that ever was contrived for concealing all personal advantages. A bulbous-shaped muslin cap, that hides all the hair and covers half the face; a long narrow dress, with the waist at the arm-pit, so fashioned that the shoulders all look equally high, the neck covered with a little square white handkerchief, pinned down before, and a pocket handkerchief, folded in a small square, and pinned near the region of the heart, or thrown waiterwise over the arm, constitute a costume that would disguise the very Goddess of Beauty."

As the first half of the nineteenth century drew to a close, the South Union Believers, who had been enjoying their most normal and prosperous period, grew conscious of the fact that their pattern of ordered living was to be broken. Although they were accepted generally as regular members of the community life, there still remained a few neighborhood enemies. Those who felt the greatest animosity toward the Shakers were the men who had never forgiven the society trustees their purchase of the Grasslands farm through a secret bidder. As the slavery agitation grew in intensity over the nation, the jealous neighborhood group began to use the Shakers' abolitionist view as the basis for open persecution.

The first of the public demonstrations against the colony came in 1843 at the Christmas season. The Believers, who did not put great stress on the holiday itself, had it celebrated for them that year by some ruffians who came early in the evening, firing guns and hurling rocks through the windows. After firing through the frame and post from which the proclaiming roll hung, the group galloped to the Cross Roads. There they called at the cabin of the hired blacks and attempted to frighten the former slaves, who were living at Shakertown as free men. As they returned from the cabin, the celebrants were "yoweling most savagely with fiddle fife and a board or old tin pan with a pretense of serenading the town." The demonstration was more than an expression of the holiday spirit; actually it was the beginning of the attempt to drive the Shakers back to the northern colonies.

Later another "parcel of half drunk cowardly brutes" visited the society premises and shot into the Elder Brother's room, "hurting no one—perhaps not designing to but maliciously threw stones, breaking some glass in the washhouse." The Believers hoped that the carousers would reflect later on the effects of "mean whiskey and low morals."

On January 31, 1855, there occurred what the elder termed an outrage. "Eight men came at one o'clock at night & took

James Richards out of his bed conveyed him to Russelville &
incarcerated him in jail to be tried for interfering with blacks
claimed by some of the party—Sd Blacks have since been
freed—"

The following May the brethren received a letter from their
antagonists, demanding that the South Union society explain
its connection with the northern orders and that the book called
the *Holy Roll* said to be in the society's possession be made
available to the public. The journal account for June 1, 1855,
interpreted the events and fixed the blame as follows: "There
has been an effort of late to raise a party in the neighborhood
to exterminate the Shakers, drive them away to the North, &
then seize the property & use it at pleasure of Mobocratic party
—One Dr. Patterson who has not been very long in the country,
it seems has been very officious, he has been riding around the
country some 3 weeks striving to enlist in the scheme—others
in this infernal crew—the word infernal sounds harsh but I
think I should be excused for its use on the present occasion—
The *causes* for this raid, or intended raid, are various—the
principal avowed cause, is said to be, the interference of *Jas.
Richards* a member of the Society, to procure the freedom of
some persons of color, illegally held in bondage by some of the
party—2nd, Ever since the Society bought the Grassland farm
by a secret bidder, some of the neighbors have been seeking
pretexts to persecute us & 3rdly—Some doubtless engage in it,
hoping thereby to get a share of the property—In fact, it is
reported that the neighbors feeling sure of success have appor-
tioned verbally the different houses to certain individuals, &
are considering how they shall divide the domain into town lots
& so conduct a city to be devoted not especially to the most
high—"

The neighbors who accepted and admired the Shakers far
outnumbered Dr. Patterson's following, and it was they who
warned the Believers of the danger of the gathering mob. Realizing that some defensive steps were necessary, the society hired

Lawyer Bristow of Elkton and accepted the volunteer services of their Lawyer Benjamin Grider.

Accompanied by their friends and lawyers, the Shaker pacifists went to the Cross Roads to meet the mob. Seeing the formidable preparation of the Believers, the mob retreated from the society property to Dr. Rhea's farm, where, according to the record, the Shakers "met the enemy on his own dunghill." Taking the chair and denying the Shaker attorney the right to speak was John Burnham of Bowling Green, an avowed enemy. The attorney, however, "put it to the crowd whether they wanted to hear him." When the majority voted yes, he addressed the crowd, appealing to their sense of right. After much speaking on both sides, Bristow demanded the vote. Those who were in favor of legal proceedings were asked to separate themselves from those who were in favor of settling the question by violence. The brethren thought the majority vote accorded their side was well worth the lawyer's fee.

Hard feelings, however, were not fully erased by the voting. Some months later when Brother Eli rode out into the country, he came across Dr. Rhea and words passed between them. "The Dr. from behind the Buggy in which Eli was riding struck Eli a blow on the head which laid him lifeless for the moment—Fearing he had killed him—the Dr. got water & bathed him & then took the buggy & conveyed him to where some of the Brethren were at work on Grassland, saying he found Eli in that condition & did not know by what means it came about so added sin to sin by lying about it."

Thus it happened that the two decades which had been otherwise notable for normal living conditions and prosperity drew to a close marked by brawls and outrages which developed from the nucleus of neighborhood jealousy and which were intensified by the rising war prejudices. Being known as pacifists had not spared the society members the neighborhood trouble; neither would it keep them from becoming deeply involved in the imminent civil struggle.

XIII

WHILE THE PEOPLE WERE AT WAR

IN FEBRUARY, 1861, AT THE TIME WHEN IT was no longer possible to ignore the impending civil hostilities, Elder Hervey Eades was living at Union Village, Ohio. Writing from Ohio to his Kentucky associates, Eades voiced his personal views on the national crisis: "It seems that Brother Urban thinks that Kentucky will go out of the Union. I entertain no such fears—Simply because I think Kentuckians have entirely too much good Sense to commit an act so insane. I have long believed the present state of things would come to pass—It has come a little sooner than I anticipated. Yet, I think that if the Cotton or Gulf States do not fire the first gun—*Civil War* may be averted with... all its untold horrors —But, if they shall burn powder against the government forces; Then... the result, it seems to me, can hardly fail to be the freedom of every African that may be left alive in these now dis-United States."

After the war changed from rumor to actuality, the Shakers found themselves in an awkward position. Living in a state where the people were divided on the war issues, they very wisely attempted to maintain a neutral position; but this, they found, was extremely hard to do. Because of their early stand on the slavery question, they were looked upon with suspicion by the southern sympathizers. Because they held to their pacific position, they were out of favor with the Federals.

Throughout the war, and especially at the beginning, the colonists' chief anxiety was whether or not their position as conscientious objectors would be accorded official recognition.

By the fall of 1861 the members found themselves in the midst of the Kentucky Confederacy. "Nov. 1, 1861 *'Way down in Dixie!'* We are now in what is termed 'Dixie' western part of Kentucky—We are in the Seceded or Seceding part."

On one side of them the Bowling Green fort was occupied by the Confederates under the direction of General Buckner; on the other, Russellville had been the meeting place of the convention which had elected George Johnson governor of the seceding part of the state. As soon as the "bogus governor" had established his residence in Bowling Green, the Shaker leaders considered it advisable to consult both Buckner and Johnson in regard to their status. They were disappointed to find the general off duty for the day, but they were able to see the governor, who advised them not to invite censure by visiting the northern colonies. He also asked them to show themselves loyal to the new government. Johnson was not to head the irregular government long; instead he entered into active service and died the following spring at Shiloh.

As the first year of the war passed, the Shakers were glad to find that their attitude of pacifism was generally respected by the people who knew them. The trustees, returning from their business trips, brought home reports of public sympathy.

One such report came from Brother Urban, who had just returned from a train trip to Louisville. According to Urban's story the train crew had reason to fear trouble from the guerillas; so as a precaution they began distributing guns to all the passengers, with the instructions to shoot if the guerillas appeared. When they came to Urban, they did not hand him a gun. This, as well as other evidences of sympathetic understanding, helped to allay somewhat the Shakers' fears; nevertheless, they still anxiously awaited the government decision, for they were well aware that theirs was a dangerous situation.

From the beginning the Believers realized they would have to help both sides; otherwise, they would be the obvious enemy of the other. "Aug. 15, 1861—*Speck of war*—A company of Rebel Cavalry called here today & they have encamped at the head of our pond in sight—We felt best to be kindly—accordingly, we gave them supper & breakfast & plenty of fruit free of charge." When the Federals arrived they were given the same treatment. The Shakers, who might well be accused of buttering their bread on both sides, soon learned that their initial policy of free food would bankrupt them; so as the troops became more numerous, the society members began to charge a nominal sum for whatever was required of them.

The price generally asked was seventy-five cents per soldier for two meals and overnight accommodations—a rate which was very reasonable in view of the soaring war prices. The newspapers subscribed to by the colonists brought the news of the prevailing food prices. The *Atlanta Journal* for March 31, 1863, listed coffee at restaurants in Richmond at one dollar per cup. In Charleston a quarter would buy only a half-pound loaf of bread, and in Montgomery bacon was quoted at one dollar per pound.

The Shakers were usually given a receipt on the government for the soldiers' expenses and for the corn fed to their horses. But many times when groups were fed, the diarists recorded such statements as these: "Fed another group. Got only a quarter from one man," or "Received $1. for feeding six soldiers." There were numerous occasions when there was no remuneration. The Shakers often deplored the fact that the officers had a "knack at drawing up their receipts in a way to get around making an honest payment." Eldress Nancy was explicit about the matter. "It seems without a chance, the officers will swindle us out of all that sugar that was made a sacrifice to accommodate the sick. We could have sold every pound of it at the Depot and to our neighbors and got the money down."

Even though the Believers were angered at not being paid

what they had charged, they expected no favor in return. "Oct. 14, 1862 Brother Jefferson went to Bowling Green with provisions to *give* the sick soldiers—80 pies, 9 loaves of bread, ½ bushel peaches, & dried beef, etc." There was also the time when the sisters of the North and Center families heeded the request of prominent citizens of Bowling Green to help prepare a New Year's dinner for the soldiers. The sisters of the separate families worked together and prepared nine loaves of bread, four baked turkeys, ten baked chickens, and an ample supply of doughnuts. They also sent along two gallons of their own apple butter and some homemade catsup.

One summer day when a company of soldiers came by the village, Eunice had just gathered two bushels of early apples. Again hospitality was the keynote as Solomon distributed the fruit around to the soldiers as far as it would go. One soldier who rushed up for the apples asked, "What are they worth?"

"Why," replied Solomon, "they are worth eating."

Not fully understanding, the soldier repeated, "What do you charge?"

Convinced at last that there was no charge, the boy again expressed his thanks and helped himself. Then he and his companions went by the well to fill their canteens with cool water and left without making any demand for eatables.

Although they intended to play the role of neutrals, the Shakers in the beginning phases of the war were more sympathetic to the Federals than to the rebels. Numerous invective remarks directed at the latter are to be found in the diaries and journals kept at South Union at the time.

Eldress Nancy was quite outspoken. "It is said Tom (the thief) was a notorious horse thief before this war came on, and such are fit subjects for rebel guerillas." Again Nancy spoke tartly when she remarked, "This looks like the work of Rebels to give such information." Even the southern women failed to escape her scorn. "The young women who were escorted by the officers were of the secesh die . . . they were very light-minded

& real squealers." Evidently she came to expect the worst of all southerners: "It is certain there is something brewing among the Rebs . . . they seem so buoyant holding such high heads and lofty airs." It was with deep regret that the eldress noted that the humanitarian attitude was being rapidly replaced by a new hardness. The guerillas were more to blame than the devil if she is to be believed. "Is not this an awful day and time we live in, that a man's life is considered of no more value than to be murdered without trial of Judge or Jury; for the mere pitiful crime of stealing his neighbor's stock. They who can do such crimes must be actuated by a good degree of the spirit of a guerilla."

When the rebels evacuated Bowling Green, another South Union journalist wrote: "Feb. 18, 1862 Aspect changed—Rebels gone and Union Soldiers constantly here. How different from the Rebs they are—who would compel us to cook for them at any hour in the night—but these Union men would not allow the sisters to be disturbed from their rest for such purpose—they seemed well satisfied with a little cold bread & meat which they ate & passed quietly on."

The members felt deeply grateful to the Federal troops who patrolled the society property for some time as protection against the retreating rebels. There was rumor that had the southerners held Bowling Green, the South Union buildings would have been converted into a base hospital. The second rumor was that the rebels had been planning to burn the village.

When the rebels began retreating from the Bowling Green fort through the village, the Believers were greatly alarmed. They thought the "bold and desperate" soldiers were coming to carry out their threats. As the soldiers approached, the women gathered quickly at the entrances of the buildings. "They gathered in such numbers occupying the front steps & yard adjacent—that there was no chance to enter without apparently walking over a few dead women—they it seems were hardly prepared for that—While a number were guarding the entrance others were busy preparing something for them to eat—which when brought most of them partook—& finally left—promising to return & 'lay our town in ashes'—as they said Bowling Green was."

As soon as the soldiers had gone, the villagers began preparing for an all-night vigil. Even though colder temperature and sleet made the soldiers' return improbable, the men spent the night watching on the outside and the women on the inside. "A spirit of prayer prevailed throughout & many knelt in prayer at their stations . . . all or most of us believing in its efficacy & of the necessity of leaning on divine protection."

Five days later when the Union soldiers who were sent to protect the Shaker property arrived, they immediately took the precaution of burning the cowpits on the railroad. The Shakers, not being told the soldiers' intention, thought the rebels had returned in disguise and were starting about their threatened business of burning Shakertown. Before the truth was determined, there was near panic over the entire community.

After a few weeks of Federal occupation, life at the village became more normal. When mail arrived for the first time in six months, a member remarked, "We are now in the United States."

Yet as the war days passed, feeling against the southerners changed, and the sharp verbal outbursts began to be considerably modified. "The officers, Rebels, as they are, keep their men in pretty good order and conduct themselves with reasonable propriety & for an army of fighting men are not to be complained of—They expect to make some compensation for what is being done for them."

On the other hand, the Believers, including Nancy, began to find some fault with the Federals. The changed attitude toward the Union army came soon after the fall of the Bowling Green fort, at which time numerous Federal troops began to pass back and forth through the village. It became apparent to the Shakers that their Federal friends could also make in-ordinate demands for food and lodging. By autumn there was a different tone evident in the daily chronicles. "Nov. 12, 1862—Last night after we had retired a company of cavalry rode up & demanded supper. These men were as obtrusive and un-reasonable as the Rebels were. War imbrutes instead of re-fines. We either had to comply or suffer for not complying."

Only a week before the visit from the cavalry company, some five thousand of General Sill's cavalry division under the com-mand of Colonel Kennedy had encamped at Shakertown. Al-though they were asked by the brethren to camp in the nearby wood, the cavalrymen spent the night in the pasture, warmed by "3 or 4 thousand campfires all burning at once." The pleasure in the grand spectacle was somewhat diminished by the knowledge that the "beautiful lights" were made with the Believers' dry white oak rails, which were later estimated as twenty thousand in number. An additional loss was laid to "the d—d Teamsters" who stole fowls, baskets, and provender.

The day the cavalry moved on was a busy one for the Shaker men, who watered all the camp fires, collected the scat-tered corn and forage, and rebuilt the fences. The sisters, too, busied themselves about the pasture as they gathered up the fragments of meat for soap grease. As for the trustees, they lost no time in presenting a damage claim to the quarter-master at the Bowling Green post. They were told, however, that the voucher would have to come directly from the army itself. Jefferson overtook the army in Tennessee and received a voucher for $378. Two or three broken down horses which had been left behind at Shakertown made the only other com-pensation.

The provident Shakers took practical measures to avert a recurrence. "The brethren are hauling wood for soldiers camp fires—being obliged to do so in order to save their fences." Giving impetus to the men's effort to get a supply of firewood was the unusually low temperature. The newspapers recorded that it was the coldest winter in years. Southern Kentuckians, who were accustomed to having the first snow in December or January, were astonished by a three-inch snowfall on the twenty-fifth of October. Part of it was still on the ground at the time the cavalrymen had pitched camp. On January 15 they were surprised even more by a twelve-inch snow, the deepest for twenty years. Such heavy snow sent Reuben Wise and Asa Ware to the top of the tall Center House to clear the roof.

The unusual weather conditions lasted throughout the spring and summer. On August 30, almost two months early, there was a frost "the like of which has not been seen in this latitude in August for more than forty years." Some weeks before the frost, a company of thirty-six Michigan soldiers had come by with their forage wagons filled with hay. The lieutenant in charge called for supper, lodging, and breakfast for all his men, stating when he did so that he would not pay for it. In the same high-handed manner, the soldiers refused to take their wagons and teams to the place assigned them by the Shaker authorities. "At least," wrote the diarist, "the Rebels generally asked where they might quarter themselves; but those Michigan soldiers up and selected their own ground. They had their guns and bayonets & looked very saucy." Without asking for permission, the soldiers took as their own quarters several of the small community houses and the loom house. As for "three of the Big Bugs" they came to the Office expecting their lodging and meals.

When the supper was ready, the brethren had to carry the food to all the scattered places. The Shakers agreed among themselves that the action of these men was worse than that of the rebels—and this was a severe indictment. Even so, the Shakers did not fail in their generosity if the meals can be taken as a measure. What soldier could complain when his breakfast consisted of biscuits, loaf, dried pork, eggs, sausages, onion, pickles, sassafras and sage tea, as much milk as desired, stewed apples, butter, and corn bread?

The next morning the self-invited guests left in good humor, saying that the Shakers would have thirty-six new friends. However pleased the army men might have been with their food and sleeping quarters, the Believers did not feel very kindly toward their visitors: first, because of the dictatorial manner shown by the officers; and second, because the army mules were "so badly abused and little cared for." Nancy remarked that their mules were the poorest skeletons of animals that her eyes had ever seen.

Though they had been hospitable to the Michigan soldiers, the Shakers felt that they had sufficient cause to complain again to the Bowling Green military headquarters. The very next day Elder Hervey, who had recently returned from Ohio, went up on the morning train to ask Brigadier General Ormsby Mitchell to put a stop to such imposition. The officer was solicitous, saying that the men had come without orders, that he regretted the occurrence, and that he would arrest the commanding officer. Furthermore, he promised that in the future the soldiers would come to South Union with vouchers and provisions in their haversacks. The society members were well enough aware of worldly ways to see that "the General was very clever" and that they would not be relieved of such future situations, as indeed they were not. Yet the Believers remained gracious to all visitors, accommodating both the Federals and rebels with food and lodging. After three years of repeated impositions from both northern and southern troops, the Shaker ministry was convinced that they should seek relief from higher sources than from the military authorities stationed near them.

Added to the continuous abuses was the constant dread of the draft. In February, 1862, the "Bogus government" had demanded that every man who was worth $500 should give a gun or $20 in lieu of a gun.

In the following May, Federal handbills were posted, ordering all male citizens who had not done so to take the oath of

allegiance to the United States Government. "Anyone failing
to comply with the order was to be arrested and sent South of
the Federal lines, not to return again during the rebellion
under penalty of death." When Eades and Rankin protested
against the Believers' taking the oath, Brigadier General
Shackelford granted them a release for the men in the society.
However, the respite was short. A few weeks later a Federal
enrolling officer came to take the names of all men who were of
draft age. Such action sent Elder Hervey to Bowling Green
to confer with his lawyer and with the army officers. Returning
from unsatisfactory conferences in Bowling Green, the elder
told his co-worker John Rankin that the time had come to seek
President Lincoln's help. This conviction was further strengthened on August sixteenth when word came from New York that
the Mount Lebanon committee members sent to Washington
had failed in their mission to get the authorities to exempt the
Shakers from military service and that twelve eastern Believers
had already been drafted. Accordingly on the same day the
two men wrote Lincoln a lengthy letter in which they described
their perilous status.

"To the Honorable Abraham Lincoln
"President of the United States of America

"Kind Friend,

" *'Strike, but Hear'*

"The armies of the South like a great Prairie fire swept
over this part of Ky. in the fall & winter of 1861, licking up
the substance of the land—We were humbled before its power
and for many months remained the quiet subjects of the Confederate Government: Obeying all its behests save *one which*,
nobly & generously, they permitted us to disregard; and that
was to take up arms in their behalf. They encamped for days
as many as a thousand at a time, in our lots, and occupied our

buildings—We chopped & halved wood for their camp fires & slaughtered our animals for their commissariat—and at all hours in the night, were we compelled to furnish diets for hundreds at a time—

"They pressed all our wagons & horses of value for army purposes; but for these they paid us a moderate price in confederate scrip—It was then we prayed earnestly 'O Lord, who art Almighty if it be thy will deliver us from our enemies!' The worst of whom were our elected and high headed rebel neighbors—This our prayer was partially answered when your loud-mouthed Ordinance was heard to open on Bowling Green 14 miles north East of us—Since that time however, we have suffered much from the ebb and flow of the tide of war, until a good part of what the fire left—The merciless and surging billows have in their turn swept away. So that we have been left, as it were, writhing sometimes under the heel of *one* power, & sometimes *another*.

"Your armies have visited us, from the small squad to 5 or 6000 at a time—Our Barns were cheerfully relieved of their contents. Our fences turned into campfires—for these we have been paid by the government—But, gratuitously, have we furnished diets for thousands of your men—Of this we complain not—To our uniform kindness (if we must say it), all your armies that have passed us—All your hospitals within our reach—All your post surgeons and commanders can bear witness—When John Morgan destroyed the Bridge on Green River and cut off your supplies—Your officers pressed our sugar for hospital purposes—Our cellars disgorged themselves of nearly a thousand dollars worth, for which, so far, in account of some informality, we have striven in vain to obtain one cent remuneration—

"We state these things now, not by way of complaint but merely as grounds (coming to your knowledge) on which we may rest a hope, that we may be treated on the sensitive point, with as much lenity & as much justice as we were by the rebels whilst we were subjects of their government—

"Is it impossible that ones friends can be as tolerant As just & generous as their enemies? Must our prayers be now reversed? & Shall we cry to the Lord to be saved from our friends? After we have uncomplainingly borne until we can scarcely bear longer—Must we receive from the friends of our choice '*The most unkindest cut of all.*' besides the derisive jeers & mocks of our enemies? Shall the main support of 150 women children & invalids be taken from them? Might this indeed be added to our yet untold sufferings? To our bitter cup of war already drunk to the very dregs?

"Hear & grant it may not be—We have yet in our Society about 24 young men between the ages of 18 & 45 years, a majority of whom would be capable of doing some kind of service in the federal army, but whom *will not* shoulder a musket, nor bear about their persons the weapons of war—who having been taught from infancy *to love & not to fight*, their enemies, would sooner lay down their lives than to aid, *even very remotely* in taking that of another. If this was respected by the *Rebel* government, can it be ignored by the best worldly government that ever existed? Tis to be hoped not—were it possible to convince us that we *could love a man & shoot* him at the same time, (!) we could hardly spare either the numbers or the few thousand dollars demanded in lieu of them—Add to this the serious fact that these young men thro us their leaders have pledged themselves (We do not swear) not to fight against the Rebel government. Must we be compelled to violate this pledge? Certainly not—Still as long as we are able, we will 'feed the hungry & clothe the naked' as an act of Christian duty, but not for the purpose of supporting War— but will cheerfully 'render unto Caezar the things that are Caezars & unto God the things that are Gods.'—

"We are aware that you are oppressed and harassed on all sides & deeply do we sympathize with you, and hence will make our words few—If you cannot exempt all the Shakers in the North who have scarcely felt the war, never having witnessed your marshalled hosts, nor the desolating nor deathly dead of an Army—Is it selfish in us to claim that *our* pledges, *our* losses & *our* sufferings & that in the midst of your enemies demand that our Society in Ky. should be the object of your commiseration & fostering care? Or can it be God's will that after having been spared by our enemies we shall be blotted from the earth by our friends?! Surely not—

"To take the lambs of the flock to sure demoralization or slaughter, or further unrest from us our means of support, with all that has been done, will seem cruel—

"Our principles are above conditions—There is not money enough in the vaults of the nation to buy them, nor to induce *one truly honest Shaker*, to engage in *any* war against his fellow man.—We do not expect that absolute equality of burden is attainable in the present condition of things—only an approximation towards it; but where it can be, it should be— We ask for simple justice, nothing more—hardly that.—We look upon you, as not only the friend of humanity and the rights of man,—but as the chosen instrument of God in time of the nations peril—But the Instrument of God *dares to do right*. Now that our young men are threatened with enrollment and draft and are only held (some of them) by the leaders, from crossing the Tennessee line—We ask, & feel almost certain you will, from the foregoing considerations grant exemptions from draft, the few young persons, at least the more *conscientious* part of our community on whom we so much depend, seeing especially, that each one, has more to do for the support of the widows & the orphan, than the only Son of a widow now by law exempt.

"With what ease you can render us the simple justice for which we pray, and enable us to hold within our sacred precincts those of whom we shall shortly be bereft, if we 'find not favor in thy sight.'—Only tell us at the earliest possible moment, consistent with your other duties that you will release them, you will have done for us a favor, equal to all the losses we have sustained & will receive the cordial and heart-felt thanks of a grateful community.

"Want of knowledge, how to address persons of your position, will be an apology for any abruptness, or seeming harshness in the foregoing—

"We will not trouble you more but humbly wait & hope & pray—

> "We are most sincerely
> "Your friends—
> "John Rankin
> "H. L. Eades
> > "Leaders of the Society of
> > Shakers at Southern Logan
> > Co. Ky.

"To the Hon. *A. Lincoln*
"President of the U.S.A.
 "Washington City
  "D.C."

The Believers waited from August until the first of the next year before receiving an answer to their petition. On the second Sunday in January, when the mercury stood at one below zero, the Believers met for their regular service, and it was then that Elder Hervey reminded the brethren and sisters that God had been mindful of them in many ways. "The last, he said, was that a telegram had been received at Bowling Green from the good President at Washington."

The society members were greatly relieved by the contents of the message which read:

"To the Provost Marshal at Bowling Green,
Sir: If. there is any religious community within your district
whose conscientious scruples adjure war, or the payment of
the commutation fee, you will parole them indefinitely still
holding them subject to any demand from the authority there.

"E. M. Staunton, Sec. of War.
"Washington, D. C. December
"30-1863"

As it turned out, the official message did not erase all of the
military problems confronting the society. On September of the
year when the message had been received by the Bowling Green
headquarters, three of the Shaker brethren—William Ware,
Achille L'Hotte, and Ed Neeley—were drafted for military
service and called up for examination. Two of the three were
released upon incompetency to serve, but the third was held
to service. Soon afterward word came down to the village that
Colonel Hobson wanted the Shakers to give "him and also Dr.
Bailey a good milch cow as a *present*, seeing they had in their
power to do our community a favor of some magnitude."

Supposing the officials were not in earnest, the Shaker leaders did not go to Bowling Green immediately, but when John
Rankin did go to see the colonel, he came home to write for
the second time to the President of the United States. The
entire case was reviewed for Lincoln, after which Rankin wrote:
"I confess to some disappointment in Col. Hobson, after what
had incidentally passed between us before—He told me on one
occasion, that if I would write to you & give a history of our
case, he thought we would be released—I see not now why he
hesitates, unless something as large as a cow has got in his
way—But this he avers is only a joke—and I cannot affirm
that it is any more—I should regret to see him superceded were
it even deemed prudent & necessary—I think him an active
and competent officer.—

But Oh! Mankind are unco weak
And little to be trusted
If self, the wavering balance shake,
'Tis rarely right adjusted.

Burns

All we want is what is right—And if we may be pardoned for a little officiousness, we would beg to suggest, that, in order to place the Col. out of temptations way—that his decision be made to rest upon the *facts*, as we have given them to you—to which more could truthfully be added."

What Rankin did add to the already lengthy letter was his personal views on the rights of the Shakers. "We bind the conscience of no one, but those who have conscientious scruples we would preserve—If there ever was a time in the world history that the shedding of human blood was justifiable, that time is now: For, never were lines more clearly defined.—The one for—the other *against*, *liberty* & the *rights* of *man*. The former *must*, the latter *cannot* succeed."

In conclusion the elder described the conditions of the society as they were in the past year of the war. "I will barely remark in closing that we number 210 Souls—Of this number there are 170 women and children, besides a number of infirm old men—The institution is, under God, a clear *charity*, & all these need good milk full as much as our friend Hobson or any other officials who are fattening at the public crib, whilst we really are losing:—Our little community are under many obligations of thanks to you for your condescension in past notice & care.—Not indeed because you are *partial*, but because you are *just*."

The journal which continued through 1877 contains no reference to a presidential answer.

There is no denying that the Logan County Shakers were in a difficult position during the war period, a position which required them to be both resourceful and persistent. Being friendly to both sides, conferring with civil and military authorities, and writing directly to the president were all means by which they helped to clarify their position; but effective as these methods may have been, the colonists probably highlighted their neutrality best simply by going about their daily business as normally as possible in what were abnormal times. Although the war cut across the society life in many ways, the journals give ample evidence that the members continued their industrial and agricultural pursuits. They gathered the cherries, threshed the wheat, filled the mows with rye and hay, gathered the beans for winter use, plowed the strawberry field, and went to Nashville for hides. Under the date of February 23, 1864, the journal contained the item: "Work in the different branches seems progressing well with the force we have—One company of Sisters putting up seeds—Another weaving—Another making Bonnets, Another Spinning Silk—Another weaving—Another ironing, Another cooking—Another hat making—Brn. at their usual avocations—carpeting, shoemaking, stock feeding, getting in logs and firewood—" Two days later Eades and McGown left for the first wartime seed trip down the Mississippi. Returning in a month, they reported the sales amount as $1,450, but the expenses had been nearly $400.

Even in wartime, the Shakers took time to combine work and play. "May 24, 1864 Fishing party—Brother Jackson McGown, Logan John, and William Booker took the teams and started for Green River for the double purpose of catching some fish and bringing home the Bark pealers."

New business opportunities created by the war were not overlooked by the Shakers. "Mch. 21, 1863 Selling milk 25¢ gal. Greens 6¢ lb. to soldiers. . . . Sept. 22, 1863 Br. Shannon goes to see military authorities in Bowling Green about supplying them with wood for the railroad. Accomplished nothing."

The attempt to carry on as usual was applied not only to business but to education and religion as well. "May 22, 1864

Elder Hervey called on the little boys and took them through a drilling in the dance to help them to a little more freedom & zeal & to learn a degree of order. . . . Jan. 21, 1863 Commenced Night School for the Young Sisters."

A second night school that year was organized for mutual improvement. It "commenced at the Garden House to be continued so long as it is orderly." The Shaker love of improvement remained constant and was expressed in various odd ways. "Mch. 30, 1861 We have lately concluded to admit artificial teeth in the Society—Accordingly we sent North for a Dentist—who is now here, taking impression—& supplying the Sisters with artificial teeth with Vulcanite Rubber base @ $30.00 per set—Sister Jency Dillon & Prudence Houston received theirs today. . . . 1863 Brother Urban brought us a nice little satchel a piece & a superb clock. Elder Hervey set up the clock in our shop room."

Although they had been advised by the Confederate governor not to visit in the North, the Shaker ministry renewed their exchange of visits with their neighboring Ohio friends as soon as the Federals took possession of Kentucky. When the Ohio ministry came to South Union in 1863, "all went out to Flat Rock—had a fine time generally. After some general recreation and partaking some repast of provisions brought along—We repaired to the North round rock held a little meeting singing & marching the slow march—After which some speaking by Elders J. R. & H. L. Eades. Returned home between 1 & 2 P. M."

The trustees, too, made whatever business trips to the north that they felt were necessary. "June 23, 1863 U. E. Johns went to Cincinnati to bring home 500 dozen fruit cans to be filled for sale. . . . Sept. 5, 1863 Brother U. E. Johns returned from New York having made the desired purchase—about $2000."

The fact that the Shaker property was in the path of the armies and might suffer considerable damage did not discourage the owners from exercising their usual care of both the buildings and grounds. "Oct., 1863—Building Repaired—repairing chimneys of Center House—putting on stone caps. . . . Jan. 20, 1864—Building a bridge by mill—Better than former one—good roof to protect it from the weather. . . . May 4, 1864—Laying of stone walk from Office to East House. Had a Bee. H. L. Eades laid most of the stones. . . . June 2, We commenced the cleaning of the upper part of the Meeting House. Eldress Jency helped us. We continued to red up and scratch out the dirt—Jackson and Eldress Jency mopped all the rooms & halls & blacked the stoves and stove pipes."

One person who was quite favorably impressed with the Shakers' care of their property was Captain McPherson, who came from the Bowling Green fort in 1863 to visit the colony. The captain, accompanied by two women of southern sympathies, came down to inspect the village and to find out more about the community. While there he remarked to his companions regarding a new stone walk: "We ought to engrave in deep letters which can never be erased, 'Laid in the year of the Rebellion of 1863. While the people of the United States were at war fighting and killing each other the Shakers remained quietly at home improving their village.' "

As he continued his inspection of the Shaker premises, the captain saw the fresh paint in the meetinghouse, the newly planted ornamental evergreens, and the lumber shop and carriage house which had been built less than a year. Perhaps he noticed too that the old log kitchen north of the brick shop had been torn down. He became more and more pleased with the neat manner in which the community was kept. "The good care," he exclaimed to his lady friends, "argues strongly against slavery." Eldress Nancy, who had been listening, added her own ardent "Amen."

During the war years, Shakertown had many military visitors who, like the captain, were genuinely interested in learning something about the Believers' communal experiment.

There was at least one exception, however, in the rough young soldier who demanded an explanation of the Shaker non-participation views. In attempting to answer the boy, Elder Brother Solomon cited the scripture: "If a man smite thee on one cheek, turn the other." Whereupon, the soldier struck Solomon. When Solomon turned the other cheek, the young soldier struck that too. Laughter from the idle crowd added to the indignity suffered by the elder brother.

A highly respected visitor was Colonel Nixon, who, according to the journal, could be styled a real southern gentleman and who deserved a chapter to himself. A New Jersey man by birth, the colonel had been residing in the South for twenty years and in civil life was editor of the New Orleans *Crescent*. While spending five days at the village, the colonel read many of the Shaker books. His hosts were delighted to hear his praises of their books and their way of life and to have him say that he could recommend Shakerism to his children.

Also expressing interest in the Shaker experiment were some Texas rangers, who were curious to know how the ninety people living in the Center House could get along without fighting and killing each other. Being told that the Good Man taught that swearing, fighting, and killing were wrong, the rangers said they did not know the Good Man, that he did not live in Texas!

"Anyway," said one of the group, "if you don't fight and kill, how do you keep yourselves busy?"

"Working for our living and for something to give the poor," replied the informant.

"But what do you do on Sundays?"

"Read and write and go to Meeting."

"Well," said the Texans in more subdued tones, "this must be a heaven on earth of peace. You are certainly a very good people."

Later when a soldier group was riding through the Shaker streets, one brother overheard two of the riders discussing life in the village. Said one, "Everything is held in common here as in the church of old. Here all work from the least to the greatest. Don't you wish everybody was like them?"

"Yes," answered the other, "in that case we wouldn't be a-fighting the Yanks."

Respect for the Believers was expressed also by the Negro who said, "Dar is no religion in dis country only what de Shakers has; de rest is all done gone up."

In their attempt to maintain their neutrality and to live as normal lives as possible even though the armies were surging back and forth across their land, the Shakers both won and lost friends. There were those who, like the Negro, admired them for holding to their religious convictions at all costs; there were others who felt they were failing in their rôle as citizens, that in dancing and singing, planting, hoeing, and reaping they were not contributing anything constructive to the war effort, but were, instead, continuing to prosper in spite of, if not because of, the national crisis.

It was such jealousy, chiefly of the neighborhood, that increased the difficulty of the Shaker position and caused Nancy to write in her diary: "Are these not perilous times?" and then give her own answer, "I think so."

XIV

ARE THESE NOT PERILOUS
TIMES?

NO MATTER HOW SINCERELY THE SHAKERS
tried to remain completely outside the war current,
there was seldom a day during the four years when they
were not forcibly reminded of the war, either by numerous
military visitors, by the constant passing of troops—both
Federal and rebel, or by attendant war evils—robberies and
incendiary fires.

Many robberies and fires were attributed to the guerillas
who were very active around the community. They robbed
private stores, burned depots of government supplies, and
wrecked Federal supply trains. At times the Shaker farmers
would discover that the railroad tracks running across their
own land had been torn loose or obstructed. In the name of
humanity, not of the Federals, they would warn the engineer
of the danger. Frequent skirmishes occurred between the
guerillas and the trainmen, one leaving a young guerilla dead
on the Shaker land. As the brethern were preparing to bury
him, some Federals came saying they would take the body to
Russellville and make the rebels do it in order to teach the
enemy a lesson. From this time on, it became a common occurrence for the brethren to find bodies on their premises. Now
and then, news came to the village that some of the guerillas
had been "shot and apprehended;" whereas others had been
hanged.

The villagers were depressed to learn that one of their neighbors "who had been thought to be respectable" had been caught and shot while robbing a second neighbor. That there was still a spark of chivalry left in the "highwaymen" was learned from the story of how they helped a stalled peddler, but robbed him immediately thereafter.

Orders had been given that the guerillas were not to be arrested or captured, but were to be shot or "hanged right up." The Louisville *Daily* carried the announcement that the death penalty would also be meted to anyone who aided them. Since so many were men from southern Kentucky, like Henry Hines and Edgar Mitchell of Warren County and Tom Mc-Elwain of Todd County, they were at home in the vicinity and were adept at dodging their would-be captors. As a final resort the Federals threatened the wives of the guerillas, hoping that fear for their wives' safety would bring the men out of hiding.

Not only were the guerillas good at evasion, but they had many tricks to use in their unconventional warfare. When Colonel Johnson was commanding one of three bodies of Federal troops in southern Kentucky, he was told that some guerillas were seen eating at Steward's near Pilot Knob, Simpson County. Rushing over, Johnson's men opened fire, killing a captain and wounding a lieutenant before they discovered that they had been misinformed and were shooting their own men. High above, perched on the knob itself, the gleeful rebels watched.

Johnson's error was an easy one to make. Many similar mistakes were made in the territory where both armies were constantly shifting and where guerilla warfare was engaged in by both sides, with those taking part dressed in almost any conceivable uniform.

Several months later in the small town of Auburn a Federal officer, Lieutenant Bennett, came suddenly upon a band of Federal foragers. Without pausing long enough to determine their identity, he fired into their midst. Naturally, the group scattered quickly. As one man rushed by a store door, his own gun went off. Believing the attackers were closing in on them, the foragers made an even more desperate attempt to escape and reach help in Russellville. When the nervous officer discovered his mistake, he sent out his courier with a white flag, but the men had "skedaddled" so fast they could not be overtaken. Later, when those pursued returned with help, the mistake was made known, and all were happy except the soldier whose gun had gone off. He was still convinced that someone had aimed directly at him. It took a dozen witnesses and his own unloaded gun to prove to him that he had been fleeing needlessly from his own gun fire.

Many instances were cited by the Shaker journalists regarding the nervousness of the undrilled soldiers. It was a drizzly, wet day in January, 1865, when fifteen guerillas dressed in Federal uniforms, "splendidly mounted and equipped, came dashing" into the village. Coming directly to the Center House, they divided, some going to the Office stable and some to the Center stable. Finding that the horses were in the pasture, they undertook to capture them. Although the horses were old, "the badly scared soldiers could not get any one they wanted."

Events happend so fast in and around South Union that the ministry were at a loss to know what was most important to record in the house journals and in their private diaries. Every day brought its new bits of excitement to the interested but somewhat terrified villagers. Often there were distressing accounts from their neighbors. There was the time when William McKerley lost seven hundred dollars and a watch but at the same time was fortunate enough to save four thousand dollars. Later their neighbor McLemore was forced to reveal the hiding place of his savings in order to keep his house from being burned. It was not until after the soldiers had gone so far as to scatter the powder around the floor and over the bedclothes that McLemore directed them to his savings. A widow in the community was robbed of her jewelry and money, but an orphan girl living in the same house protested so vigorously about the $2.50 which the men took from her own apron pocket that she got the money back. She did not, however, recover her ring and breast pin. There was the news that John McCutcheon was ordered by a major to bring out four horses for the soldiers. When McCutcheon had begun to make excuses about not being able to bring his wife's buggy horse and another one which had only one eye, the major said gruffly, "I reckon they have four legs. If so, bring them on."

Early one August morning, after the guerillas had visited him the night before, Dr. Rhea, one of the neighborhood leaders against the Shakers, sent his son to the village to implore the brethren's help in defending his home. "We informed him," wrote an elder, "of what he ought to have known before, that we would not fight to defend our own home."

Once a story circulated that ten or twelve Federal soldiers had deserted their camp and had gone into a field where there were Negroes at work. According to the rumor, the men had exchanged their uniforms for the work clothes of the Negroes, remarking as they did so that they were not going to fight for the Negroes any longer. There was much conjecture at South Union as to whether or not the Negroes dressed in Federal uniforms would be lucky enough to escape the attention of the guerillas, who would shoot at sight any Negro believed to be joining the northern cause.

Not only were there many similar neighborhood stories, but the newspapers were a source of much war news. "From the Nashville *Daily Union* January 20 we read of an awful bloody battle at Stone River between General Rosecrans army and General Braggs.... Feb. 5, 1863 We hear from the newspapers that the notorious rebel John Morgan with 5000 cavalry have made another raid on the L & N railroad tearing up the rails & destroying one bridge on this side the Cumberland river between Clarksville & Nashville at Salem." Sometimes the news concerned proposed troop movements. There was the time the Shakers heard that ten thousand Federals had been moved to Bowling Green because "John Morgan contemplated making another dash." It was Nancy who wrote: "The news prints abound with stirring events & some most awful to relate such as robbing, stealing, murdering, burning, and destroying property, houses, towns and cities. All of which is calculated to demoralize & bring poverty & suffering over these once flourishing & prosperous U.S., but now divided & in the worst possible condition." Nancy added her thanks "for the quiet and protection" which South Union still afforded in a limited way.

Often news came down from the Bowling Green fort. When General Buckner's men first took possession of Bowling Green in September, 1861, one of the soldiers had gone onto the roof of the court house in order to take down "the United States flag—the stars and stripes and to substitute the Rebel flag— the stars and bars." To express his hatred for the Union, the soldier began stamping the flag. A moment later he lost his balance and fell from the roof to his death.

But all of the topics for discussion did not grow out of the newspaper stories nor from those of the neighboring fort or community. Exciting things were happening daily at the village itself. Perhaps the event was merely the passing of the long troop trains, so heavily loaded that at times the soldiers had to get out and walk until the train got over the grade. In the early months of the war when the Confederates were being moved over the railroad, the air would reverberate "with their worse than savage & hideous yells as the cars came roaring & whistling by."

On other occasions the air was filled not with Rebel yells, but with the steady beat of feet tramping in time to the martial music of the fife and the drum. Sometimes tuneful sounds came from brass bands. When a group of Federals camped for the night, their band serenaded the town, going from family to family playing "a good many nice tunes." The next morning the Shakers "came to time" with a breakfast of "fresh loaf & biscuit, good coffee, boiled beef, fried ham, sweet & Irish potatoes, canned peaches, fresh strawberries, & butter & corn-bread & fried eggs." As the soldiers left, "they played two handsome tunes, swung their hats & cheered for South Union."

There was at least one breakfast, served when the cooks did not serve good coffee. Instead the "drink was sassafras tea and rye coffee," which the soldiers "jocosely called Jeff Davis coffee."

The Kentucky Believers found that the war gave new meanings to many words. When military agents came to take the Shaker horses and wagons by force, they were said to "delicately term it 'pressing'." Or again, a group seeking shelter for the night, "seized or as they say pressed the cow barn. The poor cows had to take the pitiless storm." As one elder quipped, the word "steal" had become obsolete; whereas "appropriate" and "press" had taken its meaning.

The army officials from the Bowling Green post paid calls now and then. "May 27—1863, *Military Visit* Gen'l Judah, Post Military Commander, & staff & bodyguard & some secesh ladies—50 noses to smell strawberries & That many mouths to eat them ... How tired we are of soldiers." The group's desire for strawberries had been particularly annoying to the economy-minded Believers because at that season the uncapped berries were selling at one dollar per gallon. Nancy complained that the military party had only pretended an interest in the Shaker principles, that actually they came "to get a feast of the good things which Shaker Town can produce." "... dinner furnished. To my notion it was extravagant— Boiled ham, baked mutton, both stew & fried chicken, cake, loaf, & corn bread, Irish potatoes, pickles, asparagus, onions, lettuce, radishes, poached eggs, butter, milk, coffee, straw-berries & peaches to grace the table where the General & ladies sat." However, not all visitors were of military rank. "June 6, 1863 Pestiferous—24 more persons here from the county for dinner. . . . June 12 What are we to do with the neighbors— 25 more here for dinner today. These besides the hirelings make it hard for the Sisters."

The Believers were not only annoyed by some who visited them, but at times they were thrown into a state of apprehension. Such was the case when some rowdies went to the Black Lick tract and called at the house where the Shakers' colored hired hands were staying while they were cutting the government timber. The vandals frightened the Negroes by announcing themselves as guerillas who had come to shoot or hang them. All the Negroes—men and women—escaped to the woods, coming back next day still very badly frightened.

One afternoon troops approaching the village alarmed one of the hired darkies so much that "he took to his scrapers and dashed over the fences thro the hen lot to get out of sight." As he ran, he startled a young sister who was gathering mulberry leaves for her silk worms.

"Lor' bless you, missus," called the darky, "the sesh are comin'—they are comin' right on us now." The girl, also frightened, "made tracks for the house."

Then on a hot July day in 1864 the Shakers were cursed and shot upon by an angry military group. It happened when some soldiers were passing through the village that two of the group, neither of whom was properly uniformed, rode up to the Shaker barn to exchange a lame horse for a fresh one. Just as the soldier mounted one of the few horses remaining at Shakertown, Lorenzo and Jefferson came up. It was Jefferson who caught up a stone in each hand, ready to use force if the supposed robber gave trouble.

"You are too fast," shouted Lorenzo. "You are not going to take them horses. We are the proper owners."

Seeing the stones in Jefferson's hands and the fire in the

eyes of both Shakers, the young fellow dismounted, explaining, "My lieutenant told me to get a fresh horse."

"It matters not who sent you. You are not going to take them." And added Jefferson, "You may as well surrender. You are our prisoner."

Stepping over to the horse, Lorenzo removed the saddle and bridle and gave them to one of the little boys standing near by. "Take it," he said, "and hide it in the woods." The sisters, who heard the disturbance at the barn, commenced ringing the big bell.

"What is the damned bell ringing for?" demanded the captive.

"It is to call the soldiers from the depot."

"What soldiers?" shouted the other visitor as he put spur to his horse and made for the lane without waiting for the answer. Hearing the brethren call for someone to head him off, the rider made the horse "spread himself" in order to get away and catch his own group. As soon as Lieutenant Phelps, who was in charge, heard that one of his men was being held, he "became furious and turned back, cursing and swearing and threatening vengeance."

Upon reaching the village, the officer became even angrier when he learned that the captive had been hidden away. After an unsuccessful search of the horse lot, the men threatened to shoot. A moment afterwards they put their threats into action by shooting three times at Averett and twice at John Perryman, who dodged behind a tree just as the bark was cut from it. The soldiers kept shouting, "We'll shoot him! Where is he? We'll shoot him!"

"Shoot him?" repeated the women, now collected in excited groups. "Are they going to shoot their own man?"

Above the general confusion could be heard the sobs of the culprit, a beardless young boy, who, because he also thought that he was to be shot, was so frightened that the muscles in his face were quivering and jerking. "Here I am," he called piteously. "Shoot me or do as you please."

But the anger of the lieutenant and his companions was directed not toward the boy, but toward the Shakers. With curses, the officer poured out his anger, accusing them of being traitors to their country and expressing his belief that rebels were harbored there, since they could be traced all around and no farther.

"You ought to be blowed out and the place destroyed!" stormed the young officer. "Here we are going night and day to protect you, and what in the name of Hell do you do for your country?"

In face of the vitriolic criticism, the Shakers, both men and women, tried to assuage their attackers. Pointing out that not one of the soldiers was dressed in proper Federal uniform, the brethren said they had believed the two taking the horse to be some of the many robbers abroad in the country, and they also explained that the women had rung the bell trying to call some Federal soldiers who were known to be near. The lieutenant could not be convinced. He insisted that the bell was a signal to call up guerilla bands.

More Shaker women began to appear in the horse lot, carrying pies, milk, bread, and apples. It was plain that the sisters hoped that appetizing food might aid in the cause of appeasement and might be more effective than gentle reasoning had been thus far. With the food before them, all of the men except Lieutenant Phelps helped themselves, but they said they agreed with the one who exclaimed, "This is damn sham kindness."

As for Phelps, he declared, "I'm too mad to eat. Go back in the house. I don't want to talk to you."

"I'm at home and don't need any one to invite me into my own home," flared Irene.

Whereas, gentler Eldress Jency replied, "I'd like to see you in a better humor before I go."

As the men prepared to leave, Phelps insisted on knowing the names of the two brethren who had captured his soldier. Being unable to ascertain their names, he rode off threatening to burn the whole place. The diarist who recorded the story concluded ". . . it was more than Lt. Phelps' proud haughty nature could bear to know that one of his armed men had been taken prisoner by our unarmed brethren."

The incident had occurred on Sunday when there were outsiders present at the public meeting. Some of these, rebel in sympathy, went about tittering, being very much diverted at the row, for they believed the vindictive marauders to be rebels. But none ever knew for certain what the intruders were, though one young Shakeress said she believed they were "Federal guerillas."

There was yet another time when the quiet of the South Union village was greatly disturbed by some soldiers who stopped to have their horses shod. Finding the service too slow, they helped themselves to all the nails and shoes around the shop. Then they started on to the next shop, lingering only long enough to question some of the little boys who happened along.

"Come here," one of the men called to the boys, "or the bushwhackers will get you." As the children came over, the man asked, "Are you ever troubled with guerillas?"

"Sometimes we are."

"What do you do when they come?"

"We drive them away."

"That's right. What are your people generally, rebel or Federal?"

"We are all Union."

"Your old horse is not worth a damn," interrupted the soldier who had been examining the boys' horse.

The soldier could have made the same comment about any of the Shaker horses, for the society had lost seventeen horses, and among those left there was none "that either the Rebels or the Federals would have." Early in the war the foresighted trustees had sent some of their best horses to Princeton, Indiana, for safekeeping. Having so few horses left at the village, they were forced to meet the farming needs by buying some mules from their neighbor Sam Bland. When the mules were placed in the stables in January, 1865, it was the first time that mules had been kept by the society. "We are driven to it of necessity," explained an elder.

Appearing one day at the Shaker blacksmith shop were two soldiers who had orders to cut the telegraph wires which crossed the Shaker farm. Needing an ax, the men began a search through the woodhouses and sheds. Not finding one, they asked several workers around the premises where they could get an ax, but no one seemed to know. By the time they approached the gardener Frederick and heard another noncommittal answer, the soldiers were exasperated enough to exclaim, "Well, how in the name of the devil do you get your wood cut without an ax?"

Hoping, perhaps, that a soft answer would turn away wrath, Frederick responded quietly, "I'm a gardener and don't cut wood."

Forced to leave their assignment undone, the soldiers rejoined their company where one of them reported, "This is the poorest damned place I was ever in. Can't afford a single ax!" After the soldiers left, the Shakers had a good laugh about the whole affair.

During the period when robberies were so common throughout Kentucky and Tennessee, when any unprincipled person could disguise himself as a guerilla and rob at will, the Shaker society was remarkably fortunate in sustaining only a few losses, and with the exception of the supplies that were pressed, even those were small. "Sept. 31—61—The Rebels took 48 yards of Blanket cloth out of the fulling mill—Worth $60.00. . . . Dec. 9—61 Grab Game. This morning being rather cool, a Rebel Soldier concluded he must have an overcoat & proposed to buy one. Offered one at $5. he said he could pay $2. in Southern scrip, but finally he disappeared with both overcoat and scrip. . . . Jan. 2—1862. Texans came—asked to buy jeans—took it saying they needed it because they were fighting our battles. Not even a thank you, Sir."

The Shakers profited from these early experiences. Afterwards the extra blankets, cloth, and clothing were hidden away. Further caution was taken in that the members rationed these items among themselves. The winter of 1861 "being uncommonly mild," they got "along pretty comfortably with a small allowance." The exercise of such caution did not save them entirely, for there are occasional later references to losses. "Dec. 1, 1864—Robbery—Someone entered the factory and cut 50 yards of flannel out of the loom. Injured loom also."

The Believers seemed to have suffered more from the constant dread of what might happen than from any actual robbery. There was the day when ". . . 4 very suspicious looking men called at the Office & said they wished to purchase some cloth, Leather, Garden seeds, etc. They first called for Gray cloth, Black Cloth, fustic drab cloth, blue Jeanes, & silk for dresses. They pushed into the sisters room after brother Jesse R. without any invitation & nothing that was presented in the way of cloth was the right thing. They appeared to want to find out what we had on hand & where it was located." The total purchase of the men was only a quarter's worth of seeds. The Shakers felt certain the men were plotting a future robbery. Although there was an immediate wave of robbery throughout the community, the Shakers were not visited. "We have reason to believe that four of these robbers were the same men who came to our office pretending to buy cloth & to find out if we had anything worth coming to take, but finding so little they turned another way & perhaps the Lord had mercy on us for the righteous sake."

The Believers had another scare the time the key to the little vault was missing. When a quick search did not reveal it, the safe was forced open. They "found the lucre all there safely; but they removed its contents to another part of the town."

Numerous warnings were received at Shakertown as to probable visitation by robbers. In the fall of 1864 the trustees were warned by an express agent to hide their account books. Two days later they again followed a warning to hide the horses and to keep the lights burning all night. Although stories about their neighbors' losses continued to come to their attention, the Believers remained relatively unmolested. The hired carder and spinner, George Copley, was convinced that the society enjoyed special protection from the robbers. Because so many intended raids had been thwarted, he felt that a charm must have been thrown over the place. The more religious attributed the protection not to a charm, but to "kind providence which has been manifest towards his heritage since the commencement of this bloody war."

Spared as they were from raids, the Shakers did not escape from heavy fire losses. There were four major fires, all of which were thought to have been set by incendiaries. One occurred just prior to the beginning of the war; two occurred during the war, and the fourth came in June following the surrender of the Confederacy. In January, 1861, the dwelling of the West Family burned to the ground. Fortunately the shutters, doors, bedding, and furniture were all saved. In September of the next year their hired Negroes warned the leaders that some of the white neighbors meant to burn out the community. Had the warning been taken more seriously, the sixty-thousand-dollar loss of factory and grist mill might easily have been averted.

As it happened there was no insurance to cover the loss estimated as follows:

Factory building—100 ft. long—3 stories high with machinery, engine, spinning jack, all carding machines $35,000.

Grist mill—75x45   3 stories high and all machin-

ery $18,000.

Wool and cloth $6,000.

                                            $59,000.

The railroad depot, filled with government-owned corn and tobacco, was burned in February, 1863. Rebuilt, it was burned again in June, 1865.

Of the many petty war annoyances the Shakers had to endure, none was regretted more than having their Sabbath days disrupted. There were many Sabbaths like the one in February when the one o'clock meeting was delayed while the sisters "gathered up a very comfortable dinner of light bread and cold meat & peach pies & milk" to feed fifteen Federal soldiers, or such as the day when "part of the 26th Kentucky Infantry (mounted) passed thro the Village about one o'clock, just after we had commenced church meeting. They loitered in the streets while listening to the singing and at the well getting some good water." Someone counted "two hundred infantry with their drums and fife and 14 wagons, ambulances, etc."

The war added its note of excitement to all the outings made by the nonbelligerents. There was the time when a group had to leave the road and hide the horses from a group of guerillas. Another group set out on a pleasure trip but was detained by the military authorities, who pronounced the passes insufficient.

The government fortifications in Bowling Green attracted parties from the society. A company made up of seven sisters and two brethren from the Center House made a sightseeing trip to the fort, traveling by carriage and buggy. As the carriage proceeded up the steep hill to the fort, a bolt gave way, causing the carriage to overturn, hurting four of the sightseers, and badly damaging the vehicle.

The war was blamed for all kinds of trivial things. Nancy

voiced the women's complaint of having too little wood to burn. This lack of fuel caused much of the handicraft to be done in the dwelling rooms instead of in the more commodious and convenient shops. Said Nancy: "It is impossible to hire hands to cut wood for us and our young brethren have been too tenderly raised to think of turning out & cutting wood as the brethren did in days and years gone by. . . . But may be they will yet come to it."

Evidently the forty brethren, some of whom were infirm, remained negligent of their tasks, for soon afterward the women were reported to be carrying cobs from the barn in order to have cooking fuel. When the cobs were all picked up from the first barn lot, the women went half a mile to the big barn and brought back six bushels of cobs. "Great management this," wrote the indignant little Civil War eldress.

The prevailing war spirit was held responsible for a growing hardness of heart and for much laxness in the younger Shakers. Nancy had once identified the lack of humanitarianism with the rebel spirit; but as the war continued, she found this spirit accompanying both armies, and she expressed the fear that the Shakers also were coming too much under the influence. She wrote: "Certainly the time has been in this place, that we could not have suffered a well man to lie down on the bare floor without bed or covering, much more to let one who is sick with ague chills & fever to come in dripping wet, & then have to dry his own clothes & then rest the best he could by the fire. How can we save our young people? These strangers, men and women, push themselves into the dwellings & shops & flatter the young sisters with their beauty & some are fools enough to believe them."

It seems only natural that in those chaotic times when so much license was being taken by everybody, that many of the Believers should have become less serious about their own rules and customs. But Nancy belonged with those who clung even more closely to their tenets, and, in so doing, found a needed security at a time when the outside world was going to pieces around them.

The laxness among the younger members became so noticeable that sermons were directed toward its correction. "Elder John spoke against so much loud, boisterous, ungodly laughing and conversation which is heard across the street by the world, who when they come here look for better things, as we are called to be an example of virtue, purity and godliness, Yea as a city set on a hill." As for the practical virtues which he meant for his charges to follow, the elder was quite explicit. "He exhorted us to be decent and cleanly & to have our surroundings in good order. . . . To be careful to shut the gates after passing thro them . . . said there was too much indifference about this thing. If a brother in passing about the premises should observe an open gate, he should shut it, and if there is a board off, or an opening in the fence wherein a hog or any animal might intrude themselves where they are not wanted or should not run; he should not rest until it is mended and made secure. And if thro carelessness by leaving the gates open, or fences marred, animals should get into enclosures where they should not be, it is unmerciful and wicked to bear, whip or abuse them by throwing stones. . . . I want all the younger part of the family to know it is a Penitentiary crime. . . . It seems that we shall be under the necessity of buying law books for the school that our young folks may learn from them what is a criminal offense."

Not only the members, but the world too received criticism for their behavior at the public meetings. The ministry observed that the outsiders "behaved badly & paid little attention to the speaking . . . they seemed to be more engaged in their courtship & plays than the preaching."

Disturbed by the shallow spirituality as well as by the evident disharmony everywhere, Nancy sought emotional release

in creative writing. In her poem "A Prayer for What I Love"
even the limping rhythm of one stanza does not eclipse her
sincere desire for release.

> I'd love to sail on angel's wings
> To where there's no resentment.
>
> Where all in harmony agree
> To love and bless each other.
> O 'tis the place for you & me
> Come let us go together.

The eastern Shakers were aware of the hardships being
experienced by their Kentucky kindred, who were caught between the crossfire of two opposing forces. Many letters of
cheer and encouragement were received at South Union in
those years. "By some fortunate wheel of Providence a letter
from Elder Abram our much beloved & spiritual Minister of
Canterbury came safe thro to us on 28 Jan. No regular mails
yet."

Thankful to Providence for the delivery of the letter, the
South Union Believers were also thankful "to be so noticed
by our gospel friends at a distance," for such letters brought
strength and encouragement. "At this time our minds are so
much carried off with wars ... it seems our spiritual travel is
greatly impeded & we need all the assistance we can get."

Another letter of encouragement came from Canterbury
from Eldress Mary Whicher. "It was directed to Elder John
but every line of it was filled with love & encouragement to the
whole lot & in fact to every member of South Union ... O
what a blessed thing it is to know we have a gospel relation in
many parts of the Earth who does feel for us in our day of
affliction & do send up their prayers to the Throne of the most
high for our deliverance and protection."

Such encouragement was welcomed during the war years;

and it was to be needed in the post-war period as well. For when the days of bitter struggle had passed, the South Union Believers found that the war had drained the colony of much of its strength and property. In fact, the prosperity of South Union leveled off during the 1860's; and by the later 1870's it was evident that a definite decline was beginning at the colony.

XV

FEAR IN THE MIDST OF PLENTY

TWO WEEKS AFTER LEE'S SURRENDER AT Appomattox three army officers from Illinois, faced with beginning their civilian life anew, arrived at South Union to purchase some Shaker cattle. Whether the officers had been there during the war campaigns or whether they had been told of the fine Shaker herd is not known, but it seems certain that the demobilized service men thought that some quick money could be made in cattle and that good stock could be purchased at South Union.

The Shakers, knowing already that the cattle business was profitable, were glad to make the sale. It was through increased cattle sales that the trustees hoped to partially recoup their own war losses. Judging from the many subsequent references to Illinois sales trips, selling the cattle to the officers proved to be a good advertisement. "1872 A journey of 500 miles with fine cattle. T. J. Shannon, William Booker & John Perryman—to Illinois. . . . Oct. 11, 1873 *Cattle Sales*—Today the Brethren Perryman, Johns & Booker returned home from Illinois. Sold their cattle for $3,600. on notes—balance cash. 36 head in all." Showing their cattle at stock fairs proved to be good advertising also. "Sept. 19, 1871 *Stock Fairs*—Brethren are attending the fairs & showing some stock—taking but little in the premium line."

Just as the cattle sales began to increase again after the war, so did the other business enterprises which had been greatly curtailed, both in production and sales, during the time of hostilities. The seed trips, for example, had been reduced in number, and were usually made over shortened routes. By January, 1866, the merchants were traveling as formerly. On the fifth two merchants returned from a sales trip with $1,800 for 30,000 seed papers. Thirteen days later two others returned from the annual southern trip "with $1,400. clear of expenses." In addition to their sales total, the Shakers brought back a considerable sum which they had collected for seeds sold before the war.

During the same spring, sales made on a newly planned trip through western Kentucky and Tennessee amounted to $1,270. Although the total seed business for 1866 was $6,807.45, the next year's sales reached $11,000. The noticeable increase was considered "good in consequence of the derangement in the South—occasioned by the reconstruction scheme in Congress which makes it much more difficult to get sales."

Seed packages were now being sold at 6 cents, a reduction of 1 cent on the original price. The following month the price was dropped to 5 cents. Presumably, the new price was fixed to encourage greater sales in the destitute southern country and to compete with some of the new commercial seed firms, such as the M. T. Gardner Company organized in 1856 and re-organized as the D. M. Ferry Company in 1865.

That the Shakers could afford to lower the original price was due to several things. One was the reduction of traveling expenses as compared to those during the war years. The first war time seed trip made in 1864 by two seed men had resulted in an expense account of $400; whereas, one year after the close of the war two other men traveling over the same route spent only $220.

In the decades following the war most of those who sold Shaker seeds solicited orders and shipped the seeds later. "Oct. 28, 1866 Orders taken on trip for 150,000 seed papers to be delivered at 5¢ paper. . . . Oct. 27, 1873 Elder Hurlburt goes South to Texas to solicit orders for seeds—John Krock on same business in Georgia." But a combination of the older method with the new was the policy followed by William Ware. "Oct. 20, 1873 *Seed Trip* Soliciting. Bro. Wm. Ware started today on southern route with garden seeds. . . . Dec. 1873 William Ware returned home from his soliciting tour—Hard time to get orders."

Recognizing the stronger markets, the women began to enlarge a number of their industries. "May, 1866—*Bee* Bonnet Making—Sisters at Center making bonnets for sale—82— about $100. worth." A few days later an observing elder wrote in the journal: "*Sisters* rather pressed with business—too many irons in the fire—Silk worm raising—preserve making— Starch making—Bonnet making—Hay-making—"

The silk worm business was "carried on some time with tolerable success." The white pocket handkerchiefs made at South Union were offered for sale at one dollar each. The industry which the sisters were able to enlarge to the greatest extent was that of canning and preserving. In August, 1867, the Center House sisters had six thousand jars on the cellar shelves; but, even so, the year's work was not finished. There remained the September peaches and the fall apples and pears "to be worked up."

Year after year the kitchen sisters, under the direction of the kitchen deaconesses, consistently carried on their extensive program. "June, 1869 1,200 jars of cherry preserves at Center this month. . . . June 23, 1870—2,330 jars of cherry preserves up to date. Again in 1871 the South Union cherry trees were loaded with fruit. Realizing the work ahead of them, the Center House women decided to get their other tasks out of the way. Accordingly, on May 2, they washed their white uniform dresses and got them ready to wear to the Sunday services. The next week four women spent three days "ironing and drawing caps." It would have been hard to find time for the laundry work later, because by the twentieth they had "made upwards of 700 jars of preserves." In addition to the crop grown on their own premises that season, the trustees had bought 114 gallons "at about $.32 for cherries, conveyance & horse feed."

On the days the women were busy canning the fruit from their own orchards, the men were riding throughout the surrounding countryside, buying fruit below Russellville and in Woodburn, Woodbury, and in the pond settlement beyond Franklin. One man furnished the Shakers two hundred bushels of peaches, gathering ten bushels each day and sending them up on the train. His charge of 50 cents per bushel included the cost of gathering and shipping.

When one realizes that in the month of May both the strawberry and cherry crops had to be preserved, it is not surprising that on the twenty-third of May the Center House stove "gave way" and had to be carried out after seventeen years in use. The next day Brother Urban left hurriedly for Cincinnati to buy a new one. The respite given by the lack of a stove was not long. June twenty-fourth found the women making 118 jars of plum jelly. Six days later they turned their attention to the making of blackberry cordial, preparing three barrels for the market. Also available for the market was the apple brandy, which was always made at the nearby Potter or Copeland distilleries with the arrangement that the distillery get half. On such an agreement the Shakers found they got one pint of brandy for each bushel of apples. One August day in 1870 the wagons came back from Copeland's loaded with 480 full pints.

In May, 1872, the women were as busy, if not busier, than they had been the year before.

Tues. May 21—320 Jars of strawberry preserves
22—488
23—400
24—132

25—626 (most ever made)
26—231 (attended a meeting)
27—475
28—310
29—476
30—172
31—287

It must be remembered that the ten-day total of 3,917 jars represented the canning of only one of the many different fruits which the Shaker cooks handled throughout a season. Too, it was the work of the women of only one family. If all the journals kept at each house were available, the total figure for all the fruits preserved and canned during one season at South Union would be astonishing.

In 1874 the strawberry canning was lighter than it had been two years before, for a drought cut the crop almost in half. Had it not been for the ingenuity of the Shaker gardeners the crop would have been even smaller. "May, 1874—Severe drought. Watering strawberries. Bro. Wm. Moore has fixed two barrels on wheels & been watering the East patch for some days. . . . June 1, 1874—1700 jars of strawberry preserves made up to this time. Expect to get 2000 only half crop." Relieved somewhat of their canning chores during the strawberry season, the women found the peach crop demanded more time than usual. "August 30, 1874 Preserve making at highest tide—about 2000 jars made also cutting & drying for home consumption."

The jars so carefully filled and labeled in the South Union preservatories were in demand over a wide territory. "Merchant in Galveston, Texas sent an order for 30 boxes of preserves. Boxes filled and shipped. . . . August, 1894 Hauled 43 cases of preserves to depot for New Orleans, Louisiana."

The gardeners, joining in the community effort to have a surplus for the outside markets, began a large-scale production of sweet potatoes. "Mch. 1865 Sales—sweet potatoes $2. bushel between 6 or 800 bushels. . . . Oct. 1866—Dug 1000 bushels of sweet potatoes. . . . Oct.—1867—850 bushels of sweet potatoes dug."

Practicing their economic precepts in the reconstruction years as they had in the beginning period of the society, the trustees took advantage of every possible source of income, offering for sale such nonrelated items as 181 pounds of Jamestown weed or "Strammon;" 1,121 pounds of honey "the most ever got in one season;" and tan yard leather, the 1867 sale of which brought $1,296.57.

After the close of the war, the South Union trustees investigated the new method of milling and manufacturing by steam. Believing it to be more efficient and thus more profitable, they bought their first steam engines in the fall of 1866. "Oct. 11 *Steam Engine*—Two steam engines arrived—one 45 horse power is to run the factory machinery & grist mill when the water is low—the other 3 horse power is to drive the pump at the North House well—so I hope we are done killing horses there. . . . Nov. 14—Steam! Grinding! no more going to Auburn I hope to get grinding done & pay one sixth of our grain for the same as we have had to do for some & most of the past summers since steam was introduced there. Both rows of stones are now grinding by steam—wheat & corn at the same time—So we shall get, instead of give, toll, but we think 1/8 is enough to take from neighbors. . . . Sat. 24, Nov. Mills running fine—will grind 200 bushels per day will consume in that time two cords of wood—We ought to have had steam 10 or 15 years ago."

The new steam engines gave added pleasure because the new method enabled the millers to increase the amount of flour and meal to be sold on the market. Again, the trustees added to the amount produced on the society farm by buying the surplus from their neighboring farmers. For example, in 1867 the amount of corn handled consisted of three thousand bushels grown on their land, three thousand more bushels bought on the outside, and the extra corn collected "by way of toll."

The operation of steam engines was not without difficulties. "Fri. 27, 1867—Bad luck—Two or 3 days since the large Boiler for the factory Engine gave way—Brooks of Auburn is now mending it—Corn & wheat passing us going to Auburn. ... 1871—Boiler burst—water shot 100 ft. in air—engine house badly injured. Bro. Reuben badly hurt. Drs. O'Neal & Halcomb called in—"

Outweighing the difficulties was the financial success of the first steam engines. Such success encouraged further investment. "Sept. 1867 Got another steam engine cost $900. to saw wood and thresh—8 or 10 horse power."

The new industrial program of milling and manufacturing and the decreased man power in the community necessitated the hiring of outside labor. Accordingly in 1867 the Shaker pay roll included the names of twenty-one colored men and boys; a miller with a $500 yearly salary; two mechanics in the woolen factory—one a spinner and carder, the other a machinist and engineer; and a dyester and finisher, all at $10 per week. The German weaver, Henry Haufs, was paid $12 a week. Questioning the advisability of so much hired help the elder wrote, "How long will it take to spend a small estate at this rate? We are making little or nothing."

After the Thirteenth Amendment was ratified in December, 1865, the Shakers began to hire more colored men and boys because they could then pay the men directly, not their masters. "Feb. 1, 1866 .. for the first time since the writer was born—nearly 59 years, can we hire men and pay *them* for their services instead of working them & paying their so called masters." The annual pay for each was $160.00.

The skilled laborers had been hired by the trustees to put the factory in operation and to "learn some of the young men." It was expected that the young brethren would soon be able to take over the manufacturing, thus reducing the expenses.

Probably the women had expressed their desire to work at the four new looms, for the journal of the time contained the statement that the authorities did not plan "to employ females there."

When he considered the cost of the factory, the equipment, and the operating expenses, the elder wrote: "I fear the concern will not much more than clear its teeth." The authorities were still questioning the advisability of hiring so much outside help. Being practical minded, one Shaker was chiefly concerned about the cost of maintenance; he was specifically concerned over the rising scale of meat production. "Oct. 1878—Hog Meat. The 18,000 lbs. of meat that was killed last November, December and January is about out. I learn that there is but one piece in the smoke house at this writing. Believers have eaten about 300 lbs. the balance used by strangers & hired darkies—Say the darkies used 10,000 lbs. that would be $1500. worth. Does it pay to hire them thats what we must ascertain."

Over a long period of years the Believers had adhered to the eastern custom of not eating meat, but the Christmas dinner of 1875 brought a change. "For the first time for many years we had meat (Roast Turkey) on the table." Even so, it can be seen from the 1878 statement that meat was still not a principal item of the Shaker diet, for the Believers had eaten only one-sixtieth of the year's total.

The amount of meat killed by the society butchers rose rapidly over a ten-year period. In January, 1867, they had put up 9,426 pounds of pork only to have the supply become exhausted before the next killing season. The next year the amount was increased to 13,799 pounds. Ten years later the annual total had reached 18,000 pounds.

Whether the ministry hoped to reduce the expense account for food and cooking fuel, whether they were conserving the energies of the kitchen sisters, or whether they were entering a new health program is not told; but in November, 1874, a new plan for meals was advanced. "Nov. 1874 *Two meals a day*—We have been thinking & talking about trying 2 meals a day at least for the winter. The ministry begin this morning, breakfast at 8 & supper at 3." After a few days' trial, the ministry announced that the new plan would be effective throughout the society for a month, but eventually they all returned to the three-meals-a-day plan.

In a further attempt to restore their former economic standing, the trustees made several trips for the purpose of collecting some old accounts. In November, 1865, Brother Urban Johns went to Washington hoping to collect from the government for sugar pressed from the society by the Federals. Returning the first of December, he reported his failure to collect, but he said that "things were in a fair way to do so." Attending May court in Nashville the next year were several of the trustees who represented the society in their lawsuit against a Nashville merchant who had refused to pay for $2000 worth of preserves. The court decision gave the Shakers $1,787.

Almost every day someone would be away from South Union on society business. Besides the collecting trips, the sales trips, and the official visits made by the ministry, there were the trips made for the wholesale purchase of supplies. "February, 1871 Bro. Urban took the train to Louisville to lay in our groceries. . . . Tues. 8, Apr., 1873—*Sisters Trading trip* Eldress Betsy & Fanny Lacy from Centre & Jane Cowan from the North started at 2 a.m. with U. E. Johns to Louisville to lay in the years supply of dry goods."

Whether at home or away, every Believer was kept busy during the Reconstruction period by the diversified economic program. "Aug. 26, 1865 Elder Asa setting up gravestones lately lettered by H. L. Eades. . . . Sept. 13, 1866—24 boarders at office beside transient visitors."

An ambitious task was the one undertaken by Believer Shannon, who was well-known as a successful merchant. "Jan. 1868 Black Lick Farm—Jefferson Shannon who undertook the business of improving the B. Lick premises—which were in the wild

woods in Oct., 1863—turned the property back. At the beginning he was given one mule & $200. cash. Now turns back

"Cash on hand	2,599.00
Previously given to S.U.	147.80
Stock on hand including provender	2,956.30
Wood on hand for sale	300.00
Deduct $200. and interest	248.00

$5,755.10"

The responsibility of managing the improved farm was given
to a newly organized Black Lick or Watervliet Family. After
a ten-years' trial, in which they were not particularly successful, the group returned to the central village, where they were
needed to reinforce the decreasing membership. "Sept. 2, 1877
Public Vendue was held today at Black Lick when a variety
of articles were exhibited to the public bid on a credit of 12
months—90 head of sheep were disposed of, 20 Sows, two
horses, one cooking stove & other articles—amount of sales
about 400 dollars."

When one recalls that the entire nation was still feeling the
effects of the financial panic of 1873, it is not surprising that
the Black Lick property had to be offered on a twelve-months'
credit basis nor that the amount from the sale was so low. The
sudden drop of farm prices had ruined many of the neighborhood farmers so that, if they attended the sale at all, they had
little desire for the property and less cash with which to pay
if they did see something they wanted.

In the 1860's and 1870's the building program was not as
extensive as in the 1830's, but it still demanded attention.
The time had passed when the Shakers could furnish all the
materials and workmanship needed for their buildings. In
1867 the East Family hired J. McLean of Auburn to build
a two-story frame house for them so that the boys, some of
whom were war orphans, and their leader might be moved from

the old log house near the cistern. After the boys had been moved, the log house was torn down, moved to the head of the mill pond, and was used as the home of the hired blacksmith. In 1868 when the society agreed to build a tavern or hotel at the railroad stop, the trustees went to Bowling Green for the bricks, paying $8.25 per thousand. The two-story building was to be 60x25 across the front and 45x20 across the back. Furniture, which was bought in Cincinnati rather than made in the village shops, was placed throughout the finished rooms, and the tavern was declared ready for its new renter, Mr. Wethered, who agreed to pay the society $1,200 per year.

Just across the road from the tavern the old frame store building had been replaced in 1872 by a store building which was to be leased also. In July, James McCutcheon and Company moved their goods and wares into the front of the store and operated a post office in the rear. The store burned and had to be rebuilt twice, first in 1884 and then in 1896.

Other construction projects were a large dwelling house for the West Family to replace the one which had been destroyed by fire during the war, a two-story frame shop (60x20x25) for broom seed, a new wood shop to replace the old log smith shop, a horse barn at the office, and a new sixteen-foot "back house for the Sisters . . . situated nearer than any we have had for them." Some months later the workers "planted 5 trees of Cedar about 6 to 8 feet high on the East of the Necessaries!"

The building of the West House in 1883 was a financial mistake for the decreasing colony. For once the trustees and leaders had refused to be realistic, for they gave no consideration to the obvious decline of membership. Instead the building was completed, and the family moved in. By 1898 it had become impossible for the weak group to maintain the family organization; consequently, they joined with the stronger Center Family. Later, when the house was sold for its building materials, it was torn down and moved away.

The clearing away of the empty dwelling house and the

turning of the premises back into well-tilled fields was quite in keeping with the Shakers' general care and improvement program by means of which they were attempting to bring their buildings up to the standard of the pre-war times. "Mch. 17—'65 Painting Sisters of 2nd Order finished painting the inside of their wash building. . . . Sept. 20—'65—Paint all shutters & blinds to the windows in Church Bldgs. & office. Done by sisters—color *Blue* all but office Prussian Blue—office ultra-marine. . . . April, 1868—Usual painting etc. White-washed rooms in Spanish whiting & Glue. Looks well & does not rub off."

Always first on the improvement program was the meeting-house. "Sept. 19, '65 Eades & 2 young brethren put 2 coats of paint on picket fence around Meeting House. . . . Sept. 1, 1866—A chandelier to hold 4 burners was put up in the meeting house today. . . . The new chandelier affords a sufficient light over the spacious room. . . . Apr. 9, 1873—New Carpeting—The Meeting House was furnished in Sept., 1872. Now for the first time the two dwelling rooms have been entirely covered."

The following spring the women honored Elder Hervey by placing a new carpet in his room. "May 8—1874—*Carpet*— The sisters have just finished & furnished the room I occupy (East end of ministrys little Brick Shop) with rather gaudy but very good carpet—its cost was $1.30 cts. pr. yd. lets see how long it will last. Will last after I leave terra firma."

That a considerable proportion of the annual income went into the maintenance program is learned from the business report appearing in the July, 1878, records.

The following September part of the seventeen thousand dollar balance was spent paying the society's taxes of $1,670 and in hard-surfacing the village streets. The leaders had been considering the project since the dry fall of 1862, when there was no rain for three months and the roads had become powdered clay two or three inches thick. Describing how the dust

Deposit in bank	$8000.	Debts to lawyers	$1200.
" " woolen miles	8000.	Smithson	500.
Note on J. L. Rowe	580.	Other debts	500.
Warren Co. bonds	8000.		
Deposit in Louisville bonds	2000.		
	$26,580.		$2200.

Net $24,380.

Spent on improvements   7300.

Balance $17,080.

enveloped them when it was windy or the cavalry passed, a journalist had written, "We are able—why not mc adamize the roads?" Sixteen years later his suggestion brought action. "Sept. 1878—Road Building—We have just contracted for mcadamizing one mile of our streets—One Jas. P. Cayne is to build a good graded road one mile for $2,956."

As might be expected, the final cost exceeded the estimated cost by almost one thousand dollars.

During the Reconstruction period when the Believers were redoubling their efforts in an attempt to restore their pre-war prosperity, unrest and disturbance were noticeable everywhere. The restlessness on the part of the world's people and their subsequent attempt for readjustment were evidenced in the constant passing of wagons filled with people who planned to try their luck in the newer territory of Missouri, Kansas, Arkansas, and Texas. The older Believers, seeing the movers stream by, recalled how the road through Shakertown had been filled once before with westward-bound wagons.

"Tues. 25, 1866—*Emigration*—For some days past, in fact I might say weeks old fashioned wagons drawn by Horses, mules & oxen, sometimes mixed in the same team, have been passing westward crowded to the top of the bows, over which a large sheet is drawn with alive & dead property—the former, women and children—the latter household furniture &—any-

thing in the world but the cross of Christ." So wrote an elder on a day when he noticed two such teams "plodding slowly along the muddy roads in the rain." Rainy or dry, the wagons continued to come. "Oct. 15, 1867 Movers—Movers—Movers! Going west. . . . Sept. 28—1869—*Movers! Wagons, Wagons, Wagons!* Have been passing westward. Sometimes a dozen per day—with their living freight, women, men, boys, girls & Babies & going to newer countries. It would seem that Kentucky would almost be depopulated if the stream is not stayed —It rivals the time when Missouri was admitted into the Union. Scarce a day for some weeks, but wagons are seen on the move." Only occasionally was a wagon seen coming back to Kentucky. Having observed a returning wagon, the elder remarked, "Nothing after all like the old home."

Numerous problems which had evolved during the war years remained problems for a long time after the war. One of these was the guerilla activity or what was frequently a robbery made under the guise of guerilla activity. Such threats continued for almost two years after the regular troops had gone from the Kentucky soil. The Believers, who had been generally protected by both armies during the war itself, found themselves without any protection. Consequently, they were in constant dread. "May 16, 1865 *Bad Scare* Eugene L'Hotte who had been watching at the strawberry field at the Knob was driven home as fast as his horse could come by what he supposed to be guerillas. . . . Oct. 13, 1866—6 men rode up—2 with their faces black as tar—claimed to be Harpers men in quest of whiskey & 'Greenbacks.' " Not many days later the same group made a daylight robbery at the South Union store.

Robberies continued to be frequent throughout the Reconstruction period. It was in 1872 that the village was visited by robbers who broke into the office, chloroformed Brother Urban, and succeeded in taking away a hundred-dollar gold watch, three hundred dollars in money, and one thousand dollars in bonds. A few days later detectives caught the robbers in Nashville and retrieved the bonds, almost all of the money, and the watch.

Beginning in 1871 there was a series of disastrous fires at South Union several of which were set by incendiaries—either by dissatisfied members or by those on the outside whose animosity of long standing was fanned anew when they viewed their own depleted resources in terms of the more prosperous condition of the Shakers. Also added to those who disliked the Shakers were many returning service men who were incensed because they felt that the society members had escaped too much of the war costs and that they had not risked anything.

Those operating against the Shakers did so either in the guise of guerillas or as members of the Ku Klux Klan. "Oct. 18, 1873—Ku Klux—Elder S. G. Hurlburt *threatened*—Rods found at shop door."

The major fires were over a period of six years, and the total loss was extremely high. "Apr. 13, 1871 An awful outrage—the darkest & foulest. The most daring & wicked deed ever perpetrated in this society or any other. It is even unparalleled among heathens. Someone set fire to the garret of the Center House. Rope to big bell severed, but news soon spread. Cistern nearly empty. Emptied the rain barrels at all the houses. They even emptied the swill and vinegar barrels & drained the water from the chicken feed. Furniture carried out. The remarkable fortitude & undaunted courage, zeal & activity manifested on the present occasion was marvelous. . . . Fire!! Aug. 21, 1873 Large bell toll'd the fire alarm a little after midnight—large grain Barn on fire. Bldg. 100x48 ft. 2 stories high—contained year's supply of wheat about 1500 bu. of 1st quality wheat worth $1.50 per bu."

The barn had housed the sheller and some other machinery. The total loss was listed as $4000. "May 1, 1875 *Fire! Fire!* —About 3 a.m. our big bell sounds—large cow barn at East Family. Work of an incendiary Thomas Burke who being expelled demanded $50.00. Not receiving it—took it out in revenge. Loss $30,000. . . . Feb. 25, 1877—Fire—large cow barn at the North Family."

The largest fire loss incurred by the South Union colony was the $75,000 loss of their factory buildings which were situated just north of the village proper and were located on either side of a small stream. Having lost so heavily, the Shakers were desperate. The elders appealed to the governor of the state, the Honorable John W. Stevenson, asking for protection from the neighborhood group who had fired the factories. They asked that the state offer a reward, but no special action was taken and no answer was written by Governor Stevenson.

The South Union society was not the only one to experience fire losses at the hands of their enemies. The wave of persecution against the Believers everywhere was comparable to that they had endured in their earliest years, except, of course, that in the early years they had not had so much to lose. "Mch. 1875 News came of two great fires at New Lebanon—started by incendiaries—Loss $200,000. I pity the wretches (incendiaries)."

Up until the time of the fires, any casual visitor at South Union would have thought that life there had returned to normal. He would have been impressed by the bustling activity in the gardens and orchards, in the preservatory, and in the new steam-operated mills. If invited to eat, he would have agreed with Shannon that the society's general fare was "the cream of the earth." Shannon had described the society fare of the time as consisting of " . . . plenty of meal & flour, milk and butter, Irish potatoes, Sweet potatoes, Apples & peaches, dried & canned, strawberries, asparagus, Lettuce, Radishes, peas & greens, chickens & eggs, Buttered waffles, fritters & doughnuts, Boiled & *baked dumplings* (or toad in the hole). Peach & apple pies & puddings & dip & Sweet Cake, Tea & coffee & Sugar—all on table in past four weeks."

In the midst of such plenty, it would have taken an observant visitor to have caught the undertone of disquiet and even fear of the future which actually existed. But probably no visitor would have realized to what extent the social and economic maladjustment of the time was sapping the vitality of the South Union community.

XVI

THE CHANGING ORDER

A S MEMBERS OF A RELIGIO-ECONOMIC SOCI-
ety, the South Union colonists found that the war
brought them both religious and economic problems. In the
Reconstruction period, the elders and eldresses who were directly responsible for the religious welfare of the community
had to work as zealously to revive the spiritual conditions as
the trustees did to reorganize the business affairs.

At the close of the war when the leaders were able at last to
hold their meetings regularly and without military interrup-
tions, they hoped the religious spirit would improve and that
the laxness and hardness would disappear. By 1866 three
services were again being held at 9 A.M., 11:30 A.M., and 6 P.M.,
the 11:30 service being the public meeting which was held
only through the summer and early fall months. "July 1,
1866—Beginning of public meeting & spectators were numerous. . . . July 8, 1866—Some of the spectators behave badly—
besides they make such havoc with the fruit orchards. We think
we shall have to suspend."

Because the zeal did improve, the meetings continued until
the regular closing time in the fall. "Sab. 14, Oct. 1866—
Public Meeting—Elder Robinson Eades addressed the spectators with one of the good discourses which he now & then
produces at a time when he felt at the beginning that he had
little to say. . . . Sab. 21, 1866—Closed public meeting until
spring."

The religious spirit was noticeably good at the church meetings during the same summer. "Sept. Sab. 23, 1866—Elder Robinson addressed the spectators—a good refreshing & lively ch. meeting at 6 about 150 attended. Strong testimony & good resolution from several Bro. & Sisters."

Spiritual conditions were so much improved at the sister colony of Pleasant Hill that the members there sent their Elder Andrew Bloomburg on a missionary journey to his native Sweden to "assist some 40 or 50 families in either emigrating here or forming a society there." The journey was made in response to a written request for instructions. After ten months' absence, Elder Andrew returned to Kentucky in August, 1867, accompanied by eight Swedes, five of whom united with the Pleasant Hill Believers.

Unfortunately, the renewed zeal of 1866 and 1867 was not to last. By the following year it began to wane. The younger Elder Eades was sensitive to the change, and many of his sermons were directed against the decreasing faith. "Sab. 9— Society Meeting—250 present H.L.E. discoursed for near half hour on the subject of *faith*—Setting forth the want of true faith in the Chh. at this time—The faith of Abraham was a living faith as it was one of obedience to the Divine light & injunction—Ours must be living by obedience to the increased light—But who among us were prepared to sacrifice our only son or all that is dearest to us?—turned from the law to the gospel of Christ in his first appearing—the forsaking he required . . . How many had in reality left *all* Mother, Brother, Sister, wives & children for his sake. Then came the 2nd appearing in Mother—her teaching & example—How far behind the mark were many of us—If Christ and Mother should walk into our assembly—How many real forsakers would they find—"

It was not Christ and Mother who walked into the South Union assembly, but the Mount Lebanon ministry who had come to investigate the war losses suffered by their western branches and to inquire into the religious condition of each society. "June 21, 1868, Society Meeting—Mt. Lebanon ministry present. After giving abundantly of their love & blessing (a hymn of welcome having been sung) we proceeded in our bungling way laboring in Holy Order—Young & old Believers mingled together—marched—danced—took sides & Elder Giles B. Avery delivered one of the best discourses for about ¾ of an hr. I have heard in many days or years—lasted from 2-½ past 4. Whole number in meeting 260 souls."

One change recommended by the visiting New Lebanon heads was that the two Kentucky ministries be combined into one bishopric. In October when the official change was made, Elder Hervey was appointed as one of the four leaders whose task would be to foster the religious affairs of all the Kentucky Believers.

Serving as adviser to the new bishopric the sixty-one-year old Hervey had a store of communal experience on which to draw. Born in 1807 in a log cabin near what was to be the South Union property, he had gone as a baby in his mother's arms to the first gathering ever held at Gasper and had become a member of the children's order before he was one year old. Growing up along with the colony, Eades learned the various trades. As a young man he served as teamster, seed grower, shoemaker, and schoolteacher. Later he bound books and worked as a tailor. In 1836 at the age of twenty-nine he was elected to the ministry. In 1844 he was moved to North Union to serve as Novitiate elder there. While a member of the Ohio ministry, he "dignified hand labor" by working at wool carding and spinning, at tin and sheet-iron work. He also learned printing, dentistry, painting, and hat manufacturing. After twelve years as elder, Eades was relieved of the office without ever learning the reason. Two years later he was reappointed, again without explanation, to his former position. In 1862 he was returned to the South Union ministry. When his brother, the senior elder, died in 1873, Hervey became the head of the colony and remained so until his death in 1892.

In the summer following the visit of the New York leaders the South Union ministry returned the visit. The Kentuckians were particularly anxious to make the visit because such trips had been considered unwise during the war, and naturally they had missed the visits.

After spending some time in New York, the ministry—composed of Elders John Rankin and Hervey Eades, Eldresses Paulina Bryant and Betsy Smith—went as far down east as New Gloucester and Alfred, Maine. This was the first visit ever made by any western Believer to the Maine society. When they returned to South Union in September, they gave a full account of their journey to the First Order, reading part of their journal and singing some of the eastern songs. At the general society meeting held later they delivered the "bountiful story of love from all the societies of the East and reported their general good time."

The following spring the Maine elders came to Kentucky looking for a new location for their "little societies" because they were wondering whether they should "leave the sterile & gravelly hills & icebergs of Maine & settle in Kentucky or elsewhere in a more fertile climate & soil." The recorder tells of their visit: "Had a delightful meeting with them. 220 present. Received bountifully of love & returned same. They both spoke beautifully & pertinently to the Believers—showed they were travelled saints."

Although the Maine visitors did not select a new location on their 1870 visit, they did not abandon the plan. During the next spring they corresponded with the South Union leaders, expressing their continued interest in buying farm land in either Kentucky or Tennessee. "July 25, 1871—Brethren make trip to Ky. River 30 miles below Frankfort at request of Maine Brethren. Won't do."

A few weeks later a similar trip was made to investigate farms around Lebanon, Tennessee. The plan to move south was finally given up and the two small societies (with only seventy members each according to the 1874 report) continued as separate societies until 1931 when the Alfred Society was combined with New Gloucester or the Sabbathday Lake group. As a combined society the Maine group was one of the four remaining Shaker communities listed in the United States in 1940.

In 1870, when the Maine delegation had been with them, the South Union leaders became more acutely aware that the religious spirit of the members was becoming weaker instead of stronger. Because the decline was apparent in other colonies as well, the eastern heads announced that the union services, customary in the earlier years, would be resumed. Beginning in July, 1870, all the Believers—East and West— met at a specified hour to join in prayer for the Shaker cause. As the year went on, conditions did not show any great improvement at South Union, so the next year's sermons were still directed toward needed reforms. "Sab. 8th—Elder Jas. spoke in a very solemn & weighty manner—endeavoured to impress the minds of all the great importance of attending to good order especially to Meetings & to meals. Brethren & Sisters should impress it on the minds of their roommates. If at any time, there was any one who could not attend they should be punctual to let their elders know it. He also spoke of the awful consequence of making sport or mock of the solemn worship of God or of any one who was under a divine influence. It was wicked and ought to be confessed."

The succeeding Sabbath, the elder followed up his sermon by emphasizing that "Mother Ann said the first step to be taken was to confess all sin. The rest was to be punctual to attend the meeting."

Throughout the year 1872 there were a few meetings in which there were "many manifestations of spirit presence" and "divers gifts & operations." But as the year drew to its close, an observant elder wrote: "Dec. 31, 1872—Thus ends the year 1872—not over stocked with living faith in the church nor society at large."

In the earlier years of the society no services had been held in the meetinghouse on rainy Sundays. Instead, the Believers had worshipped separately in family groups. Such practice had saved the scrupulously scoured meetinghouse floor from being muddied. But customs and conditions changed. In 1874 there was a "misty meeting in the Meeting House—tho a wet day." The truth was that the time had come when there was not enough active leadership to hold simultaneous family services. Too, the West Family had become so reduced in size that they could no longer have a good service of their own. Consequently, all were urged to come to a joint service at the meetinghouse even though it rained. It was pointed out, however, that all should be careful to scrape their shoes so as not to get mud on the newly laid carpet.

During 1873 the public service was discontinued altogether, and the society meetings were reduced to only two a month. Perhaps it was because of the few services at home that in August of the same year Brother Samuel Hurlburt and two of the sisters "took the cars for Cedar Hill, Tennessee, to attend a camp meeting."

The following year marked the one hundredth anniversary of Shakerism in America. The journalistic notice of the centennial contained no glowing account of the success of the movement; neither did it contain any reference to satisfactory conditions at South Union. Instead there was a brave, but unconvincing, expression of hope for the future. "Th. 6—Aug.—1874—*100 years!* This day 100 years since our blessed Mother Ann Lee & her little company landed in America bringing with them tidings of everlasting gospel to all who were hungering & thirsting after righteousness—It is to be hoped that in 100 years more the gospel will have spread to the ends of the earth."

But no improvement had been noted by October of the next

year. "Oct. 1875. Pub. Meeting—Eld. J. R. Cooper delivered a very plain strait forward testimony of about one hours duration today—Audience small as it has been thus far this season —No interest manifested in the outside world & none too much here at home."

Hoping it would offset the evident weakening of the church, the ministry was faithful in observing all the special services of the church, such as those for the reading of the covenant and making the yearly sacrifice. It had always been the custom to have the covenant read at stated times, usually in May or June. If there were those who wished to sign it after having heard it read, they were given the privilege of doing so at the next meeting. On May 4, 1871, there were forty-one individuals who signed their names. This was the last time for such a large group. Later, there were years when no signers were listed, as in May, 1875, and June, 1878.

December had long been the month when each separate family held the annual sacrifice, at which all were urged to make "the coming year an improvement on the past" and "to put away all wrong and strengthen the good." The services, first begun in 1837, were really word-of-mouth confessions in which each one set himself right with the society at large.

It was after the war that the ministry began to join the world more frequently in holding services connected with national events. Two such meetings held in 1865 were connected with the close of the war. "June 1—1865 Thursday—*Meeting* held at 10 a.m. in compliance with the requisitions of the President as well as the Governor of the State. . . . Dec. 7-65— Thanksgiving Meeting Proclamation by President & Governor of State—Thanks to God for blessing of peace."

During the 1870's special religious days were observed as well as national holidays. "Thanksgiving—1873—We observed this day by attending meeting—took seats in the meeting room —Had a good season—Br. Briggs read very nice & distinctly a chapter by Elds. Harriet Bullard in E. Lomas' pamphlet &

spoke to the point & very encouraging. . . . Christmas—1873—
A Beautiful Springlike day. Society Meeting over 180 souls
present—Have a good refreshing Season—3 letters read by
Br. Nicholas A. Briggs from Canterbury. . . . July 4, 1876—
Meeting—By recommendations of Pres't Grant—the Society
assembled in the Meetinghouse for worship & giving thanks—
Meeting at 10 a.m. lasted near 1 hour."

The problems of increasing the church attendance and of
quickening the religious spirit were only two of those which
confronted the ministry in the postwar period. Perhaps no
other group of South Union leaders ever had as many serious
problems as did those of that time.

There was also a multiplicity of small problems. One recog-
nizes that something was gnawing at the religious core of the
society when the ministry was called upon to decide such questions as whether or not allowing the beard to grow would give
immunity against throat and eye trouble. After much discussion, it was left optional with each man as to whether he would
be progressive and let his beard grow or whether he would continue to follow the eastern practice of cutting it once each
week.

Known as a charitable organization, the society had many
opportunities in the Reconstruction days to practice their precepts. "Taken by surprise—the blacksmith's wife in his absence
had two children, both females. she was too poor to furnish clothes to dress them—Sisters made and took clothes to
dress them—they have also furnished them every day with
milk & butter & various articles."

There was also the problem of the many new orphans who
had been given a home at Shakertown. During 1865 many orphans had been received. Nineteen of these, children of Georgia,
Tennessee, and Alabama soldiers, had come to Shakertown directly from the Clarksville, Tennessee, orphanage when it had
been discontinued by the government. Later the society received some quadroons from Clarksville and some other chil-

dren from Louisville. A few children came accompanied by their war-widowed mothers. "Feb. 12, 1865 Admitted Mary Austin with 8 little girls. . . . Feb. 21, 1865 Admitted Martha Charlton and 4 boys." Four children were admitted to the society's care by their father, Major William Lungford of Indiana, who either desired the Shaker way of life for his children or felt he could not provide for them during the hard times of the postwar period. There is evidence that Lungford himself spent some time at the village. "Feb. 1868—The Regulators are still around. William Lungford, a major in the late Union army, a Shaker at South Union, was frightened and considered leaving, saying that they had heretofore killed Rebels—now they feared Rebs. might kill them."

The admission of so many children was of interest to the neighborhood. In discussing it, some one remarked that rather than have no children the Shakers would take bad children. Whatever may have prompted the acceptance of so many, it was the charitable intention of the society to educate them and to teach each one a useful trade which would benefit him later.

The Believers soon found that some of their war refugees had spent little or no time in school. So in 1867 they organized a special summer session for instruction of the underprivileged. Enrolled as pupils in the Believers' first opportunity school were fourteen boys, including one seventeen-year-old and two four-year-olds. There was a similar school for the girls who had lately come under the society's care. Perhaps to relieve the homesickness and to erase the unpleasant war memories, the teachers increased the number of school outings, for such excursions seemed to have been more numerous between 1865 and 1870 than formerly. There were times when the boys went to Sinking Fork to gather pawpaws, when the little girls went to the Knob to swing and feast, and other times when some of the children took a "jaunt into the forest" to gather nuts.

In 1865, soon after many of the children arrived, a woman who had just been admitted to the East Family developed smallpox. Doctors were summoned immediately to vaccinate all the children, and an epidemic was avoided. Three years later the society was not so fortunate in curbing a spotted fever scourge. In February four children died within a few hours of each other, all dying a short time after the first symptoms appeared.

Mon.	17—Joseph Young—9 yrs.	d. midnight
Tues.	18—Gordon Brooks—11 yrs.	d. before 7 A.M.
Wed.	19—Jas. Young—12 yrs.	d. at 11 P.M.
Thurs.	20—John Edmonds—15 yrs.	d. about midnight

On Sunday, the twenty-third, twenty-one-year-old Henry Warren died, and by Monday, three deaths had been reported from the colored group. The last death, that of a thirteen-year-old girl, did not occur until the tenth of March.

A third epidemic, this time of scarlet fever, threatened but did not touch South Union. "Oct. 10, 1878—The great plague still grows worse & is now in Bowling Green. There were 8 burials there yesterday—& 7 new cases of yellow fever today— & one death at Rockfield only 6 miles down from this place." In the area affected by the epidemic the total dead for the first ten months in 1878 was reported as being 13,921. Most of these were people who lived along the river from New Orleans to Clarksville. In recounting the facts of the disaster, an elder wrote: "If it is God's judgment on the land for its wickedness It would seem that the more Northern latitude needed scourging as well as the South."

The Believers knew from past experience that they could not expect many of the orphans to become regular members of the society, but the program was administered as part of the humanitarian work of each year. There came a time, however, when an elder questioned whether or not they should continue extending charity to the orphans as they had been doing for years. "*Gone at Last!* Achille L'Hotte left clandestinely today—being the last one of a lot of eighteen boys brought from the Orphan Asylum at New Orleans & arrived here on the 5th of January, 1843—One very good & promising youth of the number & two others untried died here & their bodies interred in our burying ground—all the rest some earlier some later chose the world, whither they have gone to parts unknown—doubtless 'seeking rest & finding none.' Achille, the last to go, is 34 years old his Brother who went about a year since was a year or two older—The older of the lot was only 12 years of age—the youngest 8—they are all grown & vanished out of sight in 24 years—If all of them had remained faithful to this date temporally, as well as spiritually—they certainly would be much better off than they are now. It becomes a question, whether we are doing the best we can, or as we should, in taking in destitute children—certainly there cannot be much gain in any sense, if not one in 20 remain true to the good cause—we now have between 30 & 40—shall not one be saved?"

In spite of the questioning attitude on the part of the elder, the Believers continued to follow their usual practice for many more years. In 1873 news came that there were many orphans in a Memphis Asylum, all of whom needed homes at once. As soon as they could, four of the leaders went to Memphis. Two days later, when they returned, the journal contained the following comment. "Oct. 24, 1873—*Return*—Eld. Hurlburt & Co. Returned by the early train 2 A.M. this morning without a single baby—The distress of being overrun with Orphans there at Memphis is all bosh—A great hue & cry to get money."

The organization of the opportunity school was the beginning of a series of changes which started with a closer affiliation with the public school system. In November, 1856, William Ware, teacher of the Shaker boys, appeared before the Logan County school commissioners and was granted a first class state certificate. From then on, Ware attended the regular teachers' meetings in both Bowling Green and Russellville. One trip was made "to witness the school exhibition."

In 1867 an eight months' coeducational session was introduced. This longer term, beginning in May and going through December, replaced the two shorter sessions of former years. In the society at the time were 118 children between the ages of eight and twenty. An average attendance of only sixty-eight during the lengthened term would indicate that the older children were kept out of school when there was work for them to do.

Beginning in the fall of 1873, the Shaker school system returned to its former policy of maintaining separate schools for the boys and the girls. The term was also shortened by two months, beginning in November and ending in April. This new arrangement freed the children for work in the busy months of October and May. The boys, meeting in the frame house, were taught by Henry May; the girls, meeting in the Music Hall, were under the supervision of Mary Wann and Kate Bickford.

When the schools opened in 1874, there were some three or four neighborhood children enrolled. "Never saw this before!" remarked an elder.

Another evidence of new methods was given in the records for April, 1876. "*School session ended.* Had quite a showing off in the Music Hall last evening—Showing that much pain had been taken by the Teachers."

The Music Hall, opened three years earlier, was located in the west end of the lower floor of the sisters' brick shop. It was described as being "a room about 26x33 feet" with a seating capacity for a hundred people.

The hall had been opened to accommodate a newly organized singing school. Although the Shaker gift for singing and composing had evolved first in the Kentucky and Ohio wilderness and had been carried back east, the time had come when the South Union Believers felt that their musical talents were in abeyance and that they needed special training "to bring up the gift." Of course, popular interest in singing schools was growing everywhere. In the new practice, Elder Eades was quick to recognize a means by which it might be possible to interest some of the weaker members who were contemplating a less strict way of life and at the same time to offer needed musical training to the serious-minded members of the Church or Center Family. A few years earlier Maria Price of the Elders' Order in the North Family had moved "home to the Center family to try & bring up the gift of singing."

Eades sponsored the revival of the musical interest by starting a "musick school in the Meeting House." The first session had been held one Tuesday evening in September, 1869, at which meeting "only some dozen or 20 attended from the Centre family & occupied one hour." The following night after he returned to his room from having conducted the musical gathering, Eades wrote: "A general attendance this evening from all the families—We expect to continue teaching music & singing at intervals until all that will shall improve to either sing passably well—& learn to read & write music—It is a two year task." Eades knew from personal experience the difficulty of learning music, for he had recently trained himself in the art.

Four years passed before sufficient musical progress had been made to warrant the opening of the new Music Hall. For the opening, six dozen chairs had been ordered from Louisville. Coming as guest teacher was the eastern Believer, Brother Nicholas Briggs, who was much better trained than was Eades. "Oct. 22, 1873—*Visit Journey*—Bro. Jas. Richardson started today for Canterbury, N. H. to remain four months. This visit is made in consequence of an arrangement between South Union & Canterbury—the former to receive Bro. Nicholas A. Briggs the coming winter for music teacher. . . . Nov. 24, '73 *Music* arrangement completed—We are now organized for business—Monday, Tuesday & Friday evening from 7 to 8 learning music—Wednesday & Thursday evening from 6-7 for Voice culture & training. There is good attendance—&

Brother Briggs seems very competent and is a master of the business—an amiable, interested & industrious teacher."

The society had prepared for Briggs' school by purchasing their first piano. "Sat. Oct. 11, 1873—*Pianoforte*—is this day consecrated to the use of Believers. A seven octave chichering Piano was bought in Bowling Green on Thursday the 9th inst. Cost $240. Was brought home today & deposited in the Music Hall—Center Family." After five years' use the piano was traded for another. "New pianoforte—We put a new piano in the Music Hall this P.M. & sent the old one to Louisville paying a difference between them."

When Briggs began to get acquainted with the personnel of his singing school, he found that they had come to South Union from widely separated places. The dates and places of birth for some of the class members were listed as follows:

Logan Johns	April, 1842	Fanning Co., Texas
Zechariah Miles	Nov., 1848	Warren Co., Virginia
Caroline Loving	Nov., 1807	Plymouth, Mass.
Mary McComb	1796	N. C.
Richard Quimby	Dec., 1823	New York City
Frederic Snyder	Mch., 1820	Germany
Charles Reppler	May, 1834	Georgia
Lawrence Oscar	Aug., 1837	Switzerland
George McNally	Aug., 1846	Belfast, Ireland
W. Lambert	Jan., 1821	Rome, Italy
Lewis Forest	Dec., 1829	Corsica, France
Franz Reinfels	Nov.1, 1845	Germany
William Dupree	. . . .	. . . .
Survetus Pattillo	. . . .	. . . .

Perhaps Briggs never asked the last two members when and where they were born, for the information was lacking in the record.

Among the number who had been born very close to the colony's location were three of the older members.

Hervey L. Eades	Apr. 28, 1807	Logan County
John R. Eades	Apr. 5, 1805	Todd "
Nancy E. Moore	Sept. 1, 1807	Warren "

Born in the other neighboring county of Simpson was the younger Virginia Breedlove, who listed her birth day as May 4, 1843.

Briggs continued his singing school until March when he returned to Canterbury. "Mch. 5—1874—Our good Brother Briggs who has been teaching music—& the schools once or twice daily—started by the train this morning home."

The program of intensive musical training was followed the next year by a series of geological lectures, given by a lecturer who came and stayed a week. Many of the Shaker communities had introduced a lyceum course in which grammar and composition, declamation and correct language were the subjects. The members could also receive training in the recitation of comic pieces or in serious and didactic selections. The various new entertainment programs, as in the case of the music courses, were meant to counteract the restlessness and dissatisfaction in the colony at the time. This seems to have been only wishful thinking on the part of the ministry, for the programs failed in their purpose. Matters grew continually worse. Soon there was an open defiance which could not be stopped.

The Robert Davis affair which took place in November, 1869, may be said to have marked the beginning of the open rebellion among the Believers themselves. "Robt. Davis of East House came today after his gal—Brought two men with him—pistol in hand & demanded to see Almeta Stone—who by the way had agreed & wished to go. So there was no precious blood spilt on the occasion—So they trotted off & she married sd. Davis."

Neighbors, as well as members, were guilty of similar outbursts. "1865—A neighbor Sam McDonald 'without liberty' put his horse in our sheep barn & fed him & went to town by railroad. Returned found horse in pasture. Presumed the shepherd John Perryman, had turned him out. came and shot at Perryman, the bullet lodging in the stairway at John's feet. Half drunk—later he promised not to shoot on Shaker premises again. . . . Nov. 1869—A Shaker Chas. Johnson who had lived a few months at the North House stole a Shaker mule & rode away. Caught brought back, tried at Russelville, sentenced to 7 yrs. service in pen. Hard pay for one day's ride on a poor mule."

Another instance of stealing within the society resulted, according to the elder, "in consequence of having taken in a set of outlaws who have invented various ways to get liquor." The so-called outlaws had been spending the winter of 1871 in the Gathering Order at the North House, but with the coming of spring the "three suspicious characters" left. A checkup revealed clues left by the revelers—a bucket and coffee pot of brandy hidden in a barn hayloft, a missing five-gallon demijohn of wine from the Center House, and cut grates in the North House cellar window. The thieves had tried to conceal their entrance by replacing the grates and covering the rods with mud.

Not long after the North House affair, the Center Family had its share of excitement in a one-man revolt staged by Hugh Relner. Relner had asked frequent permission to use the new piano, but each time Elder Hervey refused to give him the key to the piano room. Angered by the elder's refusals, Relner drew a club and made loud threats. When his threats did not frighten Eades into giving over the key, he tried something else. Getting an ax, he began cutting the door to the room, until Elder Samuel Hurlburt, hearing the commotion, came in time to keep him from "cutting the door into chips." Then the enraged Believer, ax in hand, turned upon Hurlburt and "struck at him edge foremost barely marking the scalp." An onlooker said later, "One inch lower & Sam'l would have been a dead man."

When the county authorities came to arrest Relner and take him to jail, he asked to talk to Elder Hervey before leaving, saying that he wanted to compromise. His request refused, Relner committed his last desperate act of hurling a heavy glass tumbler at the elder, striking his arm. In recounting the day's disturbance, the assaulted Believer spoke with conviction: "He is either insane or a very desperate character." Later at the county trial, Relner was granted his freedom on the condition he would "leave the country."

Following this disturbance was the Barrett-Petty quarrel. "Dec. 1867—Old man Barrett, in a passion & in self-defense he says, cut Seymour Petty on the neck with a hatchet—nearly reaching the jugular vein—Dr. Curd sewed it up—" A few days later Barrett left with Catherine Smith. "*Elopement Catherine Smith*—who seems to have been using a bad influence on the Old Man—went away with him last night—Poor old fool!—" A greater source of worry to the ministry than either the Relner or Barrett affairs was the behavior of Reuben Wise. "*Reuben Wise Rebellion*—Has openly accused the lead in meeting for inquiring of another party if he had been doing wrong—It is not a personal thing but an effort in favor of independence & disorder. . . . Sab. 12—Reuben Wise asked pardon of the family for his rebellious charges." A probable explanation of Reuben's action was given later. "Sept. 27— 1875 R. Wise—Poor Bro. proposes to go to the country to work & pay off some debts he has contracted since he has been in the R.R. handle business is unwilling we should pay it for him."

The disorderly and even rebellious action on the part of so many was a matter of great concern to the leaders. They knew that some of it could be attributed to the dilemma of the post-war period and to the laxness prevalent everywhere. But the more realistic leaders had to admit there were other underlying causes.

An alarming decrease in membership was further indication

that something was amiss. From the beginning of their existence the Shakers had been accustomed to the large number of people who came for a while and then left. The leaders had tried to guard against their leaving by selecting the prospective members carefully and by asking those that were admitted to the Gathering or Novitiate Order to consider the covenant and its requirements thoroughly before signing it and becoming members of the Church Order. Even so, there had always been a high number of "Winter Shakers." But from 1870 to 1885 the number of departures was much higher than for any previous periods. March and April, 1870, saw many people leave.

March,	Mon.	7	Absconding—2
	Sab.	13	Taken away—Mary Ann Austin came & took her 7 girls after our expenses of raising them.
	Thurs.	24	Leaving—Matilda Cooper.
	Tues.	29	Still going—Permila Woodall
April	5—		Absconding—2
	Tues.	12	Going 7 people

Some who left did so because they were asked to leave. "Absconding—Oct. 26, 1871—George Gallisharn and Elizabeth Rust from the North Family—Were sent off for bad conduct. . . . Oct. 28—1871—Absconding—Nay sent away—Henry Burns & Nancy Wright—the former this evening, the latter goes tomorrow."

The records for the next several years contain frequent notices of people who were leaving. It was in 1872 and in July and August, 1876, that there was almost an epidemic of departures. "The New Year—1873—Whole number of souls 200. Decrease by death and departure since 1st of January, 1872, 64 souls. I have no previous record of so great a decrease in any one year—Whether are we tending?

"Centre family	Brethren	38	Sisters	63	101
West "	"	7	"	8	15
East "	"	14	"	29	43
North "	"	17	"	24	41

200"

One small ray of hope had shone forth briefly on Januray 17, 1873, when three members were admitted. It was one of few such entries for the year. Occurring much more frequently were items concerning those leaving. "July, 1873 Karl Andler, the German painter leaves today. . . . Aug. 23, 1873—*Backsliding.* Belle Bates took her boy—they and America Sorrel left for the world. They went to Auburn." One left because he thought fortune was elsewhere. "Mch. 1874—Gone—Sidney Hopton left for England professedly to settle up an estate." Four months later, Sidney was back at the colony. Even the schoolmistress Mary Wann left the North Family for life in New York City. But like Sidney, Mary came back. Another who left, but did not return, was Frances Buchanan, who, it was written, "now gets a pension for the services of her husband in the war—& this is worth more to her than Christ."

Of greatest concern to the leaders was the number of turnbacks who had been prominent at the colony for many years. Chief among these was Jefferson Shannon, who had helped establish the river trading trips and who, only four years before, had turned back the Black Lick farm to the general society after having spent five years putting the farm on a profitable basis. "June 24—1872—*Terrible Backsliding!* Thomas Jefferson Shannon who was brot up here from a mere boy & who has lived here for more than 60 years has been one of the most executive business men, has so far abused his privilege that now at 71 years of age feels compelled to turn his back & withdraw from Society. He left about 3 p.m. and his Dulcinea Sarah Woodward left also by the 2½ train for Auburn expecting to join him there. Alas! Alas!"

Three years later the community lost another prominent merchant, Asa Ware. "Dec. 22—1875—Absconded—Asa Ware denied the faith & left today—gave him $50.00. He had been here about 23 years."

The question arises as to why Jefferson and Asa, after sixty years or even twenty-three years of service, should renounce the life to which they were so accustomed and undertake to start private businesses. That each was capable of succeeding in a new life is apparent, but why had they not left earlier if they felt an urge for individual independence rather than communal independence? Had the time come when the society was more filled with drones than in the 1840's and 1850's? Were Jefferson and Asa tired of exercising their talents to support the less resourceful members? Was the religious spirit decreasing to the point where it was no longer the magnet for holding such an economic experiment together? Had religion always been the sole force? Had the war losses been so great that the business minds of these two failed to see a successful future for the experiment? Or were these men caught up in the rebellious spirit so prevalent at the time?

In February of the following year Eades listed in the house journal what he chose to term the first real rebellion. "Feb. 1, 1876—*Rebellion*—1st to occur—Lorenzo Pearcifield & Jackson McGown refuse to remove from the West family—gave our consent for them to write their grievances to headquarters in Ohio—they agree to abide by their decision. A large team must have a wide lane to turn in. . . . Sab. 20-Feb.-1876— It was announced in this meeting that the two Brethren would remove in accordance with the gift from the West to the Center family on Wednesday next—This much obedience is commendable even without repentance. . . . These things perhaps should not be recorded but as this is the first outstanding rebellion that had ever taken place in this society & I fear the end is not yet—I thought best to make a note of it. Lorenzo was born at the East family & W. J. McGown received into society at about 21 years of age. . . . Wed. 23 *Move*—Lorenzo & W. J. removed (as desired of them 3 weeks since) to the Centre from the West."

Unlike the rebellious two was the ministry who, when they realized the time had come for greater consolidation, moved without hesitation from their living quarters in the meeting-house to the Center. Discouraged by the open rebellion in the church relation, the ministry was further discouraged by the few members who were either capable or desirous of assuming the leadership, which, considering the advanced age of the ministry, was soon to be theirs. Before the turn of the next century death was to come to three outstanding members, all of whom had spent their entire lives at the village. Dying at the age of seventy-six was the trustee Urban Johns; at eighty-two, Nancy E. Moore; and at eighty-five, Elder Hervey L. Eades.

At the age of sixty-seven, eighteen years before his own death, Eades had expressed himself concerning leaders who held their office too long. "June, 1874 Old Battle-Scarred veterans—Why dont you all resign? Why not & then simply hold up & support some younger ones & see them prospering, before God suddenly calls you away when the young will be compelled to go forward without your support—How silly they all seem to this writer—I may also be as foolish when I arrive at their age." In a note added ten years later, Eades confessed: "I am just that foolish now—nearly 78 & cannot find any one to take my place yet. Sorry I am."

XVII

HOW DIFFERENT NOW

PUBLISHED POSTHUMOUSLY IN THE APRIL, 1892, issue of the eastern *Manifesto* was a letter from South Union's Eldress Nancy E. Moore. In the open letter, which was addressed to her "beloved Companions" everywhere, Nancy had commented on her own death, which she felt was near. Her chief concern, however, had not been for herself, but for the colony, whose condition, she wrote, was "... not one of well being. The people have suffered from the war ... It is now dark, very dark! Yet we have the promise & wait patiently for the better day when peace shall dwell in the land and righteousness in the hearts of men." Writing out of the fullness of her own heart, Nancy brought her letter to a close with the words: "In tender regard for all of the human race, Farewell."

The better day longed for by the little Civil War eldress did not come to South Union. The written records kept from 1892 to 1922 are sufficient evidence that the community did not regain its early vigor and prosperity. The signs of decadence are evident not only in the content of the journals, but also in the careless manner in which many of the records are kept. The pages are not written with the characteristic neatness exhibited in the older journals. Too, there were days and even weeks when recorders neglected to make a single entry.

In contrast to the former accounts, which almost always

concerned the general welfare of the community, the late records are filled chiefly with personal items.

Mch. 22, 1889	The tailor cut my hair after dinner.
Oct. 28, 1895	Patched my mittens.
Mch. 18, 1898	My bowels ran off fearfully all last night.
Jan. 5, 1911	A Syrian peddler was here. Carr got 1 pr. of socks, 25¢.
Sun. July 16, 1911	Kay Wilson . . . took our picture with a camera.
Aug. 11, 1912 (Sun.)	Very pleasant all day and harmony reigns supreme. Carr put on his new pants.

Further change is noted in the many trivial events which appear as the only item of the day or week. When such items as the following are written into the permanent records, one surmises either that there was little of importance to be recorded or that the journalists did not take their duties seriously. "Jan. 1914 Put the old rooster over with the young chickens and the white rooster and him had a royal fite. The white one whipped him. . . . Jan. 1915 The old brown cat disappeared last Wednesday and has not made its appearance yet, and its little kitten feels lost without it."

Perhaps the inclusion of such unimportant domestic bits may have resulted from the fact that Elder Logan Johns and Eldress Lucilla Booker were ashamed to keep complete records in the days when bickerings and petty jealousies were common. Pride in their heritage may have caused them to ignore such details.

Although a complete picture is not given, a great deal can

be read between the lines of the items that do appear. In reading the entry for August 26, 1912, one learns that "Carr bought a cape to wear on his shoulders for 50¢ from Sabrina Whitmore." But one also learns that at least two Shakers, a man and a woman, were managing their own pecuniary affairs, evidence that the old days of absolute communal living were over.

The personal purchase of a victrola by one of the Shaker women, Josephine Thrall, is added proof that the society had departed from its earlier plan. The staunch Believers at South Union never approved wholeheartedly of the victrola, but visitors from the outside always made up an eager audience. Josephine, or Miss Josie as she was known to the world, loved good music, and her records were among the best to be bought at that time. "May 23, 1913 Outside Company. Josephine Thrall played on her victrola for them. . . . Sab. Aug. 16, 1914 Five girls came to Center House this afternoon and visited in J. Thrall's room to hear her play the victrola. Shakers don't approve of it on Sabbath."

Another clear indication of the changing order is found in the many references to the Shakers' attendance at events on the outside. From the beginning of its existence the society had maintained a consistent separation from the social, political, and religious affairs of the world; however, from 1870 on, there was growing evidence of change.

First to show change was the social pattern; the Shakers began to seek their entertainment away from the village. "March 6, 1871 Bro. Reuben went to Bowling Green. While there he went to the Odean [Ogden?] Hall to see the Davenports perform their strange exhibition. . . . Aug. 7, 1871 *A show at Auburn* A number of wild beasts exhibited at Auburn. Some 4 or 5 of the young brethren attended (Went on their own footing)." In September, 1894, four of the sisters went to the Warren County Fair, and a month later some of the members went to a circus in Bowling Green. On another occasion when Nicholas, Sabrina, and Josie attended a circus, they reported it "a great affair." On the second of July, 1909, several of the Shakers went down to the neighboring town of Auburn to join in the celebration of the Fourth. Since the holiday would fall on the Sabbath, the townspeople had decided to celebrate on Friday preceding the holiday itself. How strange it would have seemed to the early Believers to stand and watch the Methodist Sunday School children marching to band music. Certainly it was a change from the days when they themselves had marched and danced while the world had watched.

As time went on, many of the remaining Shakers began to attend baseball games and chautauqua programs in Auburn. At least one of the men is known to have made a trip to Louisville to see the running of the highly advertised Kentucky Derby.

Not only were the Shakers participating in the pleasures of the outsiders, but they were beginning to tolerate and even to admire the gayer fashions of their neighbors. This new, lenient attitude was a definite break with the former Shaker belief that too much ornamentation was a worldly indulgence. As early as 1871 a group from Shakertown had visited their friend Barkley in Russellville. At his house they found: ". . . all that we could desire—nothing appeared to be wanting to complete an earthly paradise—on calling for water, a beautiful silver pitcher was filled with pure ice water . . . and silver cups to drink out of. The parlor where we first entered was decorated in the most magnificent splendor. Drawings, portraits & photographs of many distinguished men being present." The principal item of interest was the oval frame containing a floral composition. They learned that on the evening before she died the late Mrs. Barkley had walked in her garden and had gathered flowers for a bouquet. The family had sent this bouquet and a few of the funeral wreaths to Chicago to have them framed. The visitors were no less interested in some frames in which Mrs. Barkley had arranged "little curios" such as shells and locks of hair.

Soon after the Russellville visit with the Barkleys, a group from the village visited the family of Captain Woods in Auburn. There they were entertained by the five Woods girls, who "sang several Sunday School songs and selected several from their musick lessons." After a pleasant visit, the Shakers left for home, taking with them a bottle of choice wine, which they were told to compare with their own best.

Not long after the Shakers commenced visiting their neighbors regularly, they began to add the brighter colors of the outside to their own quiet tones of blue, green, grey, and black. By 1915 even an eldress had turned to gaiety. "Lucilla very busy sewing in her room today. She made a turkey red table cloth for her room table & cut off two red flowered curtains for her room windows."

It happened that out of the small number who came late to join the Shakers three of them were already imbued with a love of color and festivity. "Dec. 1915 Mary Finke & 2 little girls, Ethel and Gertrude (late from L-ville to join Shakers) are making little trinkets to put on a Christmas tree. They are kinds of toys & baskets & butterflies & Roses of all colors & pictures of various things to tie on the tree." The Christmas tree itself was a departure from the time when the twenty-fifth of December passed almost unobserved.

The fact that the Shakers took early advantage of the twentieth-century mechanical improvements is not due altogether to their increased contact with the outside, for in their economic life they had always had dealings with the world. It was rather because of their established policy of buying the latest labor-saving devices so long as they proved to be of practical value.

The modern age could be said to have arrived at Shakertown when telephones were installed in 1910 and bathrooms were built in the Center House in 1916. A gasoline engine was bought to pump water to the kitchen where it could be heated for the bathrooms. This was an improvement over the limited water system which the trustees had installed in 1838 when water had been piped from the mound cistern to the kitchens of the Center and North houses. There had also been an earlier installation of the telephone, a limited interhouse system which George Caldwell had completed in 1878 between the ministry's shop and the office. "We can easily converse with a person in the office & vice versa without the trouble of going there."

Caldwell, who came to South Union from Ancora, New Jersey, had been responsible also for the installation of an electric call bell in the hall of the ministry's shop. The journalist, evidently intrigued, explained: ". . . that by the cooks pressing a small button at the office the bell is rung instantaneously in our shop—Electricity generated in our office cellar."

The modern invention which created the greatest amount of excitement was the automobile. From the first written mention of a car in 1911 until 1915 when the society bought their own, the recorder was quite attracted by the new mode of traveling. "Aug. 20, 1911 Auto here this evening. . . . Feb. 3, 1913 Mrs. Carrie Coke & children drove down in their auto last evening & got auto stuck . . . walked to Center House—got mules to pull it out. . . . Apr. 27, 1913 Mr. Watkins and his wife Lilly here in their auto this P.M. over at the office. . . . Sep. 20, 1914 Everything quiet but the autoes and they go past at full speed. . . . Feb. 22, 1914 Some automobiles running by here today. Weather not fit to run them yet hardly."

Although some of the comments imply disapproval of the new machine, the salesman who first approached the society about buying an automobile had little difficulty in making the sale. "April 16, 1915 Mr. Thomas Hamblin came to Centerhouse this A.M. in his automobile & wants to sell one to Logan Johns for this society. Mr. Hamblin came back with his chauffeur & took some of the sisters a short ride this aft. & Wm.

Bates.... April 27 A. L. Johns bought automobile. Lucilla, Sabrina, & Josephine Thrall took a ride in it & Wm. Bates too this afternoon.... April 29th Third day of owning car. Wm. Bates & chauffeur & John Perryman riding in our new automobile all day all over the country. Can't tell where they went to learn Wm. Bates to run it." The all-day lesson was evidently sufficient, for the next day Bates "took the chauffeur (Mr. Clarkson of B.G.) home."

While John Perryman was "riding all over the country" in the car, he probably was thinking how travel had changed since the days when Daniel Boone had walked the early Wilderness Road. Perryman had thought a great deal about Boone since the day when the younger John Slover had presented him with Boone's knife.

With the purchase of the car the Shakers became the owners of one of the first automobiles in their county. They evidently enjoyed the novelty offered by the car, for the next few days' accounts are filled with short trips, such as, "went for a ride in auto after supper tonight & brought mail in" or "took company to Russelville this afternoon just to see how it rides. They think it is just fine."

The automobile age came on apace. By October, 1915, the elder could write "*Fourteen* automobiles passed here this afternoon going west through Auburn."

Unlike the Mennonites who believed the automobile to be the work of the devil, the Shakers accepted it because of its practical value. No Shaker could call the new automobile wicked if it offered cheaper and more rapid transportation to market, for in the Shaker mind to save time and money was to serve the Lord.

Although the economic virtue was still strong, change in the religious life of the members was becoming quite pronounced. Concerned with the loss of spirit, an eldress wrote: "The religious interest is very low and the power of conscience seems to have lost its power for good." Attendant to this decline was an ever-increasing laxness in observance of the church services. Very few public meetings were held after 1900. In fact, few services of any kind were held during the last twenty-five years of the colony's existence except the singing meetings and the special services required by the official visits from the eastern ministry. "April 5, 1896—Easter Sunday—No meeting—a beautiful day.... Sun. May 26, 1907 A beautiful day. Had no meeting—but singing and talking in the front room at the office at 2 p.m. Bates took Elder George Baxter Buggie riding after the meeting."

In 1910 the Ohio ministry stopped for a short visit enroute home from a business trip to Florida. During the next two years the Canterbury, New Hampshire, and Whitewater, Ohio, elders came. From 1910 to 1920 the most frequent visitor was Elder Arthur Bruce of Canterbury. Bruce seems to have been a trustee at large, being responsible for the official business of South Union as well as that of other societies. He was often at South Union on his way to and from the new Shaker ventures at Narcossee, Florida, and Camden, Georgia. Both colonies, established in the late 1890's, proved to be failures. It was in October, 1915, that Bruce and the Mount Lebanon ministry met at South Union to consider the possibility of selling the society property. The neighboring Kentucky society had been sold five years before.

Even as late as this the services honoring the various ministries were still being held. The visitors always spoke, giving encouragement and good counsel as well as dispensing love from the eastern societies. But the time had passed when the Kentuckians returned the visits. Instead, the elder sent minute reports of the colony's welfare to the eastern leaders. In the summer of 1890 the eighty-three-year-old Elder Eades was sending the reports. "July, 1890.... Have an 18 in. lawn mower. The mower is more fatigueing than the scythe, but much nicer. Wish you could see the ministry's yard now. You would be delighted.... Aug. 1890—This has been a great fly year & a fruitful year for rabbits. In the evening the rabbits are running around the yards almost as tame as cats."

The eastern Shakers continued to show their interest in the faraway Kentucky Believers, not only by visits, but in sending gifts from time to time. For Christmas, 1915, there was a package containing sleeping socks for the brethren and sisters. These were the gift of the New York eldresses M. Allen and Sarah Burgher. Arriving by express were two stands of bees "of the Italian variety," a welcome gift.

In spite of all the encouragement given by the easterners, the local religious leadership continued to decline. By the early 1900's the society began to invite outside ministers to conduct the funeral services at the village, many of the funerals being conducted by the Presbyterian and Baptist ministers of Auburn. It became necessary to have help in the song service at the funerals. But the society members never asked the outsiders to join them in the special closing hymn. "Wood Hall from Auburn preached her funeral & did it well. There were several neighbors did most of the singing during the funeral."

One November Sabbath in 1908, a year in which no meetings had been held by the society, a colored baptism was held in the creek on the society farm. Although they had never practiced baptism themselves, the Shakers had given their consent for the service to be held on their property, and they attended the service, being part of "a large congregation of white and colored people." In the journal it was stated that it was the largest crowd ever there and that the preacher was a good one.

Along with the decline in religious leadership and spirit came economic retrenchments. In spite of the fact that the trustees were in no way any less ardent in their attempt to get "the one thing needful" than their predecessors had been, they still had to make a great many economic adjustments. The Shakers, who had been among the first Americans to change from a household scale to mass production, knew that the machine production of the twentieth century was on a far bigger scale than the society could hope to attain. After losing their factories by fire and being faced with a dwindling membership and changing customs, it seemed even less expedient to enter into competition with the commercial concerns; so after the turn of the new century, very few garden seeds and preserves were prepared for the market. The manufacture of bonnets, hats, and cloth was discontinued entirely, as was the business of making and selling coffins.

In the last twenty-five years that the colony operated, the chief source of income was from the continued sale of farm and garden products, poultry, sheep, and cattle. Added to the farm crops was tobacco. Among the garden products the sweet potato had come to be one of the most profitable. Not only did the gardeners sell the matured potatoes, but they did a good business each spring selling and shipping the potato slips.

From 1870 on, the raising of sheep was practiced on a considerable scale. In 1890 Eades reported that the farmers had sheared six hundred sheep, averaging six to seven pounds of wool, which they had sold at twenty-three cents per pound. Also, they had sold two hundred lambs at $3.50 per head.

With so many of their industries discontinued, the Shakers found it necessary to patronize the neighborhood stores for their clothing, groceries, and other supplies. Very frequently they paid for their purchases by exchanging butter and eggs, fresh meat and chickens. Never having tolerated cheapness and imperfection, they bought only high quality merchandise. The older members accepted the new practice of buying on the outside, but not without regret for the passing of their former economic self-sufficiency. "May 31, 1916 Center family had their first green beans & peas this year. The sister bought them in Bowling Green yesterday. This is strange to say."

The time finally came when the membership was so small that it was not practical to pay the salaries of a dentist and physician. It was then that the Believers closed the little building known as the dentist and doctor's shop and turned to the outside for their needed medical and dental care. "Mch. 28, 1908 William Booker went to Auburn this afternoon . . . and . . . had his mouth looked at by Dentist Freeman. . . . Nov. 2, 1908 Dr. London came with his electric battery & gave Lucilla the battery on the shoulders, arms & hand." One February day Brother Jefferson went to Russellville for the double purpose of supplying the merchants with garden seeds and getting "some repairing done to Annie Booker's teeth."

There was still a community fund for paying all the general expenses even though a few of the members were handling their private funds and satisfying their personal wants. The account books carried many entries such as:

2½ yds. veiling	$4.40
9 straw hats	1.85
6 pair girls shoes	7.35
2 dozen sisters stockings	5.40
6 small shawls	2.70
Suspenders	.75
Larkin's for "Sweet Home" soap	5.43
Cutting hair, tea, soap	1.30
Bedstead and springs	5.50
Broom and oil	1.00

Also appearing were such miscellaneous items as "J. R. Cooper's teeth fixed for $6.50" or "bought two coffins from W. Stagner $8.50 and $6.00."

There were two business transactions in the late years which added to the community treasury. In 1908 the trustees leased their lands for five years to a company interested in testing for oil and gas. In October, 1912, they sold the unoccupied West House. The nine hundred dollar sale was made with the understanding that the house would be torn down and the materials hauled away. Before the house was finally razed, several transactions took place. "April 19, 1913—Began to tear down the front part of the West House. Mr. Vick bought this part of the house from Mr. Johnson & he bought it from Allen Jones and he bought it from the Shakers."

As long as Shakertown remained, it was a magnet for all the people in the country about. The quiet village was the ideal place to go on Sunday drives, to have picnics, or to take visitors. It may even be that the village was all the more attractive as a picnic site in the days when there was not so much activity as before. "April 19, 1907 A picnic party from Potters Ladies College was here today. 12 ladies & Mr. Madison the driver all in one wagon. . . . August 1, 1909 Some few parties in buggies came to South Lane & hitched their horses & are going over the place *taking pleasure*. . . . July 14, 1915 Mr. Whit Potter & his wife & Preacher Dulin's wife and another lady & two children came in an auto to the Center House well and took their lunch."

Many organizations selected Shakertown as the place to hold their annual social affairs. In September, 1913, the Odd Fellows from Russellville came to have a picnic. The program consisted of public speaking and band music. The next year a bankers' "get-together" was held at Shakertown. Bankers from several counties came for the picnic and the lecture on business affairs. "They were seated on chairs in Center House dooryard. Had hired colored men to make squirrel soup in our grease house. Largest crowd ever here. Some few ladies, mostly men."

From the population peak of 349 in 1827, the colony membership had dropped by 1911 to 17, of which 10 were at the Center House, 3 in the East House, and 4 at the Office. In addition to the 17 Believers, several of whom were not very ardent, there were 10 hands hired by the month and 2 hired by the day. The society also had business arrangements with the 3 men who rented and operated the village blacksmith shop, located at the cross roads, and the store and tavern, located at the railroad depot.

As the population declined and the life of the colony drew to a close, the atmosphere at the village was caught and reflected in the pages of the house journals. On New Year's Day, 1911, the journalist at the Office wrote: "There is only four of us at the Office—Frances & Mary, & Joseph and Jas. Carr. We have quiet and peace and plenty—and are thankful for the same." A later entry sounded a note of reminiscence. "Sab. 14, 1915 No visitors today from outside at Center House. Seems quiet here like Shakers used to be. But alas that day has passed away. How different now."

No doubt she was writing literally, but Eldress Lucilla Booker struck a prophetic chord in one of her late daily entries. "Very dark. Can't hardly see how to write now in the South window of my room."

In a letter written in 1895, addressed to the *Manifesto* readers, James Carr of South Union had analyzed his society's chief attribute when he said, "We are with a full supply of muscular energy, a force which is very useful in many an occupation." He recommended that the eastern Shakers leave their homes and come to Kentucky where they would find a "more genial climate & fertile soil." And, he added, they could "blend their mental culture with our muscular energy." This, he thought, would result in a society that would be a beacon upon a hill.

But that was not to be.

September 26, 1922, was hot and dusty, typical of first fall days in Kentucky. The early morning found most of the women in Auburn up early frying chickens, preparing salads, and baking pies and cakes; for it was the day when the church women of the town were expecting to sell their food to the thousands of people who would attend the opening of the great Shakertown sale. The women were not disappointed. From far and near came the crowd, made up of people interested in buying farm land, farm machinery, and cattle, or choice pieces of Shaker furniture. Others came not to buy but to visit for the last time an institution which they had long known and admired. During the two days of the sale the large crowds roamed over the grounds and through the now vacant buildings from cellar to garret. Many people went home carrying books, as well as copies of the *Manifesto*, which were scattered carelessly about the empty rooms. Most of the more important manuscripts—house journals and diaries—had been given previously to certain of the Shakers' antiquarian-minded friends from the world.

At the end of two days, the Shaker holdings were in the possession of outsiders. The land and all the buildings were bought by an investment company that was mostly interested in the large northern tract of virgin timber. Later when this timber was cleared and sold the company realized the price of its original investment. Then, not wishing to keep the real estate, the owners subdivided the land into some sixty farms and arranged a second sale, at which the land averaged fifty-six dollars an acre. The largest single tract contained the buildings, and it was bought by a member of the company, O. S. Bond, who began the operation of a model farm.

Responsible for the welfare of all the Shaker colonies, the New Lebanon authorities had come down to oversee the original sale. It was they who offered the remaining nine Believers a choice between a life home at the Mother society and an outright gift of ten thousand dollars. There had been a time when the members would undoubtedly have gone to the eastern society. But the situation in 1922 was different. Only one, Elder Logan Johns, refused the money and chose instead to finish his life among Believers.

The elder, now too sick and feeble to make the eastern trip alone, was provided with drawing-room reservations and was accompanied by the hired farm manager, Joe Wallace.

One who had left the colony only two years before the sale was Sabrina Whitmore. Although she had lived at South Union for years, she was not allowed to share in the monetary arrangement. Another who did not have the right to choose was Josie Bridges, who had been a mental case for some time. Josie was taken east by Elder Walter Shepard, who had come to make arrangements for the sale.

Choosing life in the world were seven members two of whom moved to Louisville and five to Auburn. Of the latter five, two —William Bates and Lizzie Simmons—married. In addition to beginning married life with a combined bank account of twenty thousand dollars, they also came into possession of the Shaker's automobile. Another of the five was Mary Wann, a little Scotch woman, who moved to the home of friends in Auburn, and later moved to Florida. Another was Mrs. Bass, who had lived somewhat irregularly at Shakertown over a period of years. The last was Mrs. Josie Thrall who, boarding first with acquaintances, finally moved to the home of Mrs. Bass.

Those who selected Louisville as a home were Miss Annie Farmer and her mother. There Miss Farmer became an active worker in a Baptist church.

It was Logan Johns who regretted most leaving the community. As the train pulled away from the South Union depot, the elder looked for the last time at the fertile acres stretching away in all directions from the train windows. To the left, in the distance, he could see the cluster of large substantial buildings. Leading away from this group ran an avenue of tall maples, shading the neatly laid stone walk that connected the central buildings with the East House. Last to pass from view was the East House itself, a building which, along with a small house and the large cattle barn, was destined to be badly damaged the next year by a tornado, as though nature herself could not endure the forsaken and lonely structures.

The Logan County Shaker enterprise had come to an end. Reviewed from its beginning in 1807, it becomes apparent that the life of the colony was like that of any normal individual, having its birth, growth, maturity, old age, and death. In terms of communal living, few American communities have been as successful. This success, as well as that of the other seventeen Shaker colonies, was attained under nineteenth century conditions—conditions which gave rise to a wave of sixty or more different Utopian plans, each of which had a varying number of separate communities. It was a period when many Americans were enthusiastic about communal experiments and when large numbers were allying themselves with some plan, expecting to gain economic security, to establish a new religious faith, or, as in the case of the Brook Farm members, to practice a "share-the-work" plan in order to have more time for high thinking.

The Shaker way of life has made a real contribution to American culture. First to be accorded recognition has been the contribution to American art. Functionalism, as practiced by the modern designer, is merely a contemporary application of an old Shaker idea, for every society craftsman was governed by the utilitarian principle. No one of them felt that he worshiped God aright unless he was satisfied that the article he was making was needed, would fit the purpose, and would last. Such criteria led to the use of the best and most suitable materials at hand and to the creation of designs pleasing in their simplicity and economy of purpose.

Not only the handicraft worker, but the gardener, the farmer, the merchant, and the kitchen sister, all performed their tasks according to the tenets of their religio-economic creed. The satisfaction of having done things right and having dealt honestly with their fellow man gave rise to their sense of composure and to their harmony of living.

As a people, the Shakers have helped to preserve the best virtues of our early colonizing spirit: simplicity, honesty, self-reliance, fortitude, love of industry, and the capacity for holding fast to convictions.

BIBLIOGRAPHY

PRIMARY MATERIAL

Manuscripts

Record A (1807-1835) Kept by the ministry. Copied by H. L. Eades. Contains autobiography of John Rankin, Sr., 1746, and a portion of the early Wabash Journal of B. S. Youngs.

Record B (Oct. 1, 1836-1878) Kept by the ministry.

Journal of a Voyage from South Union, Kentucky, to New Orleans, Louisiana (Oct. 6, 1831-Feb., 1832) Kept by T. J. Shannon.

Journal of Eldress Nancy, The (Saturday, January 17, 1863-Sunday, September 4, 1864.)

Diary of a Journey to New Lebanon and Watervliet, New York (July, 1854-September 10, 1854.)

Necropolis: A List of the Names of the Brethren and Sisters Who Have Died in This Society Since the Year 1810.

Fulling Mill Ledger begun in 1814.

Account Book (1888-1897)

Annie Ingram's Account Book (1901-Oct. 20, 1910)

Account Book for 1911

Journal of the Centre House Family (1871-1872; 1890) (1913-1916)

Journal of the Office Family (Mch. 1, 1905-Aug. 31, 1906) (Sept. 1, 1906-May 27, 1908) (1909-1910)

Shaker Publications

Avery, Giles B. *Sketches of Shakers and Shakerism*. Albany, Weed, Parsons & Co. Printers, 1883.

Bates, Paulina. *The Divine Book of Holy and Eternal Wisdom*. 1849.

Brown, Thomas. *An Account of the People Called Shakers: Their Faith, Doctrines and Practice, Exemplified in the Life, Conversations, and Experiences of the Author During the Time He Belonged to the Society*. Troy, Parker & Bliss, 1812.

Eades, H. L. *Shaker Sermons: Scripto-Rational Containing the Sub-*

stance of Shaker Theology. Shakers, New York. The Shaker Manifesto, 1879.

Evans, F. W. *Shaker Communism or Tests of Divine Inspiration.* London, J. Burns, 1871.

McNemar, Richard. *The Kentucky Revival.* New York, Reprinted by Edward O. Jenkins, 1846.

Robinson, Chas. E. *A Concise History of the United Society of Believers Called Shakers.* East Canterbury, 1893.

Stewart, Philemon. *Holy, Sacred and Divine Roll and Book; From the Lord God of Heaven, to the Inhabitants of Earth: Revealed in the United States at New Lebanon, County of Columbia, State of New York, United States of America.* In Two Parts. United Society, Canterbury, New Hampshire, 1843.

Wells, Seth, ed. *Testimonies Concerning Character and Ministry of Mother Ann Lee and the First Witnesses of the Gospel of Christ's Second Appearing.* Albany, Packard and van Benthuysen, 1827.

————. *Testimonials Concerning the Life, Character, Revelations, and Doctrines of Mother Ann and the Elders With Her.* Second Edition. Albany, Weed, Parsons & Co. Printers, 1888.

————. *A Brief Exposition of the Established Principles and Regulations of the United Society of Believers Called Shakers.* Improved Edition. Albany, Hoffman and White, 1834.

White, Anna and Taylor, Leila. *Shakerism: Its Message and Meaning.* Columbus, Ohio, Press of Fred J. Heer, 1904.

Youngs, B. Seth. *The Testimony of Christ's Second Appearing.* Published in Union, by Order of the Ministry, Lebanon, State of Ohio, Press of John McLean, Office of the Western Star, 1808.

Manifesto, The, VIII (March-May, 1878), XV (Jan. 1885-Dec. 1899)

SECONDARY MATERIAL

Andrews, Edward. *The Gift To Be Simple.* New York, J. J. Augustin, 1940.

————. *The Community Industries of the Shakers.* Albany, University of New York State, 1932.

Andrews, Edward and Faith. *Shaker Furniture.* New Haven, Yale Press, 1937.

Buckingham, J. S. *America, Historical and Statistical.* New York, Harper & Bros., 1841, Vols. I, II.

Chase, Daryl. *An Experiment in Religious Communism.* Part of a Dissertation, University of Chicago, Private Edition, University of Chicago Libraries, 1938.

Dow, E. F. *A Portrait of the Millennial Church of Shakers.* University of Maine Studies, XXXIV, Second series, No. 19, August, 1931.

BIBLIOGRAPHY 273

Finch, ———. *English Woman's Experiences in America.* 18—.

Hinds, William A. *American Communities and Colonies.* Second Revision. Chicago, Chas. Kerr and Co., 1908.

Howells, William Dean. *Three Villages* "Shirley" Boston, Jas. R. Osgood and Co., 1884.

McLean, J. P. *A Bibliography of Shaker Literature With an Introductory Study.* Columbus, Ohio, Fred J. Heer, 1905.

———. *Shakers of Ohio.* Columbus, Ohio, Fred J. Heer, 1907.

Melcher, Florence. *The Shaker Adventure.* Princeton, The Princeton Press, 1941.

Nordhoff, Charles. *The Communistic Societies of the United States.* London, John Murray, 1875.

Noyes, John H. *A History of American Socialisms.* Philadelphia, J. B. Lippincott and Co., 1870.

O'Brien, Harriet. *Lost Utopias.* Boston, Perry Walton, 1929.

Sears, Clara E. *Gleanings From Old Shaker Journals.* 1916.

Sweet, W. W. *The Story of Religions in America.* New York, Harper & Brothers, 1927.

INDEX

ADMISSION of children, 39, 115-16, 169, 240, 241, 243
Alfred, Maine, 236, 237
Arkansas River, 124
Army worms, 98
Asiastic cholera, 78-79, 115, 169
Atlanta Journal, 179
Auburn, Kentucky, 162, 199, 221, 222, 225, 251, 262, 264, 266
Audubon, John James, 128-29
Automobile, purchase of, 259
Avery, Elder Giles B., 235

BACKSLIDING, 54-55, 73-74, 76, 163, 250-51
Baptists, 7, 16, 26, 31
Barren River, 82, 161
Barrett-Petty quarrel, 249
Bass, Alice, 268
Bates, Issachar, 10, 20, 22, 27, 33, 36, 81
Bates, William, 260, 261, 268
Baton Rouge, La., 127-128
Belknap, Morris, 120
Bilious pleurisy epidemic, 169
Bloomburg, Elder Andrew, 234
Boat race, 132-33
Bond, O. S., 267
Bonta, Sam, 28
Booker, Lucilla, 255, 258, 266
Booker, William, 193, 216
Boone, Daniel, 260
Boston, Mass., 10
Bourbon County, Kentucky, 24
Bowling Green, Kentucky, 79, 82, 110, 161, 162, 176, 180, 181, 182, 186, 190, 202, 211, 226, 243, 256
Bowling Green, bank failure, 87

Bowling Green, *Gazette,* 79
Breedlove, Virginia, 247
Bridges, Josie, 268
Bridges, Nicholas A., 240, 246, 247
Brook Farm experiment, 269
Brown, Thomas, 7
Bruce, Elder Arthur, 261
Buchanan, Lucetta, 147
Buckner, General Simon Bolivar, 178, 202
Busroe, Indiana, 33, 37, 52
Butler County, Ky., 49

CAMDEN, Georgia, 261
Camp meeting, 16, 238
Canaan (South Union), 103, 172
Cane Ridge, Ky., 16, 24, 27
Canning industry, 48, 111, 112, 160-61, 218-20
Canterbury, N. H., 69, 139, 173, 214, 245, 261
Carr, James, 255, 266
Cartwright, Peter, 12
Celibacy, 5, 25
Center House, construction of, 88-90
Christmas, celebration of, 86, 223, 240, 258, 262
Cincinnati, Ohio, 21, 70, 153, 165, 170, 194, 219, 226
Civic opposition, 24-25, 50, 174-76
Civil War events, 177, 179, 180, 183, 184, 185, 199-200, 201, 202-03, 203, 204, 204-07, 207, 208, 211
Clarksville, Tennessee, 105, 113, 118, 240